VIEW FROM THE SHORE

VIEW from the SHORE

Roger Pilkington

The Book Guild Ltd
Sussex, England

This book is sold subject to the condition that it shall not, by way of trade or otherwise, be lent, re-sold, hired out, photocopied or held in any retrieval system or otherwise circulated without the publisher's prior consent in any form of binding or cover other than that in which this is published and without a similar condition including this condition being imposed on the subsequent purchaser.

The Book Guild Ltd
25 High Street,
Lewes, Sussex

First published 1995
© Roger Pilkington
Set in Palatino
Typesetting by Acorn Bookwork, Salisbury, Wiltshire

Printed in Great Britain by
Antony Rowe Ltd
Chippenham, Wiltshire.

A catalogue record for this book is
available from the British Library

ISBN 1 85776 017 4

CONTENTS

Foreword	9
The Quarry Hills	11
The Schwaighofstrasse	20
Two Professors	26
The Summer Term	33
Reinhold Borstmann	42
The Meteorite	49
The Editor	57
Hans Spemann	62
Sky High	68
To Climb by Night	79
The Byways Club	88
Prone to Accident	96
Mr Wendon	99
Father of Chemistry	103
Lab Life	112
The Riddle of the Sands	122
Princeps Botanicorum	132
Farewell to the Desert	138
Plus and Minus	146
Arno Piechorowski	151

Fritz the Forester	158
The Golden Raven	166
Master Matthis	173
The Night Mail	181
The Ville	186
John Poynter	193
Thirty-Ninety-Eight	198
No Waiting	202
Floating Voter	207
Harvey Flack	212
Lady Rhondda	217
Life in the Lower Case	224
Billy Graham	229
Stanley Spencer	234
Twelve Good Men and True	239
Friendless	248
St Stephen's	259
Kicked out of Bed	270
Sweet Repose	276

Some of the material in this book has appeared at one time or another in the following journals and periodicals, to which grateful acknowledgements are made:–

The Guardian
The Sunday Telegraph
The Spectator
Time and Tide
John o'London's Weekly
History Today
Family Doctor
Air and Space
Der Schwarzwald

FOREWORD

This is not an autobiography. After all, I am not a general, a trades union leader, or even an unsuccessful politician who has to find a means of occupying his time between an electoral defeat and (with luck) success at the next General Election.

That is what this book is definitely not. It is, on the other hand, a collection of essays covering a period of sixty years or more, a period during which things have changed beyond imagination, not only in science but in our way of living. I am not making any great social judgments about these changes, but merely regretting perhaps that while the lot of the poorest has vastly changed for the better, the excitement that could be experienced when one constructed one's first wireless set and actually managed to contact, with twenty yards of aerial wire slung between trees, the voices of the suave announcers broadcasting the evening news bulletin – for which they were impeccably dressed in their dinner jackets – is no longer there.

Some of the earlier essays concern the very first year of Hitler, and for that I make no apology. The Nazis had still a certain bumpkinish atmosphere about them, and Hitler had not begun on his fearful rounds of conquest and extermination, and the persecution of the Jewish people was only a faint stirring. The seeds were there, certainly, as I hope the reader will discover for himself. But the simple clownishness of much that went on immediately after Hitler's usurpation of power in Germany is little known.

The rate of change has accelerated, and I hope it is leading somewhere sensible – though often enough I have my doubts. But as it is not my business to be a forecaster on either the economic or political scene, I shall leave that also to others.

This is just a book which dips into the years past, and not so past, as experienced by one who can never be grateful enough for the privilege of living on the wonderful planet that has for better or worse been offered to us, for eighty thrilling and varied years.

Montouliers, 1995.   Roger Pilkington.

THE QUARRY HILLS

It was a chill day of February when we drove from Heathrow north-westward towards the Midlands. As we passed through the rather uninteresting village of Newbold, it all came back to me vividly. The derelict factory building with the leaning chimney, the miniature mountains with their field-grey surface of sticky clay furrowed by miniature river valleys where the rain had run down toward the chalky-blue lake. I turned into a lane and left the car beside a building of the local council school.

'You must see it,' I said to my wife. 'It is . . . well, just come and see. We might find something. You never know.'

The whole area was now laid out as an 'amenity'. There was a notice-board with pictures of newts and marestail and various other things to be noted by visitors. And there was a neat path which rose in carefully graded steps, up and up until it wound through a copse to come out on a little plateau with a picnic area, and seats, and a notice warning one not to walk over the edge and fall down into deep water. Apart from this one clearing, the whole area was woodland, not very beautiful woodland but the kind of copse of which a local authority is usually proud; unkempt, self-strangling, and devoid of all charm whatsoever. But the derelict factory? The range of grey hills? All that had vanished.

'After all,' I said to Ingrid, 'it's sixty-five years since I was last here, so one must expect a bit of change.' I glanced at the ground, now covered with the well-trodden leafmould of decades. There was not even a trace of grey in it. 'We shall not find anything here. You'll just have to imagine how it was all that time ago.' And disappointed, we walked down the amenity path, back to the car.

Sixty-five years back. On Sunday afternoons we were allowed to cycle out as far as we wished, provided only that we were back in time for evening chapel and call-over. So one day I left Rugby by the road which crossed the stripling Avon and passed by what was then the small village of Newbold, little more than a hamlet at the edge of the allotments of the railwaymen who worked in the main-line junction of Rugby. I noticed a ruined factory building with broken windows and a cracked furnace chimney, and behind it the little range of hills forty or fifty feet high, a waste heap of battleship grey. Like the colliery tips around St Helens the clay provided a foothold only for marestail and coltsfoot.

Something prompted me to stop, leave my cycle beside the hedge, push open the rusty gate and scramble up the hill which, having been formed by dumping, was naturally at a critical angle so that the spoil slid down under my weight almost as fast as I could scramble up it. Reaching the top I found myself on a ridge from which I could look down on a great pit filled with chalky-blue water. I could see that the place was a deserted cement works, and that the hill was the spoil heap of the softer and clay-like material which could not be processed and baked to form cement.

I began to walk along the top of the mound when my eye was caught by a kidney-shaped object about an inch or more across, and almost as thick. I picked it up and examined it. The thing had the appearance of bone, but yet it was as hard as stone. I realised that it was some kind of fossil, but of what I had no idea at all. Searching further along the heap I found a number of miniature, whitish, five-pointed stars (which in fact were sections of the stems of fossil crinoids or stalked echinoderms), one or two small curled ammonites of great delicacy, and a few shells of an oyster-like mollusc. The whole place was dead, deserted, a relic not only of days when trucks clanged and steam-shovels scraped and scooped at the layers of stone below the Warwickshire clay, but of times still further back, probably, I thought, before there had been any Rugby at all, or even ancient Britons. I searched further and before it was time to cycle back to the school I had found altogether some thirty broken pieces of fossil bone, some of which fitted together to make longer, curved pieces, tapered at one end. I had no idea what these could be, but a few rounded disc-like objects dished on either side were at least recognisable as vertebrae. I stuffed the finds in my pockets, slid down the hillside, and cycled quickly back to school.

That same evening I packed up the pieces that appeared to be some sort of fossil bones, and after padding the parcel carefully with newspaper I waited for a chance to slip into town and mail the packet to the British Museum. I enclosed a letter which was short and to the point.

'*Dear Sir,*' it ran. '*Please tell me what these are and how old and send them back.*'

A week later the parcel was returned to me, and in the greatest excitement I carefully opened it. There was a letter enclosed, from the office of the Assistant Curator, Palaeontology, British Museum of Natural History, South Kensington.

'*Dear Sir,*' it began – and as a fourteen-year-old schoolboy I was very flattered to be thus addressed – '*The specimens you sent for identification are ribs, vertebrae and a wrist or paddle bone, all of* Ichthyosaurus, *a large marine reptile. They are separately labelled for your convenience and are returned herewith. The date at which the* Ichthyosaurus *lived cannot be precisely determined, but would be approximately one hundred to one hundred and fifty million years ago.*'

I put away the treasures in my locker, where later they were joined by other finds from the Lower and Middle Lias, the strata of which were so obligingly laid bare in the many quarries around Rugby by the diggers of Rugby Cement. One, a splendid specimen of a huge bivalve named *Lima gigantea* is still used by me as a paper-weight sixty-five years later. But the letter made an enormous impression upon me, for if I had a vague notion about fossils derived from the colliery tips near our home, I had not yet reached the school level where I would abandon Latin grammar and political geography for a more extended history of the earth and the life upon it. It was not that I had been primed with any rigid and obstinate fundamentalist doctrine, but merely that like most boys I accepted the world as I found it, without questioning or thinking any more about its origin and infancy than I did about my own prenatal development. At the same time I was brought up in staunchly Nonconformist surroundings, and so as a child I was certainly much more familiar with the Bible than my Church of England companions. And of course the Bible which had been presented to me on my sixth birthday by my Pilkington grandmother had the famous dating from Archbishop James Ussher's *Annales Veteris et Novi Testamenti* at the top of the reference column on every page. I had seen the date 4004 BC for the creation and had worried as little about that as I had about the means by which it might all have come about. And now, with the bland statement from South Kensington about the age of my finds, I began to wonder. I had a curious sensation of being suddenly in touch with a world that had existed at a time so long past that its very age was unimaginable. The ruined workings with the stilled chimney were a relic of a past that had gone perhaps a mere ten or twenty years since. That was a past that I could visualise, a time filled with the clanking of steam-shovels and toiling, dusty workmen. But this – at least a hundred million years earlier, a million centuries away. And the letter spoke of a marine reptile too, so where there now was land there must once have been sea. An ocean, with my own *Ichthyosaurus* swimming in it, but no human on the whole length of its long-vanished shores.

My whole view of the world was jolted, and the solid daily life of school with Latin, chapel, the shop with its strawberries and cream, the house with its little studies and long dormitories – all this seemed now to have a strange impermanence, to be as it were a single frame taken from a two hour reel of a movie of which I myself could not hope to see either the beginning or the end. A slow-motion film stretching from a past infinity to . . . to where? To eternity, or perhaps to the end of time itself.

I had had the good fortune to be given a vision of a world of living things that extended back from the present into the dimness of an almost unimaginable past. And then came the time when my view of the universe was extended far out into space as well. My own particular confidant among the Rugby staff was H.P. Sparling, the chief mathematician. I happened to be good at mathematics, but that was incidental. What particularly drew me to Sparling was his somewhat aloof position as resident astronomer in the Temple Observatory, a small brick house behind which some steps led up to the observation room with a rotating roof and what seemed to me to be an enormous telescope, complete with its complicated clockwork gear for keeping it aligned upon a star or planet while the Earth, upon which Rugby so securely stood, rotated about its own inclined axis. Looking back it astonishes me that so few boys haunted that magical space around the telescope. Perhaps none of us had much time to spare in the dark winter evenings, but again and again I would sign out of Whitelaw House to slip round to Sparling's before dusk and talk with him until dark and we could open the big roof, crank it round, and set up our observations.

One day at the end of a calculus session Sparling asked me to stay behind for a moment. What he had to say was more exciting than I could ever have dreamed of, for he explained that we were closer to Saturn than we would ever be again for a great number of years, and he thought we should take the chance. It was certainly going to be a clear night, and he intended to ask my housemaster to let me attend at the observatory at two o'clock in the morning.

Permission was granted, and I lay awake hour after hour in the silent dormitory for fear of missing the great adventure. I glanced every now and then at the luminous dial of my watch until at last the time came when I could dress and creep quietly along the corridor and down the stairs to let myself out into the garden, which backed on to the wall of the observatory.

It was a brilliant night of crisp starlight. Never in my life had I been out and about when the world was asleep, and the weird hooting of an owl in the trees of the school close seemed to emphasise the strange otherness of the small hours. There was no further sound except the faint rumble of a night train far away on the main line to Euston. Rugby lay in a frozen sleep.

I climbed over the wall and tapped on the door below the observatory dome. Sparling was already there, half crouching beneath the upturned telescope, and he welcomed me in his usual abrupt but cheerful way. A faint glow came from a lamp beside the sidereal mechanism, and the scene had something of unearthly magic about it. We began the tracking. It was a while before we had located our remote prey, but when at last we had pinned it down we set the clock in motion to keep it continually in our field of view. Saturn, orange gold and wearing at an angle its astonishing halo belt was there before us, so real that it seemed almost as though we could lean out into space and touch it.

We were both enormously moved. I had often seen pictures of this strange planet, but I could never have imagined its sheer beauty. I tried to speak, but could not. Four hundred million miles further out than the mighty Jupiter, Saturn spun there in the brilliance of the light of the sun, a thing of fantastic, glorious grace, seemingly displaying itself just for us two tiny remote mortals.

That glimpse into the hugeness of the universe did more than anything else to widen my vision of nature. I had seen far out into space, and I had seen a beauty that was unearthly, mystical, divine. And all this for the benefit of man, the only creature that could be humbly aware of the wonder of the creation.

But Saturn and the *Ichthyosaurus*, however much they awakened in me a desire to know more about the wonder of the whole creation, were nevertheless remote in both space and time. I could have a vivid impression of each of them, but no more. I could not lay my hands upon their actual being, and it was left to a place called Ainsdale to provide the intimate personal contact with the real, vibrant world of nature of the present.

On the seaward side of the old Lancs and Yorks railway track from Liverpool to Southport there was a vast belt of wasteland, a few hundred yards or so of pine-woods not unlike those of Les Landes near Arcachon, followed on the seaward side by a mile or more of dunes dotted with marram grass and dwarf willow a mere foot in height. A belt of balsam poplar edged the dunes on the woodland side. In all this great tract of wild country there was only one house, a one-storeyed building put there as a shooting-lodge for a former owner. My father had bought this so that we could retreat from the tuberculosis-laden air of St Helens at the week-ends, and to me – as to him – it was a place of inexhaustible discoveries. It seems hardly credible that within the shadow of what was then a great mercantile city and port, such a wonderful desert could have existed, but somehow it had survived.

During the following years we were to spend many weekends and holidays there, and we had the sole and unrestricted run of the huge area of several square miles of rough country, a haunt of long-eared owl and sparrowhawk, of newts courting in the shallow brackish water of the slacks, and of natterjacks whose mysterious caterpillar-tread tracks led over the mountains of blown sand. In spring the marshes were white with *Pyrola*, bog cotton grew all across the wetland, and the sandhills were a paradise for rabbits. But more than anything else the area was a homeland for birds, some of them resident, others migrating northward or southward. Among those that nested in the dunes were the handsome shelduck, always ready to take over the tenancy of premises abandoned by rabbits, and in spring the terns and plovers laid their eggs over the short grass and sand in such numbers that one had to walk, like Agag, delicately. There were nightjars pretending to be rotten logs, and woodcock and bee-eaters flashed through the pines. But my own greatest delight was in the belt of the strong-scented, sticky-budded balsam poplars, for it was on their branches that I could discover the poplar hawk caterpillars, green and solid and well camouflaged, but betrayed by the tell-tale droppings on the clear sand immediately beneath them. There were puss-moth larvae too, which would raise their huge black and red heads in defiance and lash with the pinkish filaments which they could extend from their forked tails when disturbed. And there was a whole catalogue of the prominents, those caterpillars so astonishing in their clever mimicry of bark and twigs. I learned to paint a patch of sugary treacle on a tree and watch at night in fascination as oak eggar and magpie moth and a dozen other species would come to savour the feast.

'Windy Gap' would never have been acquired by my father just as an escape from the dust-laden and chemical atmosphere of St Helens. Certainly it was near the sea and the air was fresh and clean, but it must have been the closeness to nature and the sheer beauty and variety of the flowers in the wilderness of woodland and dune and marsh which attracted him most of all. My father was not a biologist, he was chairman of Pilkingtons. But he loved nature, and wild flowers above all. Appropriately, the memorial window to him in the church at St Helens has *Gentiana verna* and other alpines tucked away in the border, for always he was conscious of the beauty of flowers, and the divine wonder of the excellence of their intricate form and brilliant colour.

I do not believe my father would ever have wished to be a botanist in the sense of one who pulls flowers to pieces to count the stamens. He just appreciated them for their beauty, even if he knew them all by their Latin names. But I was more curious than he. I wanted not just to admire, but to understand. Certainly I did not wish to become a cataloguer and classifier, a systematic taxonomist in the tradition of Linnaeus. I wanted to dive deeper into the mystery of life. I was inquisitive, yet even at that early age my curiosity was somehow tinged with a kind of reverence. I would never knowingly have trodden upon a flower.

THE *SCHWAIGHOFSTRASSE*

In the nineteen-thirties scientific papers were written either in English or in German, and just occasionally in French – in which event they were not read. Hugh Lyon, the headmaster at Rugby, suggested that I should leave a term early and go to a German university to perfect my scientific German. I might even decide to stay on there, he suggested, instead of going up to Cambridge. Thus it was that I alighted one afternoon on the platform of Freiburg-im-Breisgau, ready to attend on the following day the matriculation ceremony of the Albert Ludwigs University.

It was not my first visit to Germany – we had had family holidays in Bavaria and the Black Forest – but my immediate impression was of a kind of mass hysteria. A man with a brown shirt, black boots, hunting breeches and swastika armband rushed toward me and thrust a newspaper at me with a demand for ten pfennigs. I bought the paper. A few yards further ahead another individual in a brown shirt and with the same style of armband pushed a similar newspaper under my nose. Tactfully I bought that too. By the time I reached the station exit I had five identical evening papers, four of which I dropped into the litter-bin before pushing my way through a singing and dancing crowd to the taxi rank. A driver in smart black uniform with silvery facings beckoned to me and opened the door of a big black Horch, very similar to a stately Rolls. I climbed in.

The driver informed me that his name was Stehmann. Alfred Stehmann. As we drove out toward the suburb of Günterstal I asked Stehmann why the streets were thronged with swaying lines of people with linked arms, some of them obviously drunk. Alfred drew in to the kerb. I did not know? No, I had only just arrived, I said. But today was the twentieth of April. That I knew; but what of it?

'*Heute ist des Führers Geburtstag!*'

I said I was sorry not to have known, but inwardly I was relieved that the maniac behaviour was not necessarily to be expected every day.

Stehmann turned to face me over the back of his driver's seat. He rolled up his left sleeve.

'See!' In the flesh of his forearm were displayed the weals of a swastika, about two inches across. 'See! I did it for him, the *Führer*. I did it with this!' He pulled out a dagger and flashed it with pride. 'Yes, I am an SS-man! To become that I had to ride a motorcycle to cover one hundred kilometres in an hour, and ride through a fire, too. Not everyone can do that.'

'No, of course not,' I agreed. 'Well done.'

'And my fiancée, she is proud of me . . .'

'I'm sure she must be.' I was hoping he would drive on, as the meter was ticking away merrily.

'I made her take out all her savings, and I have bought her a part share in a firm that makes flags. We have a new flag, you know. Red, with a *Hakenkreuz*, like all these you see.' He pointed along the street. 'Every house must have at least one. A large one. Many people have several. It is a good business.'

'Very good idea,' I said.

To my relief Stehmann put away his dagger, rolled down his sleeve and set the Horch on course for the Schwaighofstrasse, where I was to lodge with Frau Geheimrat Hofrat Professor Doktor Axenfeld in one of those vast houses that abound on the edges of German cities and seem to have been devised to accommodate families of fifteen or twenty.

The Frau Geheimrat was the widow of Professor Theodor Axenfeld, the eye expert who devised the test still widely used to identify failures in colour vision by having a series of cards printed with a mass of peas in various colours of the spectrum. All that an ophthalmologist needed to do was to flick over the cards and ask the patient what number he saw marked out in peas of one colour against a background of peas of another. Sufferers from various deficiencies saw either an incorrect number, or no number at all.

Left at the professor's death with the large house and a fair-sized family, Frau Axenfeld had sensibly decided to take paying guests, all of whom were students. There was Grace, an Oxford undergraduate who would never touch a glass of beer, let alone wine, and whom Frau Axenfeld genially called *'mein kleines Milchkühlein'*. Then there was Herr Zornbra (his name was actually Thornborough) from Trinity Cambridge, who was so absorbed in the classics that he still thought of the universe and the world around him in terms of earth and air, fire and water.

Petit the Swiss was a strange addition to the household and was hardly a student in the ordinary sense. He was a railway fanatic, and from after breakfast until supper-time he haunted the Freiburg station, train-spotting. Sometimes he would tell us excitedly that he had seen a 4-4-2, and he knew exactly where it had been built, and what were the special characteristics of its boiler. Then there was Leonard, a shy and retiring young man who had been picked by the Foreign Office as one who had the qualities necessary to rise high in the Diplomatic Service, and after his Oxford days had been sent out to Germany to become fluent in the language. Last in the list of paying guests from abroad was myself, but there was also one German. His name was Reinhold Borstmann, and he was nearing the end of his medical studies. He was extremely superior toward foreigners and took no great pains to conceal the fact, whereas the Frau Geheimrat's son Helmuth, a post-graduate medical, was as kind and courteous as could be.

All these, with three grown-up daughters, two domestics and the ageing family nanny Luisa had their own rooms, study-bedrooms in the case of the guests, and all these opened off the balconies which ran round three sides of the vast central hall, on the first and second floors. The establishment was a large one in every way.

Frau Axenfeld was ample in every direction, and she had a natural aristocratic charm. She had a sweet and kindly face, and I could see that as a girl she must have been good-looking. In the drawing-room she held informal court, sitting alone on the sofa, for to sit on the sofa without being invited to do so was as much of a breach of etiquette in Germany as it would be to poke the fire in another's house in England.

Dinner on my first evening in Freiburg was at seven, earlier than usual. The meal proceeded pleasantly and informally, although Borstmann sometimes interrupted the conversation to speed the meal along. He kept looking at his watch and saying that we must be quick, and he even peremptorily told the maid that there would be no time for coffee. But there he was wrong. Frau Axenfeld ordered the coffee to be brought in, but to avoid open unpleasantness we drank it somewhat hurriedly.

It was nearly eight when we adjourned to the sewing-room, a bleak little work-room with an elderly sewing-machine, the second-best chairs, and a wireless. I could not understand why we had to be crowded into this small space, and the Frau Geheimrat seemed to sense my perplexity.

'He will be speaking in a moment,' she said quietly, as she signed to one of the others to turn on the wireless.

'He, Frau Geheimrat? Who?' It seemed to me a natural question, but it caused Borstmann to explode.

'Who? Who do you think?' His voice rattled like a machine-gun.

I simply could not imagine. After all, I had only been in the country a few hours and I had no idea who were the celebrities in radio, or football, or films. I said as much to Borstmann. He clicked his heels sharply with a sound like a pistol shot, raised his arm toward the chandelier and shouted at me.

'The *Führer*!!!'

One or two of the family escaped on some pretext or other. The rest of us waited uneasily and Petit the Swiss passed me a bottle of beer. 'You'll need it,' he whispered. I sat on the floor and leaned back against the wall. After a crashing of brass bands, The Voice began. It was guttural, rising to crescendos and falling away again, rather bumpkinish but at the same time curiously mesmerising. I drank the beer and closed my eyes.

What awoke me after fifty-four minutes (Borstmann had timed him) was that Hitler had come to an end. There were tears on the Frau Geheimrat's face. Borstmann was glaring at me with death-ray eyes. His arm shot out toward me.

'You were asleep!' He too was, I very soon discovered, an SS-man, one of the adoring elite who would carry out any order *unbedingt und gehorsam*, unconditionally and obediently. He could not comprehend that anyone, even if they had been sitting up all night in a train as I had, could possibly doze through Hitler's birthday speech. Nor indeed could the Frau Geheimrat. She was genuinely distressed by what I had done.

'You do not understand,' she said. 'It is a new Germany . . . a new world . . . a new age. The old order is gone. A new spirit is born.' She broke off and quietly left the room. The others had all left, except for her eldest daughter, Dorothea.

As soon as the door was closed Dorothea began to shake with suppressed laughter. Then, seeing my bewildered expression, she shook her head.

'No,' she said. 'I was not laughing at you. It was just . . . the relief after all these weeks. Four months, nearly.' Suddenly she became very serious. 'What *is* it? Why does it take people that way? Good people, honest people like my mother, like the others down the street. Why? Borstmann – I am not surprised about him. He has nothing up here.' She tapped her forehead. 'Nothing. No, but everyone else. They are not stupid, and yet this . . . this *Führer* has them in his hand. How? Why do they lose their reason the moment he speaks? You heard what he said – no, of course you did not hear much of it because you slept. But I can tell you that there was nothing, nothing but hatred and lies. I too was listening to him, and I had to fight to prevent myself being drawn out of myself. And then I looked round and saw you were asleep. You actually snored!'

'I'm sorry,' I said.

'No! No! Please don't say that. For eleven weeks since the *Machtübernahme* we have all been mad. Mad. But tonight, on the *Führer*'s birthday, to see that there are still people in the world who can go to sleep while he is shouting and raving – do you know, that is the only happy thing that has happened in this house?' She paused, and sighed. 'My mother talks of a new age. Yes, yes. Certainly. But not an age fit for humans to live in . . . unless . . .'

'Unless?'

'Unless they are like Borstmann,' she said simply.

TWO PROFESSORS

As a new student I had to be properly enrolled at the University Registry. The first step was to acquire a Certificate of Arian Ancestry, without which it would not be possible to enter the university except under circumstances which were less than pleasant. I had to write down the names of all my grandparents and swear that they were not Jewish; my word was then taken for the facts I gave, and a certificate was issued. This procedure took no more than a few minutes, but as the student behind me in the queue was a Japanese I waited outside the door to see how he got on with proving himself to be of pure Arian ancestry.

Sure enough, he came out a minute or so after me, with the certificate in his hand.

'Are you classified as an Arian?' I asked him, surprised.

'Sure.' He showed me the certificate. It only differed from mine in that 'Honorary' had been inserted before the word 'Arian'.

Next I was given a cursory medical examination and provided with a certificate of fitness to follow any sport that I might wish. In fact the university did not have any organised sports, but it was pleasant to know that I could have played them if they had existed. Then, with these formalities accomplished we were given a list of all the university lectures available, and told that a student might choose those that he wished, and make up his own timetable. The only exception was that one particular course of lectures was compulsory for all foreign students. It was somewhat naively entitled 'German History for Foreigners', and it consisted of weekly lectures by Professor Heinrich Felsentraeger.

Felsentraeger was a rather angular individual with receding hair and sunken cheeks. Aged about forty, he was one of the new-style professors of the Third Reich. In the introductory session he stressed to us the vital importance of a proper understanding of Germany history, pointing out that it was by no means a matter of dates and the periods of successive governments. The real history could only be properly grasped within the philosophical concepts of National Socialism, and so he intended in the succeeding lectures to deal in detail with the pioneers. During the following week we would go back, not to the very beginnings – that was reserved for the second week – but to consider the life and work and philosophy of the second in the train of great National Socialist thinkers.

So the next lecture was to be on National Socialist Number Two, and as the days went by I wondered who this was going to be. The bombastic Hermann Goering perhaps. It could hardly be Ernst Röhm (he was soon to be murdered in the Night of the Long Knives), because none could seriously think of him as a philosopher at all. So could it perhaps be dear old Hindenburg, fresh from laying hands on a seventh child of a seventh child?

I discussed the matter over a glass of beer with other newcomers, but none of us could be sure of the answer. Some said Nietzsche, others Schopenhauer. And what chance Immanuel Kant? These were the only philosophers we had heard of. But none of us guessed aright, for at the lecture next week National Socialist Number Two turned out to be none other than William Shakespeare.

We listened spellbound to a lecture which was anything but boring. Felsentraeger proved his selection by one quotation after another, drawing particularly heavily on certain passages in *The Merchant of Venice*, and though I cannot recollect all the twists and turns of his reasoning, I was determined not to miss the lecture in the following week, when we were to be given the run-down on National Socialist Number One.

During the next few days we again discussed the probabilities of who this might be. As the original founder of National Socialism he must obviously pre-date Shakespeare, something that took us far back into the murky Middle Ages. We agreed that for tactical reasons he would have to be of German origin, and the only candidates that sprang to mind were old Friedrich Barbarossa of the red beard, he that was reputed to rise from the dead once every century to see if the ravens were still flying around – in which case he could relax for another hundred years because Germany was safe – or Attila, chief of the Huns, victor over all nations from the Rhine to China. Or maybe the mighty Hermann who massacred the Roman legions in the Teutoburger forest. None of these seemed a safe bet, so we had to wait. Once again we were in for a surprise. The real genuine founder of National Socialism turned out to be a man of whom I had never heard, a hydraulic engineer and fountain-builder who later took to painting. His name was Mathis Nithardt, though as official painter to the Archbishop Elector of Mainz he became known as Matthias Grünewald. He lived in the early fifteen hundreds, not too far in advance of Shakespeare, and various of his paintings still existed, one of them actually in Freiburg itself. But his greatest work of all, Felsentraeger explained, and one which illustrated vividly the birth of National Socialist philosophy, was the polyptych painted for the altar of the Monastery of the Antonites at Isenheim. He was the one who introduced into art the sheer truth and realism which were to be the great hallmarks of National Socialism.

Professor Felsentraeger expanded for the rest of the hour upon this theme and also explained that the villainous French had robbed Germany of the pictures under a clause in the Treaty of Versailles and had spirited them away to Colmar. (This of course was patently untrue. Isenheim, where the monastery of the Antonites lay for which Grünewald had painted his most famous work, was then as now in Alsace. So was Colmar. The Germans had captured Alsace in the Franco-Prussian War, but they had been forced to return the territory to France in 1919, and once again in 1945.)

Though I did not follow the whole of the argument, there remained firmly implanted in me, probably in my subconscious, a determination one day to see the Isenheim altarpiece for myself. But it was to be more than a quarter of a century before this wish actually came true.

The list of optional extras handed out at matriculation contained few that particularly appealed to me, my days at the Zoological Laboratory in the Katharinenstrasse being already well filled with lectures and practical work, but there was nevertheless one which seemed to suit my interest in all things living, and so I enrolled for *'Einheimisches Tier – und Pflanzenleben'* (Indigenous Fauna and Flora). It was to be a course of weekly lectures conducted by Professor Asschenheimer. Not formal lectures, as it turned out, but excursions. It was not a class-room affair at all, but a practical demonstration and commentary upon the plants and animals of the region.

Early in the morning we would assemble at the Schlageterdenkmal at the end of the Adolf Hitlerstrasse, formerly the Kaiserstrasse. Albert Leo Schlageter had been a student who ended up being shot by the French for derailing trains, and had thus become a national hero about whom Hitler's favourite playwright had written a play. There, at the memorial, we were to await the professor.

Professor Asschenheimer had a beard larger than Charles Darwin's, and a high domed head which hinted (correctly, as I soon discovered) at immense knowledge and wisdom. He was as polished as Linnaeus, but more modest – he was not, like that eminent Swede, accompanied by trumpeters who blew a fanfare when he was about to speak. He was as gentle as Gilbert White of Selborne and as reverent as that early member of the Royal Society John Ray. He wore a deep black cape and a broad-brimmed hat that would have suited the Quangle-

Wangle-Quee. He was almost a caricature of the old-style naturalist, yet even to smile at his appearance would have been impossible. His mere presence commanded instant and genuine respect.

The professor would arrive just as the clock struck eight, and sweep off his broad hat in greeting. To the girls he would bow with such genteel courtesy that they were impelled to curtsey rather clumsily in reply. He would then draw out an antique gold watch, study it curiously, listen to make sure that it was going (it had never stopped during the half century that it had been in his pocket) and replace it. Then with a soft 'So!' he would turn and head off briskly toward the edge of the town, with us at his heels.

From the moment we set out, the professor never stopped talking for more than a few seconds. His voice flowed gently in the most perfect high German that was a sheer joy to hear, and never for an instant was he boring. At nearly eighty his sharp ears picked up the slightest sound – a distant willow-warbler, the hesitant footstep of a hedgehog in the undergrowth, the faintest click of the elytra of a beetle. Nothing escaped his notice. The smallest insect, an aberration in the veins of a leaf on a wayside bush, all these he noticed and discoursed upon as he forged ahead in the hot sunshine with ourselves struggling to keep up with him.

Sometimes we covered only a few miles, but on other occasions our circuit might be twelve or fifteen. Always at exactly the right moment he would stop, with another soft 'So!'. Then he would draw out from under his cloak the spotless white serviette which contained his lunch. We flopped down on the ground to rest, but the professor invariably continued to stand, interrupting his meal to explain the chemistry of the pigment of an orchid or the mating behaviour of a curious worm that he had seen under a bush.

It was Asschenheimer who introduced me to *Gordius*, the worm so-called because it indulges in the peculiar habit of tying itself in a knot as complex as that of the Phrygian king. It was he who managed to find a pair of *Helix pomatia*, the edible snail, engaged in the curious erotic stimulation produced by firing a little crystal arrow, the *Liebespfeile*, into the flesh of the hermaphrodite suitor. And it was he who took us to see the ant-lions in the sandy banks of a vineyard track. The ant-lion, *Myrmeleon formicarius*, was not a giant mammal or even an ant-eater, but a neuropteran insect. Somewhat like a dragonfly in the adult, the larva had the engaging habit of wriggling its thick rear end into the sandy soil and digging deeper by throwing up the sand with a jerk of its flat-topped head. In this ingenious way it would make a crater, the walls of which were of course at the critical angle of stability, and at the bottom it would burrow down, tail-end first, until only the pair of sharp jaws remained protruding from the sand. Sooner or later an ant would blunder over the edge of the crater and try to scramble out, merely dislodging sand-grains as it did so. The ant-lion would then jerk upward the flat top of its head and fire sand at the ant until at last the victim slid right down into the waiting jaws. After it had been sucked dry of the juicy contents, the hard exterior, which was all that now remained of the ant, would be fired right out of the crater by the spring-like flat head. The whole process was extremely ingenious, and of course it raised problems for those who really believed in the step-like mutation mechanism of evolution. The ant-lion's crater and ejection mechanism, the jaws and flat head-top had all to be working together before the creature was in any way efficient, and it was difficult to see how any one of these components could have been selected without the others.

Since then I have often encountered ant-lions, because I had learned to notice the little craters which they make in suitable ground, but without Asschenheimer's introduction to them I would probably never even have noticed them.

Professor Asschenheimer was a figure from the past. Within his immense head he held a complete library of knowledge which covered the most astonishing details of every living thing that walked, crept, flew or rooted in the ground. He was never stumped, not once. He knew the group, class, order, genus and species of everything that we encountered, its behaviour and life-cycle, its haunts and habitat. I knew even then that this gracious man would probably be the last of a dying race, for already the complete naturalist, the 'Natural Philosopher' of earlier times, was almost extinct. So much had science expanded that even by that time the scientist who hoped to reach the top had to concentrate upon his own ever narrower line to the exclusion of others, with the result that his knowledge of even adjacent matters might be quite sketchy. Besides, the style of science itself was changing fast. The habit of observing nature was rapidly being replaced in so many fields by the tendency to dissect, to isolate an organ and to study the reactions of fragments rather than the life of a whole intriguing creature.

Whenever I was there among Professor Asschenheimer's flock I had a sense of this changing pattern of knowledge, and I had a fear that he would die before the next weekly outing, his immense store of wisdom and knowledge perishing with him. Yet every week he was there again, with his watch and his white serviette and a vigour that shamed the newer generation that accompanied him on his walks, and whom he filled with a reverent interest in their fellow-creatures which would remain with some of them throughout their lives.

THE SUMMER TERM

An academic term at Oxbridge began, as I was soon to discover, without any shouting or tumult. There was Term, and there was Full Term, and it was when this latter began that lectures also started. But there was no ceremony, nothing beside obscure committee meetings of dons or sports and dramatic societies. To the outside world the dividing line between vacation and term-time was hardly visible.

But in Germany things were very different, and on the first day of term we had to go to the Aula, the main university building. As I went in I was approached by a pleasant, tall young man, who told me that his name was Friedrich, and he was one of the students appointed to single out the foreigners and see that they were at home in what went on. The Aula was packed to capacity and beyond, and Friedrich led me up to the back to perch on the sill of an open window – a very wise precaution, because during the next couple of hours the carbon dioxide content of the air increased by several percentage points.

The proceedings were opened by the *Rektor*, Martin Heidegger, who addressed the students at length. He was Hitler's favourite philosopher, although I doubt if Adolf the Great could make any more head or tail of his philosophy than I could. Indeed, the Biographical Dictionary remarks rather pointedly that 'some British philosophers have found his linguistic innovations such as "nothing noth" insuperable.' He was, apparently, not concerned with personal existence, though he talked for a long time about the synthesis of various types of human existence or *Dasein*. At least I think so, but after forty minutes of not paying much attention I fell asleep, and so did

Friedrich. We were awoken by the thunderous applause, probably of relief that he had come to an end.

Next the university orchestra played Brahms' *Academic Overture*, with its well known final chorus of *Gaudeamus Igitur* – which, curiously enough, I knew well enough because we used to sing that ditty at the end of term at my prep school in Worcestershire. Then came the *Horst Wessel Song*, and finally *Deutschland über Alles*, to Haydn's splendid tune 'Austria', which was more familiar to me as the melody of John Newton's hymn *Glorious things of thee are spoken, Zion, city of our God*. Actually there is nothing offensive about that national anthem. It does not mean (as so often asserted in Britain) Germany on top of everything; it means I love Germany above everything.

A lot of brilliance was added to the ceremony by the student societies, many of which attended in groups wearing their special colours and with great tasselled standards held by their leaders. These so-called *Verbindungen* were newly re-established in their original form. They had formerly been to a great extent duelling societies, and under the Weimar Republic duelling had been at first discouraged, then forbidden. But Adolf the Great considered duelling a manly activity which developed the sort of character he wanted to see developed, and he rescinded that particular law. But duelling was not a compulsory activity, or I would have been on the first train bound for Britain.

The *Verbindungen* were of three types. There were the *Schlagende und Farbentragende*, duelling and colour-wearing, and it was they who made most of the colour at the ceremony in the Aula. Then there were the *Nichtschlagende und Farbentragende*, who were decorative but did not duel, and finally the *Nichtschlagende und Nicht Farbentragende*, which were not colourful and led an ordinary peaceful existence like any university or college society in Britain. Some of these were actually religious foundations, and Friedrich belonged to such a one and frequently had me come along to their meetings at which we drank beer and chatted. We did not even *Heil Hitler* when we met together.

The duelling was a curious business, and probably appealed to the worst kind of Junkerish student. A member had to fight a certain number of serious (no visor worn) duels with a rapier every year. The only way to get into a position where one could fight such a duel was by insulting a suitable person (that is, another *Schlagende und Farbentragende* man) so that he threw down a glove, of which he was sure to carry one about his person for just such an occasion. The glove was then picked up, the challenge was accepted, seconds were appointed, and a date was fixed for the duel about six weeks or a month ahead, in the private duelling gymnasium of one of the *Verbindungen* involved.

I only once saw the glove-throwing business. It happened in the Friedrichsbau, my favourite beer-haunt in the town. A student (wearing his coloured cap) collided gently with a waiter when he was bound for the toilet. The bump caused a little beer to slop from a tankard the waiter was carrying, and it landed on the jacket of another student, who similarly belonged to a *Schlagende* society and no doubt was itching for a chance to issue a challenge. Which he did. He leapt to his feet, a picture of outraged dignity, and flung down the gauntlet. I used to watch for these two in the street after a few weeks, and eventually I saw them again. They both had received satisfactory gashes on their cheeks; at least I presume so, because they were covered with sticking plaster.

Now one might think that the object of a duel was to slash the opponent and remain unscathed. But no. It was essential during the course of one's student career to acquire three or four or more slashes across the cheek. Salt could then be rubbed into the wounds to make them heal badly and leave unsightly weals, of which the owner was proud. Such disfiguring scars can be seen in photographs of German diplomats or military men of earlier days; but I never saw such marks on an academic. Not even on Felsentraeger.

I happened one day to come across my taxi-driver SS-man acquaintance, Alfred Stehmann. In the course of conversation he told me that he had been challenged to a duel. A member of a duelling society had asked Stehmann to take him somewhere in his taxi, and at the destination this man had jumped out and run off without paying. Alfred gave chase, overtook him, and seized him by the collar, at which the student produced a glove and threw it down.

I thought it rather disgraceful, and certainly not cricket (but maybe duelling) to challenge an untrained member of the public, and I said so.

Alfred shook his head and smiled, 'Maybe you are right, but I took up the challenge.'

'You're an idiot. He only did it to pick a quarrel and fill up his duelling quota. You should have socked him on the jaw.'

Alfred shook his head. 'I am not afraid,' he said. And he went on to explain that he had opted for sabres as weapons.

Stehmann happened to know that this young man's *Verbindung* was almost literally daggers drawn with another such society, so he had gone round to their clubroom and told them what had happened. They at once suggested that they would give him two hours' expert tuition every evening for the next six weeks, then he would be a formidable opponent.

A little more than six weeks later I saw Alfred sitting in his Horch outside the railway station.

'Well, how did it go?' I asked. I could not see any cuts on his face. 'Did you give him the slashes across the cheek that he wanted?'

'No. I side-stepped, and I sliced off his nose with my first blow. Then they stopped the fight.'

*   *   *   *

Although Friedrich was nominally a Commander in the Storm Troops, this probably signified no more than that he was a mature student and somewhat senior. He was not one to rave about the party congress at Nuremberg, nor was he in any way anti-Jewish. He was just a pleasant and very ordinary fellow. But every now and again he had to dress up in his outfit, as did many others, because it was some special day in the National Socialist calendar. And it was on one such day that he invited me to go with him to a concert. I had no hesitation in saying yes, as it was Furtwängler conducting Beethoven's *Ninth Symphony*, and Arthur Schnabel playing the *Emperor Concerto*.

'Wonderful,' I murmured inadequately as we emerged from the hall and cut across the Platz into the darkness of the park.

'Yes. But then Furtwängler is a great man. Shall we wrestle?'

Storm-troop Commandant Friedrich Klempe's jackboots were so highly polished that they reflected the moonlight as we walked. He clinked a bit, too, with all his buckles and brass.

'Wrestle?' Wrestling was hardly my idea of a conclusion to an evening of culture. Besides, I had no idea how it was done, but as he had paid for the concert tickets I did not like to decline.

Friedrich said that he was going to represent his *Verbindung* in a wrestling contest. It was to be Grecian wrestling, of the kind we sometimes watched in the Friedrichsbau, a reasonably clean game with no grabbing below the waist. Friedrich said that in fact he was not a wrestler at all, or not really – although he had tried a few bouts now and then. However, he was sadly out of practice, and so he was asking me whether I would mind giving him a few minutes of wrestling, just to loosen him up.

'Try and throw me, and then hold me down. Here, between these bushes. Then we shall not be seen,' he said.

Unwillingly I took up my position and a moment later we were locked in a friendly clinch. Panting and heaving we swayed backward and forward until at last Friedrich lost his balance and I forced him down on the grass and thrust his shoulders over the edge of a flower-bed. Suddenly he relaxed his grip on me and whispered urgently. 'Let go. Let me go.'

Thinking that he must be hurt, I released my hold, and he wriggled clear. To my astonishment he leapt up and disappeared between the bushes. At the same moment a sharp shout from behind made me jump.

'*Hände hoch*! Hands above your head and turn round.'

Automatically I obeyed, and turned to see a thick-set policeman in a cape and wearing the sort of inverted coal-bucket headgear that was then current. He was pointing a stubby revolver at my stomach.

'Drop your hands and I shoot,' he exclaimed. 'About turn, and quick march. I shall direct you. *Los!*'

It was about a quarter of a mile to the police station and before long my arms were beginning to ache, but I kept them up. As we passed along the streets a few people paused to watch, but they showed no great interest. I wondered vaguely what was going to happen, and remembering how Jerome's Harris had got into trouble for stepping over a park fence, I thought that perhaps the Germans didn't like people to rough-and-tumble on the municipal grass.

Inside the police station I was searched for weapons and led before the inspector. A dozen policemen were in attendance and I was at last allowed to drop my weary arms.

'Very serious business, Sir,' reported the constable. 'He was attempting to strangle a senior officer of the Storm Troops. Yes, to strangle him – *so*.' He demonstrated in the air in front of him. 'Fortunately I heard the sounds of struggling, or the officer would not have been able to escape with his life.'

I discovered later that it would have been most undignified for Friedrich to have been seen in such a position in uniform. The situation had a curious unreality about it, but I was not scared. I knew that it would only be a matter of a short while before the police could ring Friedrich and discover the truth.

The inspector strode over and for a moment I thought he was going to strike me, but he merely peered closely into my eye and smelt my breath. I giggled quite involuntarily.

'Quite sober,' the inspector pronounced professionally. 'You have disarmed him?'

'He had no weapons, Sir. He was attacking the officer with his bare hands.' Once again the policeman made strangling motions in the air.

The inspector looked at me with interest. 'A dangerous type of assassin, obviously,' he pronounced. 'Your prompt action was very commendable. Have him locked up.'

At this moment a voice from near the door interrupted the proceedings.

'There is a mistake.' The policemen all turned round to see who had spoken. It was a man of about thirty-five, wearing a macintosh and a trilby hat, and he was quietly confident. 'The constable must have taken the wrong person,' he continued blandly. 'I have known the prisoner for many years, and he would never do such a thing. He is heart and soul behind the *Führer* and the *Reich*. The constable has made a mistake.'

I had never seen the man before in my life, but I realized that this was not the moment to say so, and I tried to look as though dedicated heart and soul to the *Führer*.

Rather to my surprise the inspector treated the man with obvious respect and addressed him as '*Herr Doktor*'. He then looked dubiously at the constable whose prompt action he had so recently commended, but the constable stood stiffly by his assertion.

'There can be no mistake, Sir. He was carrying out a murderous assault, and I arrested him at pistol point.' But my advocate was not to be put off. He smiled condescendingly and shook his head. 'The constable is mistaken, Inspector. My friend would never do such a thing. His loyalty is quite beyond question. I will vouch for him personally.'

The inspector nodded. 'Of course, *Herr Doktor*. Clearly there has been a mistake. Perhaps the darkness . . .'

A minute or two later I was walking up the Adolf Hitlerstrasse, no longer a dangerous assassin but a free man. I walked three blocks before stepping into the doorway of a cafe to wait for my benefactor.

'Come and have a glass of wine,' I suggested as he came up.

Over one of those good German glasses of Kaiserstühler which only make just three to a bottle, he introduced himself. He was a *Privat-dozent*, a species of university don. He had seen the constable marching me through the streets and he had simply followed out of curiosity and had come into the police-station behind us.

'Weren't you taking a very serious risk to vouch for a total stranger?' I asked.

He smiled modestly. 'Life is full of risks,' he replied.

'But you had no idea at all what I had been up to.'

He dismissed the matter with a wave of his hand. 'I do not wish to know. It is no business of mine.'

'Well, I can assure you that I was not trying to strangle a high-ranking officer of the Storm Troops as the policeman alleged.'

He nodded. 'Yes, I thought there had been a mistake.' With a sigh he helped himself to some more wine. 'It was perhaps just the faint hope that it was really true that prompted me to speak.'

I asked the *Herr Doktor* for his address, and he gave me his card. And that was to prove very useful, because about a month later I was walking home around midnight when I saw a body lying in the flowing gutter. (Freiburg had some of these, similar to the Pem and the Pot of Cambridge). I crossed the road to have a look, and rolled the body on to the pavement. It was my friend the

Herr Doktor. He had not been murdered; he was just plastered to the state of unconsciousness.

One good turn . . . I thought. And then I had an idea. I went to a nearby phone box and summoned SS-man Stehmann to come up from the station with his taxi.

Alfred looked at the unconscious man, who was snoring and gasping.

'Do you know who he is?' he asked.

'Yes. He is a Party member,' I said. He is absolutely devoted to the *Führer*. But just now he is incapable, and we have to take him home to his lodgings.'

We loaded the *Herr Doktor* into the Horch and drove him home. He had two rooms on the first floor of a lodging house, but together we managed to carry him up the stairs. He was rather a wet burden, still dripping from the rivulet in the street, so I thought we should undress him, wrap him in a clean blanket, and ease him into bed. The whole time he never regained consciousness, but his breathing was regular and satisfactory.

I left a note on the bed:– *Undressed and put to bed by Roger with the help of SS-man Alfred Stehmann.* I thought he would like that.

And Alfred was very decent about the incident, too. He refused any payment for the services of his taxi in taking the *Herr Doktor* home.

REINHOLD BORSTMANN

It was a few weeks after my arrival at the house in the Schwaighofstrasse that Leonard, who had been reading the handbook of diplomatic procedure issued to Foreign Office trainees, invited me into his room.

'That chap Borstmann,' he said. 'I suppose he's quite a good sort really.'

'What makes you suddenly think that?' I asked.

'Nothing really. Of course he's not one of my particular friends.'

'No?'

'But he's – well, clean in a way,' Leonard said. 'Mind you, he ought to be, with all those cold baths. But I've a sort of feeling he's not overbright.'

'No, I suppose not,' I agreed.

'Of course he's not so easy to get on with as . . . well, Thornborough, and Petit.'

'No. He's a curious fellow,' I said, trying to keep within Leonard's officially correct mode of expression. 'In fact I sometimes wonder whether he isn't a bit conceited.'

Leonard took some time to reply. He rummaged in his desk to find a bag of toffees. 'I think that on the whole you have a point there,' he said at length. 'Tell me, what do you really think of him?'

'Well, if you really want to know, I think he's about the nastiest cold-blooded reptile that ever crept.'

Leonard looked out of the window, as though pondering his reply.

'I'm glad you think that,' he said. 'That has been my feeling about him for some time. We must do something about it. Get rid of him.' He saw my surprise. 'I don't mean murder him or anything of that sort. Just . . . well, in a case like this,' Leonard continued leaning back in his chair like a specialist doctor, 'in a case like this, the current practice in diplomacy is to soften up the subject with repeated pin-pricks. Not actual pins, of course, but minor attacks of a mild yet profoundly irritating form which can prey upon the nerves.'

'Such as?'

'Well, I happen to have purchased this gramophone record.'

He opened his desk and carefully lifted out a ten-inch disc. Leonard went on to explain that Borstmann leapt to his feet and stood at attention with arm raised whenever the *Horst Wessel Lied* boomed out of the wireless, and we could well take advantage of this habit.

And so we did. In the hall there stood a radiogram. Every evening when Borstmann was due to return to the house one of us was there with the machine ready to run, and Leonard's ten-inch of the *Horst Wessel Song* played by the massed bands of the SS all set to go.

The first evening Leonard released the brake as soon as Borstmann entered the front door, and the strains froze him to stiff attention on the mat. Clearly he thought it was good for us to hear such a piece, because he complimented Leonard on buying the record.

The next night we let him reach half way up the first flight of stairs before we struck him to a halt, and the third evening we froze him on the gallery, just outside his bedroom door. By this time Borstmann's suspicions were aroused, but his loyalty to the *Führer* was such that nothing would have induced him to move during the playing of the sacred song. Instead, he tried to beat us by stealth, or speed. Once he came in through the front door and took the first flight of stairs four at a time in an effort to reach his room before the needle had hissed its way round the silent introductory grooves, and another time he came in by the back door and through the kitchen.

After a few days we varied the system by introducing other and quite harmless records, and this unnerved him considerably. He had to run, in case it should be the *Horst*

Wessel Lied, yet if it were merely a yodel he looked extremely foolish; and since he could never admit that we were amusing ourselves at his expense he always had to have a reason for his lightning ascent of the stairs.

'*Mein Gott!*' he would exclaim, brushing the Frau Geheimrat out of the way as he met her on a bend of the flight. 'I must hurry for my bath.'

We kept this game up for a week or more, and Borstmann carried it off with considerable ability. Nevertheless the strain was beginning to tell, and I saw what Leonard meant by repeated pin-pricks which could prey upon the nerves. Then one night Borstmann left the house very quietly at about ten o'clock, and Leonard decided from the evidence – the stealth, the special dose of hair-oil and the clean trousers – that he was meeting a young lady. This meant that he would probably be returning very late.

We checked on the family and the guests. Everyone was already in, except Petit and an Italian lady. At half-past eleven Petit returned. He was anxious to tell us all about the locomotive of the night express to Berlin, but we gave him rather a cool reception, so as to get him off to bed. Shortly after midnight the Italian lady returned alone, and somewhat drunk. We eased her up the stairs before we settled down to wait.

As expected, we heard the Frau Geheimrat open her door. She leaned over the balcony, an imposing figure in her flowing dressing-gown.

'Not in bed yet?'

'No, Frau Geheimrat. We both have important work to do.'

She sighed in a kindly manner. 'You poor things. All this study. Good night then.'

She retired to her room, and the house was ours. I tiptoed upstairs to bring the clothes line which we had procured for the occasion, and taking off our shoes we got to work to set the stage for Borstmann's return. We moved the radiogram to near the front door and put the massed bands in position, setting the dial to 'repeat'.

Leonard produced from his pocket a packet of needles marked 'Extra loud. For public performance and outdoor work.'

It need much trial and error to have the mechanism perfect. On the inside handle of the front door we placed a loop of string, from which hung two heavy dictionaries. When the outside handle was turned the loop would slide off, the books would fall and jerk violently another string which passed over the back of an armchair to the brake release on the radiogram. Then we braced the clothes line across the centre of the door so that it could open an inch or two to allow the relay to work, but not far enough to admit an SS-man, and then with a final burst of inspiration Leonard climbed around on the furniture and removed the lamps from every light-fitting in the hall and up the stairs. Then we retired quietly to our rooms to wait.

I stayed awake until two, waiting for Borstmann's return, but eventually I dozed off. It was a quarter past three when the massed bands of the SS struck up. Leonard's special needle was magnificent. The tubas could have been in my bedroom.

Almost at once there were sounds of movement. Then came the voice of the Frau Geheimrat, loudly raised against the blaring of the brass.

'Who is it? What is it that is happening?'

We were all out on the balcony by now, but as none could turn on the lights nobody seemed inclined to venture down below, for the booming of the band was accompanied by queer scrabbling noises from the corner by the front door.

There was still no answer to the Frau Geheimrat's call, so she repeated it in a shrill, demanding cry. 'Who is it that is down there?'

'It's me, Reinhold.' He sounded out of breath, and his voice lacked its usual bounce and confidence.

'You, Herr Borstmann? Then you will stop making that noise! You have woken the whole household.'

No answer came, however, except that the brass bands struck up a fresh verse. The scuffling sounds near the door grew louder.

'Are you out of your senses?' The Frau Geheimrat's voice was shrill with anger, tinged with alarm. 'Stop that horrible din!' But the music still played.

'I cannot, Frau Geheimrat,' came Borstmann's voice rather faintly through the music. There followed a rattling as he tried to squeeze through the door.

It was too much for the Frau Geheimrat. 'He's drunk! He's drunk!' she exclaimed in horror. 'To think that one of my own guests should make this drunken din and wake us all from our beds!' And with that she retreated to her room and slammed the door.

By now the domestics had joined the rest, and fifteen people were peering over the rails into the gloom below. The record came to an end, and began the second round.

'For heaven's sake, man,' cried Thornborough into the void, 'take your accursed brass band away. We don't want to hear it all night.'

Now Borstmann, being an SS-man, had a ceremonial dagger about his person, and he had the sense to pull it out and slash vigorously at the clothes line which barred his progress. Bursting through the door he fell over a chair, and swore. One of the maids screamed.

'It's shocking,' said Grace. 'And in front of ladies, too.'

Thornborough had slipped back into his room and he now reappeared with a bicycle lamp. Its thin beam revealed the terrifying spectacle of a dishevelled Borstmann scrambling to his feet, in his hand a dagger.

The house-maid and cook-girl shrieked, and in the dim light thrown back from Thornborough's beam I saw the nanny crossing herself. It was the Frau Geheimrat's son Helmuth who took charge of the situation.

'All the ladies return to their rooms,' he instructed. He then took the lamp from Thornborough and advanced to the head of the stairs as the SS massed bands struck up once more. Keeping the lamp trained on the creature below, Helmuth spoke authoritatively.

'Reinhold! Put down that knife,' he ordered.

The SS-man obeyed, and dropped his dagger.

'Now turn off the gramophone.' He did so, meekly. 'Upstairs to your room immediately, and not another sound. Stand back, everybody, he's drunk.'

With surprisingly sober step Borstmann marched up the stairs, head erect. I fancied there was a rather unpleasant look in his eye, but he said nothing as he turned past us along the balcony toward his room.

What he had to say, he said in the morning. He was waiting in the hall when Leonard and I came down to breakfast together. Six people already had reproved him for his inebriate and unseemly behaviour, we discovered.

'It was you!' He darted his steely eyes at each of us in turn. Then, as we did not deny it, 'An SS-man would never do such a thing.'

'No,' said Leonard cautiously. 'Probably not.'

Borstmann seemed at a loss how to proceed. We waited for it, standing on the bottom stair, and at last it came.

'I do not wish to be friends with you any longer,' he hissed. He clicked his heels, turned round sentry-fashion and departed.

Unfortunately the whole household was very amused by the figure he had cut on the previous evening, and so he had to ostracize the entire company. He would march past with head erect and gaze averted, and the only member of the household with whom he tried to establish good relations was the Frau Geheimrat. But she never accepted that there was any explanation other than that he was revoltingly drunk.

Yet Borstmann stayed on in the Schwaighofstrasse, and he was still there when I left. I never saw him again, but twelve years later I had a letter from the eighty-five year old nanny Luisa Fleig, who in the cellar of the small house that she had bought with her savings in the little Black Forest town of St Georgen had survived the savage bombardment which came just before the end of the war. She sent me news of all the family.

'*I do not know if you will remember Herr Borstmann,*' she added in a postscript. '*He was in Stalingrad and did not return.*'

And that, I felt, was probably the memorial he would have wished for.

THE METEORITE

The main reason for most of the guests staying with the Frau Geheimrat in the Schwaighofstrasse was that they wished to perfect their German. To satisfy their desire for conversation the Frau Geheimrat employed an impecunious German student, who was somewhat older than the rest of the student household. Joachim Stiegler had a rather unhealthy complexion, but he had no doubts whatsoever about his ability in conversation. He was given two marks a day and his supper, and in return for this meagre salary he was expected to make conversation from after lunch until late in the evening, when he left.

Stiegler certainly earned his money from the point of view of talking, but it hardly amounted to conversation because nobody else had a chance to speak. He ran like a long-playing record, tirelessly and monotonously, and if we quietly slid out of the door to escape he would pursue us without apparently pausing for breath. On one of these occasions Petit the Swiss and Grace and myself were so desperate that we ran out of the house and boarded a passing tram in the Günterstalstrasse nearby. But Stiegler just managed to scramble into the trailer wagon, and as we were forced to get out at the end of the line he was there, ready to continue.

Stiegler had of course not just to talk but to talk about something, and we thought that he sat up all night reading a popular encyclopedia to be ready, tanked up to capacity, on the following afternoon. He was actually a chemistry student, but he would bore away by the hour on music, country customs, geology or economics. He was omniscient, or so he assumed. We would often discuss how we could get rid of him painlessly, but we never managed to think up a satisfactory strategy. His humiliation, when at last it came, was utter and final, and yet it was entirely accidental. He blundered into a snare which had been good-humouredly laid for another.

From time to time the hot sunshine of the South German summer would be interrupted by tremendous downpours of rain. There was no radio weather forecast in those days, but the approach of one of these heavy storms could be foretold without difficulty because the portents were always the same. After a week or two of bright weather there would come a morning of absolute stillness. Not a leaf moved, and the air was damp and heavy with apprehension. Jackets and ties were stripped, windows were thrown open wide, and doors wedged ajar with piles of books. Borstmann remained almost continually in the cold bath.

In the late afternoon a breeze would spring up, and if one climbed up the Schlossberg behind the cathedral one could see the clouds forming far away on the French side of the Rhine. Suddenly the range of the Vosges would disappear from view, dissolved in sheets of rain, and I learned by experience that it needed only forty minutes for the deluge to race across the Rhine plain to smash against the hills of the Black Forest and drop its load on Freiburg.

Late one evening a storm arrived. It was exceptionally violent, and the sky was continually lit up by vivid flashes as the trees moaned and shivered in the downpour. We were all soberly impressed as we watched through the French windows, but Thornborough seemed almost supernaturally affected. Every peal made him start as though he had actually seen Jove fling his sight-outrunning arrows. Then came a loud swishing sound followed by a sharp crack and an immense rending noise. The whole house shuddered. It turned out later that the tram-wires had been struck, and a nearby tram had taken the force of the discharge – though nobody was actually hurt.

With the shock, all Thornborough's classical folk-lore surged within him, and he yelled the one word 'Thunderbolt!'

'What do you mean?' enquired Petit the Swiss, startled.
'A thunderbolt. Thank heaven we're still alive.'

The Frau Geheimrat had heard his yell, and she came bustling in to see what had happened. We assured her that nobody was hurt.

'It's a thunderbolt!' Thornborough insisted. 'It's out there, somewhere. It must have missed us by inches. I heard it strike the ground.'

Stiegler intervened.

'Herr Zornbra means a *Meteorstein*, Frau Geheimrat. I think it most unlikely. Meteorites are known to fall, but there is no reason that one should fall at the same moment as a flash of lightning.'

But Thornborough would not give up his belief, and he continued to speculate about where the divine dart had struck the ground until the rest had drifted off to bed. Even Stiegler left early. Meanwhile the storm had vanished and the stars shone clear in the deep, cool sky. Leonard and I were sitting alone in the hall, but he looked thoughtful.

'Suppose there really were a thunderbolt in the garden,' he said mysteriously. And then, in a cautious whisper, 'That stone on your desk is just the thing.'

We went up to my room. The stone he referred to was one I had found in the crater of an extinct volcano a week or two earlier. It glistened with metal and sulphides, and had obviously been subjected to immense heat. Here and there clear crystal domes overlay bubbles caused by the vaporising of some of its constituents in the volcanic furnace.

'It looks right to me,' Leonard said with a smile. 'Of course I'm not an authority.'

By good fortune none of the bedrooms but our two looked out over the garden, so after giving time for the household to be asleep we got to work. The lawn at the back of the house was about ten yards square, and we chose a site roughly in the centre. Leonard had a sharp knife to cut the turf, and we dug a hole nearly a foot deep with the help of kitchen implements. Then we collected all the ashtrays from the hall, sifted out the fine grey dust of the ash, tipped it into the hole and rubbed it on the sides too. The *Meteorstein* was placed in position and rammed down tight, and using matches we scorched all the grass around the edge of the hole. Satisfied, we crept stealthily to bed.

The idea of choosing the centre of the lawn was that Luisa the nanny always hung out the washing on a line which passed over it, and we thought that that simple soul would be the best person to make the discovery. But as we watched from Leonard's room in the early morning, we saw her come and go repeatedly over the very obvious hole without noticing it. Later in the morning our intended victim, Thornborough, ensconced himself in a deck-chair within a few feet of the thunderbolt, but he was entirely occupied with a volume of Greek verse.

Suddenly Leonard whispered to me. 'Stiegler!'

Stiegler had evidently noticed Thornborough peacefully studying in the sunshine and was advancing upon him to indulge in one of his one-sided conversations. The hole lay immediately between him and Thornborough, and he simply could not miss it. He stopped suddenly, fell on his knees, and began to grapple in the hole, digging with his claws like a dachshund.

'The *Meteorstein!*' he exclaimed excitedly. 'Look, Zornbra. You were right. I knew it! Look!'

Thornborough looked up from his book, but he seemed only mildly interested. 'Yes, I thought there was a thunderbolt,' he said quietly. 'Do you know, I've never seen one before.' And with that he returned to his Greek verse.

Within a few minutes Stiegler had rounded up the whole household, including Leonard and myself. We squatted in a circle on the grass, staring awestruck at the thunderbolt, which Stiegler had laid reverently beside its hole.

'Just think,' said the Frau Geheimrat proudly, 'that of all the gardens in this road, in Freiburg, in Baden, in the whole of the Reich – just think that mine should have been the chosen one. The stone could have landed next door . . .'

We all congratulated the Frau Geheimrat on the great honour thrust upon her, and to mark the occasion she ordered a special tea to be served on the lawn. Strawberries were provided, with cream, and a wine from the Kaiserstuhl. We all drank her health, and that of the meteorite too. After a while Leonard leaned over to me and whispered, 'He's gone.'

'Gone? Who?'

'Stiegler.'

During the evening neighbours were invited in to see the wonder that had so nearly visited their gardens but selected the Frau Geheimrat's instead. Some were interested and shared her excitement, others were clearly envious and cool in their attitude. But the Frau Geheimrat had her whole attention fixed upon the stone beside the hole, murmuring again and again her wonder that her garden should have been singled out by divine lot.

I began to be worried. 'Sooner or later the myth will surely be exploded,' I whispered to Leonard. 'It will break her heart when she discovers that it's a fake.'

Leonard agreed, and we decided to soften the blow by spreading doubts. He stood up and declared his conviction that a meteorite of such a size should surely have been embedded much deeper in the ground. I said I thought so too, and was the stone not of the wrong consistency? But every objection was countered by the Frau Geheimrat with a demand for an explanation as to how else the stone could have got there. Was not the ground scorched, too, and the hole filled with fine, grey ash?

'Perhaps somebody put it there just for fun,' I risked.

It was at that moment that Stiegler returned, pushing his way to the front, crammed to the brim with new knowledge. He heard my suggestion, and it gave him his cue.

'I know something of meteorites,' he said modestly. 'There can be no question but that this one is genuine.'

Enormously relieved, the Frau Geheimrat glanced around the circle.

'Herr Stiegler will tell us all about meteorites,' she said with a smile toward her ally. 'It will be fascinating, I am sure.'

So Stiegler began where the encyclopedia began. We heard all about the rotation of the Earth, of fragments of rock lying around in space, of the tremendous force of gravity and the incredible speed with which fragments hurtled toward the Earth, of the terrific temperatures generated by atmospheric friction. The audience was spellbound, and when after a little more than half an hour he came to the end the visitors shook him by the hand and congratulated him on the brilliance of his exposition. Stiegler purred in the glow of their admiration.

Next day brought a surprise. Stiegler came importantly into the garden after lunch and held up his hand for silence.

'I have phoned the *Münchner Illustrierte*,' he declared. 'The photographers will be here tomorrow, and I have agreed to explain the whole matter to them. A reporter will also be coming.'

The Frau Geheimrat was beside herself with excitement.

'My *Meteorstein!* In the papers! It will be famous!'

Just before supper Helmuth returned from a course in a regional hospital. The family and guests dragged him across the hall and out into the garden. His mother embraced him wildly.

'Look, Helmuth! In our garden of all the world, a meteorite!'

Helmuth looked at the object which Stiegler lifted up and thrust under his nose. Then he laughed. There was a shocked silence.

'You don't really believe that this stone has fallen from the skies?' Helmuth looked at the circle good-humouredly, then laughed again.

Stiegler jumped on the incipient heresy, but Helmuth only laughed the more, and eventually Stiegler faltered.

'You think it is not a meteorite,' he broke off angrily. 'But I *know*. I happen to have knowledge of these matters.'

Helmuth smiled. 'That may be,' he said. 'But I've seen that stone before. It's been on Roger's desk for some time. He uses it as a paperweight.'

Stiegler went very white. He looked around, then advanced rather nervously across the grass until he stood in front of me.

'Is this . . . true?'

'Yes,' I said. 'I told you somebody had probably put it there for a joke.'

'And you *knew* all the time?'

'Yes, we put the stone there, Leonard and I.'

'You and Leonard! And the two of you sat there these two days . . .'

It was Thornborough's delighted laughter that rang out, followed by that of Petit the Swiss. The ripple of merriment spread over the whole assembly.

'Herr Stiegler, you had better cable the newspaper not to come,' advised the Frau Geheimrat, unintentionally adding yet another humiliation.

Stiegler disappeared through the French windows. We never saw him again. But I was more concerned about the effect of the disillusion upon the Frau Geheimrat, now that she had been robbed of her unique present from outer space. That evening when we were alone together I could see that she was trying to summon up the courage to say something.

'Tell me, Roger,' she said gently. 'The *Meteorstein* – you know Helmuth said it was not real, that it came from your room.'

'Yes,' I said. 'It was . . .'

She held up her hand. 'But he only said that because of Herr Stiegler, didn't he? And you only pretended you had put it there, to get rid of Herr Stiegler?' She put her hand on my arm. 'It will be a secret between us two, just you and me. It really was a real meteorite, wasn't it?'

Her lips trembled, and I realised just what it would mean to her if her hopes were dashed.

It was a lie I have never regretted. 'As a secret, I'll tell you. The meteorite was genuine. A real thunderbolt, right there in your lawn.'

THE EDITOR

In the first year of the Third Reich there were three newspapers circulating in Freiburg. There was the somewhat ordinary and unsensational *Freiburger Zeitung*, then once a week we were also treated (though not at the Frau Geheimrat's) to *Der Stürmer*, the official organ of the professional Jew-persecutor Julius Streicher. Not much education was needed to be editor of that newspaper I suspect, for on one occasion it appeared with a banner headline to announce the sensational discovery:– JESUS CHRIST WAS A JEW! *Der Stürmer* circulated throughout the country, but the third of the newspapers was more local, restricted to the south-west corner of the land. It appeared twice daily, and morning and evening it was thrust through the letterbox of the Frau Geheimrat, its headlines printed in blood-red gothic characters heavily underlined. They had the appearance of being written with a dagger steeped in the blood of some victim or other of the editor's virulent attacks. *Der Allemanne* took its name from the early barbaric tribes which inhabited that part of the world, and it did much to live up to their record.

A week or two before I was to leave Freiburg something prompted me to seek out the offices of *Der Allemanne* and ask to speak to the editor of the Freiburg area edition.

Climbing a bleak stairway I found a door which was marked as the editor's office, and I knocked on it boldly. It was opened by a pale young man with straw-coloured hair who was wearing an open shirt with a suitable emblem on the sleeve, and a pair of brown breeches. He Heil-Hitlered me vigorously, and I heiled him back. 'I would like to speak to the editor,' I added.

He led me in and sat down on a bare trestle table, motioning me toward a plain wooden chair.

'I am the editor,' he announced briefly.

I tried not to appear surprised, but instead of sitting below him in the chair I perched beside him on the table. He mistook this for an indication that I was politely offering him the only chair, and he seemed to think that some explanation was needed to account for the lack of furniture.

'We do not waste money on luxuries,' he said.

He was right. There was not much else in the room but a desk with a typewriter, a wire filing-tray, a cardboard box to serve as a waste-paper basket, and a gigantic picture of the *Führer*, who looked as though he had been caught in a bad mood.

'I am an Englishman,' I began. 'I am leaving for England shortly, after many months here. I have seen your paper twice daily.' I did not say that I had read it, as I had been brought up to be careful with the truth. 'I thought,' I continued boldly, 'that you would wish to have an English correspondent.'

The idea that there were parts of the world outside the bounds of the Reich seemed new to him. He appeared to think for a moment, then he shook his head.

'It would not be of interest,' he said at last.

I was not to be put off so easily. I knew enough about Germany to be aware that for some inscrutable reason there was one feature of English life which was always closely followed in the more respectable papers.

'I would write for you an account of the annual aquatic battle between Oxforrd and Cambrritsch,' I said.

It was my trump card, and it gained the trick. To have a correspondent who could actually understand the technicalities of this famous institution, with its fixed pins and swivels, Barnes Bridge and Mortlake Brewery, would put him on a par with the editor of the *Berliner Tageblatt*, to say nothing of the *Hamburger Fremdenblatt* and the *Frank-*

furter Zeitung, all of which always gave the Boat Race considerable coverage.

The young man thought for a moment, then jumped down from the table and extended his hand.

'It is agreed,' he exclaimed enthusiastically. And then, 'What else would you write?'

'I thought it would interest your readers to know the impressions which the Third Reich has made upon a visitor from overseas.' I stressed the overseas, as I was not absolutely sure that he knew where England was.

He considered. 'Yes, that would be good. You will have been greatly impressed, no doubt.'

'Very much so.'

'Then it is good. Very good. You will write for us once a fortnight, yes?'

This was much more than I had hoped, but I was careful not to appear flattered. Once a fortnight was agreed. The editor looked at the blank wall opposite, so as to avoid meeting my eye.

'There will of course be no payment,' he said.

'No?'

'No.'

'I see,' I said in what I hoped was a dignified voice.

'Everything is for the *Führer*. He saluted the photograph which scowled down upon us from the end of the room. 'The need of the community takes precedence over the need of the individual,' he continued, quoting a favourite party slogan, *Gemeinnutz geht vor Eigennutz*.

'Of course,' I agreed with all the enthusiasm I could muster.

'Workers of the fist and brow,' he went on, 'the *Führer* needs the unhesitating devotion of both. We . . .' he tapped the space between his hair and eyebrows as though sounding for traces of a brow, 'you and I, are workers of the brow, yes? And we dedicate our cranial contents to him without thought?'

'Unconditionally and obediently,' I concurred, snatching the cliché he was about to use. '*Unbedingt und gehorsam!*'

'But, we would send you a copy of all the papers containing your articles,' he conceded. 'There would be no charge.'

'That is indeed generous,' I said.

Back in England, many weeks later I was hard at work on the first newspaper article I had ever written, the article which was to mark my debut as the foreign correspondent of *Der Allemanne*. I had already agreed to write in German because I judged mine to be quite adequate for the readership. As my setting for the first article I chose the early morning scene, and I described the contrast between the joyful German sunrise and its uninspiring counterpart in Britain. At home I habitually awoke to no other sound than that of my alarm clock, but in Germany my sleep sweetly dissolved each morning as a full chorus of men's voices floated up to my bedroom window, singing in unison some sweet melody, perhaps *Volk ans Gewehr* (Man the guns, people!). The sturdy voices were those of the forced labour gangs marching off at six o'clock, spade and pick on shoulder, to cut a roadway or prepare a range for grenade-throwing.

No, in England there was nothing to remind one of the great forward march of civilisation, no singing from the forced labour squads, and perhaps this was due to the fact that there was no forced labour. True, we had had something like the *Arbeitsdienst* in feudal times, but it was gone and forgotten. And since Wilberforce . . .

I also dwelt at some length upon the curiously stupid English habit of playing games like cricket and rugby football just for enjoyment, without a thought for their usefulness. In Germany things were very different. Had not everyone in our laboratory gone out once a month to carry a massive pack to the top of the Schauinsland? Such healthy activities, I pointed out, were not provided by English universities, which hardly seemed to care whether or not their young men could carry the wheels of field guns up mountains or throw a grenade accurately enough to be sure of killing half a dozen men at a single fling.

I wrote about fifteen hundred words and posted the article. Ten days later my free copy arrived, and there beneath the bloody headlines was the article of 'Our British Correspondent'. A short blurb said that the writer had been deeply impressed by National Socialism, so much so that he found many things in the life of Germany which were sadly lacking in his own country.

I could hardly believe my eyes. In the highest of spirits I sat down to write my second article, which touched upon the treatment of racial minorities. I did not do so very forcefully, but what I wrote was enough to rouse the editor, and he must have re-read my first article, which he had published so easily.

He wrote briefly to say that he had been instructed by the Minister of Public Enlightenment (Dr Josef Goebbels) to inform me that my employment as special foreign correspondent was terminated. Oddly enough, he did not express a single word of gratitude.

HANS SPEMANN

The zoology lab was on the northern side of Freiburg, in the Katharinenstrasse. It was a friendly institution, where work was pursued in a leisurely if conscientious way and the New Spirit was only felt, and not particularly welcomed, once every month, when all German students and even the professors and assistants of reasonable age had to shoulder a pack of twenty kilos or more and stagger on foot up to the summit of the Schauinsland, a Black Forest dome which raised its head to some four thousand feet. Female students had also to take part in this exercise, though their packs were slightly reduced in weight. The only members of the laboratory who were excused from this healthy occupation were Kitching, a post-graduate research worker from the United States, and Pink – which was the nearest that the chief laboratory assistant could come to pronouncing my name. We two carried on as usual, in company with the director of the institute, Professor Hans Spemann.

Spemann was a kindly, quiet Swabian. He never raised his voice, but his expression was continually tinged with a strange melancholy, as though he were carrying some weight of sadness in his mind. He would come on his rounds to see how the students were progressing with whatever they were engaged in, would murmur a gentle word of approval, and then retire quietly to the peace of his microscope and his own work. Two years later he was to be awarded a Nobel Prize for the embryological research on which he was already engaged, and which established the existence of the Organisation Centre, which he first located in the developing egg of the newt *Triton alpestris*.

There were, Spemann discovered, two classes of eggs in the animal world. There were those in which the whole of the future development seemed to be mapped out in the greatest detail from the very beginning, as though there were contained in the egg a detailed blue-print of precisely which bit would turn into what; and there was the other kind which somehow had the ability to adjust – at least in the early stages – to form a proper whole and balanced individual from however much egg material was available. Insects were typical of creatures in which the development was already mapped out, and these eggs were 'determined' from the start. If a tiny piece were burned with a hot needle before development had proceeded, then a structure corresponding to the area of the damage would be lacking in the grown creature. But certain other creatures had eggs which behaved quite differently, the egg having the ability to 'regulate' and go ahead to produce a complete individual from however much material was at hand. (The human ovum is of this 'regulation' type. A fertilized ovum can cleave in half at an early stage in its development and yet each half will go ahead to produce a complete child – the two individuals being identical twins because the later and final developmental details are determined by the same genes which are present in both halves.)

Hans Spemann discovered that there was an area in the blastula (hollow ball) stage of the developing newt embryo which was vital to the regulating mechanism. If this area were chopped out or damaged, the organisation of the development ran wild or failed altogether, whereas if that particular area were left untouched and material was removed from elsewhere, the embryo would adjust itself to make a complete and normal individual. This vital regulating area was Spemann's 'Organisation Centre'.

German universities were different from British ones in many ways, but particularly in the arrangement of their research. At Oxbridge a research student could pursue almost any hare that he wished, even if it were natural for some main umbrella theme such as animal behaviour to occupy several workers in a loose and undefined team. In Germany it was quite different. It was a case of Professor So-wie-so and his 'school'. The professor master-minded a plan of campaign on his own pet subject and dealt out the problem in pieces to the researchers, each of whom concentrated upon a small area of the same puzzle. So I too was engaged on some minor problem concerned with biological organisers and through that I came to know the gentle, softly-spoken Spemann.

The Frau Geheimrat had spoken of a New Spirit, and this spirit was certainly abroad. I doubt if any who did not directly experience the early days of the Third Reich can ever appreciate the sense of hope, of purpose and unity which pervaded almost everything and everybody. Germans had known defeat, humiliation, starvation, reparations, and a slump and inflation which annihilated their savings. Now, all at once, with the neatly creased breeches of the brownshirts, the singing in pubs, the shiny swagger of the SS-men and the remarkable willingness of ordinary people to serve and to help, the terrible past seemed to be blown away. People willingly saved one mark and had hotpot for lunch the first Sunday of the month, trusting that this would help to alleviate the lot of the poor. Youths joined the Hitler Youth, girls flocked to the *Bund deutscher Mädel*. Not all, of course, but the dissenters were not conspicuous in their absence. There was a heady, intoxicating feeling in the air, and I wrote of it enthusiastically to my parents in England. Their wise reply was to mail me the *Manchester Guardian Weekly* as a corrective.

This was Hitler's first six months in power. Jews came and went without any obvious interference, or so it seemed. No roughs were as yet smashing their shop windows or hounding them out of their homes and livelihoods. Not obviously – that is the point. If the *Manchester Guardian* had its doubts, I had none, not until one evening when I cycled back from a day of newt embryos in the laboratory.

I had to pass a level crossing and when I came to it there was a body lying beside the track. The roadway was stained with blood. A woman was seated in the road, holding on her knees the head of the dead man, the rest of whose body had been covered with a macintosh. One or two bystanders were hovering nearby, embarrassed, not knowing quite what to do.

I dismounted. 'Is there anything I can do?'

The woman looked up and shook her head. Then she patted the hidden face of the dead man.

'He is dead,' she said simply. She was not weeping, which struck me as strange. She seemed to sense this.

'I do not know him,' she explained. 'He lived in those flats over there. They persecuted him, made his life a misery. Always they would come, perhaps in the middle of the night.'

'They?'

'The *Geheime Staatspolizei*. This time he fled from them, and the two men chased him. A train was coming. They chased him under it . . .'

I could not speak. Quite suddenly the whole facade of song and beer, flags and uniforms, which up to then I had merely regarded as perhaps rather comic was stripped away. The evil stood before me, stripped naked in the glare of that fearful event. Nor was it long before even the trusting Frau Geheimrat began to feel the hidden hand, for her doctor son Helmuth had become engaged to a girl graduate who had Jewish blood. Before June was out, Helmuth was in a mental hospital recovering from a breakdown, but even there the plain clothes men sought him out to torture him.

I had already been accepted for Cambridge, but now my letters home began to show the growing disillusion which struggled with my great affection for so much that I had experienced of friendliness in Freiburg. When in July my parents came out for a week to the Black Forest I had no difficulty in saying that my period at the Albert Ludwig's Universität should come to an end, and that I had told the staff at the laboratory that with the greatest reluctance I had decided, after this summer term, to pursue my studies at Cambridge instead.

On the last evening but one in that frail summer of 1933 I was invited up to Spemann's house on a hill at the southern side of the city, in a pleasant residential suburb gay with blossom in springtime, and in the later summer bright with herbaceous borders and rose-beds.

I had been invited alone. Spemann sat for a while, talking of his work and his newts. We discussed some of the difficult technicalities of embryological genetics as we drank a glass of wine from the slopes of the Kaiserstuhl. Yet all the while Spemann seemed to be waiting, as though avoiding something vital, and I noted a greater tinge of sadness than usual in his eyes.

At about eleven o'clock he rose to his feet, and I stood up also. But it was not the signal for me to take my leave. There was something Spemann had to tell me.

'So, Pink, you are leaving us,' he began in his quiet and deliberate voice – he could speak my name perfectly well, but he preferred the nickname which had been given me in the laboratory. He led me over to the window, and we looked out together across the dark of the pines and the silent roofs to where the lights of the city sparkled in the distance under the warm night air. Dimly the spire of Freiburg's cathedral stood out against the starlit sky, and beyond it and a little to the left we could just make out the lights of the Katharinenstrasse where his laboratory lay. The scene was intensely beautiful, and yet there hung over it an intangible sense of tragedy.

Spemann was silent as two or three minutes ticked away on the clock behind us. Then he leaned over and pulled the heavy curtain deliberately across the window to shut out the view.

'Already it is too late,' he said simply. 'I can do nothing. You can do nothing. In ten years all that we have seen out there, lying so peacefully at the foot of the hills, will be destroyed. None can prevent that now.'

He sat down at his desk, and looked straight at me with his large, sad eyes. 'You have come to love Germany, Pink,' he said. 'But there will come a time when you will find it very difficult not to hate Germany. And then always, always you must remember these months that you have spent in Freiburg. Remember the happy things, the good things; in those you have seen the heart of our people. The cruelties and foolishness, the stamping boots and coarse voices of command, the pitilessness of the people toward those of different belief or race – when you recall those things, Pink, remember that they are the symptoms of a disease. When a person has a terrible disease you may easily be revolted; but if that person is someone you love, then you know that under the disfiguring symptoms the true person is still there. Possibly in very great pain. You forget the symptoms, except in so far as you can help that person you love to be rid of their sickness and recover.'

Ten years, Spemann had said. He was not far out in his estimate. It was just on eleven years later that wave after wave of the vast force of bombers came over the Rhine, high in the night sky. In the morning Freiburg lay in smouldering ruins. Of the buildings in the Katharinenstrasse no trace remained, and only an acute observer noting the brilliant wings of exotic butterflies lying in the rubble could have guessed that once there had been a laboratory there whose director had won the Nobel Prize.

Mercifully, Hans Spemann had died a few months earlier.

SKY HIGH

It was on my way to Freiburg that I first went up in the air. I flew with my father to Paris and took the train to Freiburg. In 1933 it was a really exciting venture to go by air. We were to fly from Croydon. We just had to turn up twenty minutes or so before departure and walk out over the tarmac to where the giant plane was waiting. At least it seemed a giant, even if by modern standards it would not have been an enormous aircraft at all. Its body was not smooth and glossy, but ribbed like a French farm-truck. It was a biplane, and its name was *Hannibal*. It belonged to Imperial Airways, the forerunner of British European and later British Airways – but at that time Britain was still decidedly imperial.

A flight at that time was much more interesting. There were no radio beacons, radar had not been invented, nor had the jet engine. The plane lumbered along in a satisfactory fashion but not at an enormous speed, and we flew at only a few thousand feet above the ground. That was partly because the navigation had to be done entirely by eye, aided by a compass, so the captain had to have the scenery in view all the time and fly from one prominent landmark to another. The first landmark was Bodiam castle in Kent, very distinctive with its moat full of water. It looked a very pleasant place to live if one was of the upper crust and had a plethora of servants. Leaving Bodiam behind, the plane next headed for Dungeness, a point of land projecting into the English Channel. Once that was left astern one could, with luck and good visibility, make out Dungeness' partner, Cap Gris Nez, between Calais and Boulogne. And then . . . one was over France! Two cathedrals, Amiens and Beauvais, and Paris was straight ahead and already easily visible. Le Bourget airfield was situated on the near side of the capital, and the biplane began to glide down toward it. The flight was over. The fare, I remember, was seven pounds ten shillings return.

Seven pounds ten shillings was not too much to pay for such an adventure, even if the third class return rail fare from Victoria all the way to Freiburg was only three pounds nineteen shillings, channel crossings included. At least, my father evidently thought it reasonable. But a fare of that size invited competition, and soon another carrier was offering flights to Paris for only four pounds ten shillings return. This was Hillman's Airlines, and their plane (though I think they had more than one) operated out of Epping. The next time I went out to Freiburg at the end of a vacation I decided to be economical and fly Hillman.

Hillman was a bus operator who ran pirate double deckers into London from Romford and Ilford. At least, the London General Omnibus Company reckoned he was a pirate. He undercut their fares, and his chocolate brown buses were popular with people living in that area. When he decided to go into the air travel business he chose Epping airfield, probably because it was cheaper, and it was handy for his bus operations. The plane in which I flew to Paris was a Fokker and it took seven passengers beside the pilot, who sat in the front of the cabin but was in no way shut off in a holy of holies as he would be nowadays. There was of course no radio operator, because there were no beacons, no need to call up an airport, because I doubt if they were equipped with a transmitter, and in any event there was no need to take up an allocated position in a queue of aircraft waiting to land. It was just a matter of landing, with maybe an eye cocked for an unlikely other plane in an otherwise empty sky.

All began as usual. Bodiam castle, Dungeness, Cap Gris Nez, Amiens. But no Beauvais cathedral. It seemed to have disappeared. It was a perfect day with bright sun and good visibility, and I noticed that the sun had got into a curious habit of walking slowly round the plane, shining first through a window on the left, then going round the nose, walking along the right side of the aircraft, and disappearing round the tail to start another circular trip. The pilot had lost Beauvais, and so he had lost Paris too.

Now Paris was not such a small city that one could easily overlook it, and after several wide circlings a smudge of smoke appeared, far away. 'Ah,' the pilot exclaimed. 'That must be Paris.' And it was.

The seven passengers were met by Hillman's French representative, who asked how they enjoyed the flight. I said it was excellent, but I wondered that the pilot should have had to search for Paris for more than twenty minutes.

'Oh that,' said the local manager. 'He hasn't flown here before. You see our Paris pilot is ill, so the Isle of Man pilot had to take over the flight.'

When it came to return on the other half of the ticket there was misty rain and something of a wind. The sky was cold and grey, and the clouds were so thick that they seemed almost to be on the roofs of the nearby buildings. I wondered how our man would find the landmarks. But he did.

That is, he found the first two, and we roared across the French countryside so low that whenever we came to a wood he pulled back the stick and we rose to take the trees in a long leap. Eventually we reached the coast, and the pilot turned right to follow along the line of the shore. The weather had improved somewhat, so we could fly a bit higher and have a better view. It was more than half an hour before we reached the shore of a broad river estuary. Even I knew enough basic geography to be certain that this could only be the Scheldt. And it was.

The pilot sat in the front seat, with what appeared to be a road-map on his knee. He turned the plane and headed back along the coast, passing a number of ports, large and small, until we came to the place where we had first reached the French coast. He continued for a while, glancing continually at the map and peering down at the landscape. After a while a curving and muddy-looking estuary came up.

'That's it!' he exclaimed genially. 'That's what it says in the notes. Leave the French coast at an estuary shaped like an umbrella-handle!' And that was exactly what it looked like. I recognised it in later years as the creek leading up to Montreuil-sur-Mer.

With the umbrella-handle safely behind us we struck out over the Channel. We had good weather now, and although I was still rather apprehensive I was relieved when I could make out the dim line of the English coast ahead. Dungeness, then Bodiam castle, and Tower Bridge, confidently and magnificently indicating exactly where we were. And then, surprisingly, we were lost. However, the pilot was resourceful enough. After flying straight ahead for a while he saw a small island roundabout in a road below. I knew exactly where it was, as I had passed it several times when driving between London and Cambridge. It was on the rather grandiosely called Great Cambridge Road. The pilot got the island in his sights and dived at it. There was a yellow AA signpost in the middle of it, with lettering about three inches high. As we pulled out of the dive I could read the signpost myself. The pointer to the right bore the message 'Epping 8 miles'. The Fokker banked sharp right, and a few minutes later we had landed.

But Hillman was dogged by bad luck, or the results of adverse publicity. First there was the occasion when two young lovers who had made a suicide pact opened the door during the flight and threw themselves out. Then came the incident of the Paris gold.

It is a curious fact that the Bank of France, which was transferring a cargo of gold bullion bars to the Bank of England by air (for every minute or hour saved in transit meant money in interest), should have chosen to save three pounds by using Hillman's instead of Imperial

Airways. The Paris plane set off for Epping with four or five passengers and a pile of gold blocks stacked in the tail. When the plane arrived in Epping the bullion van drove up to collect the gold, but what the guards found was a hole in the bottom of the tail area where the floor had given way under the weight. The gold had gone.

When the loss was reported, all enterprising citizens whose homes were situated more or less on the line between Paris and London spent the week-end in a gold rush. The police interviewed the passengers and asked them if they had heard a cracking noise, or felt a sudden lightening of the plane. One man said he had, he felt the plane suddenly rise as though it had gone over a hump, and when asked if he could say about where this sensation had occurred he was only able to reply that he was not sure, but perhaps it was about half way over the Channel. A sad disappointment for the gold-hunters.

The gold was not found. Not, that is, for more than two years, when a peasant woman walked into the market at Beauvais bearing a bright yellow brick. She asked if anybody could tell her what it was, because up there in the wood the ground was covered with such bricks.

So the gold, or nearly all of it, was recovered from where it had been lying unnoticed for a couple of years, and the Bank of England generously (as they thought) awarded the woman a reward of £2,000.

Not long afterwards, the end of Hillman's came in an unexpected way. Hillman was in bed with influenza at his home in Romford, when his drivers had decided to strike and had agreed to stop their vehicles at twelve o'clock precisely, wherever they might be. Twelve noon came, the buses stopped, the drivers sat in their cabs. Somebody brought the news to Hillman, who jumped out of bed, put on a dressing-gown, ran down the street until he found the first of his buses, opened the door of the cab, dragged the driver out and knocked him senseless. Jumping into the cab he drove the bus himself for the rest of the day, then went home. He at once went down with pneumonia and died. So did his brave little airline.

Two years later I had another remarkable flight. My brother's wedding gave rise to the trip, which fitted ill with the regulations of Cambridge University where I was an undergraduate, having left Freiburg a few months after Hitler took over the management of Germany, leading that country inexorably toward destruction.

My brother had arranged to be married in Toronto in early June, and I was to be best man. But in order to take my degree I had not only to have passed the necessary exams but also to have 'kept' nine terms, each of which was to consist of fifty-six nights' residence within the college. No aircraft as yet had the range to cross the Atlantic, and the sailing of the various liners happened to be timed in such a way that I could not possibly reach Toronto until after the wedding.

No aircraft? That was not strictly true. There was indeed one, and it was leaving Frankfurt on a most convenient day, giving me the chance to keep the vital number of nights and also to reach the other side of the Atlantic in time.

The idea was my father's, and he decided that he and I would fly over in the German airship LZ129 *Hindenburg*, which was about to make her second scheduled flight, to Lakehurst, New Jersey, whence we could easily make Toronto by train. The fare, I remember, was the same as second class on a ship, so two tickets were secured.

We flew Imperial Airways to Paris, this time aboard the *Heracles* – the aircraft all had classical names beginning with H. Next morning we were out at the airfield to enter the hangar and go aboard the Zeppelin. Because it was inside the hangar I did not immediately appreciate its true size, but in fact the airship was about one sixth of a mile in length, two-thirds the size of the *Queen Mary*. Her average speed on this trip was only sixty-eight knots and she needed just under sixty hours for the flight from Frankfurt to Lakehurst.

The *Hindenburg* was the only airship ever built to serve as a regular passenger carrier on a particular route. As I went aboard up a little stairway in the bottom of her huge gleaming hull I had to step on a weighing machine so that my weight could be taken. I turned the scale at eighty kilograms – and sixty years later I still do – and as I mounted the steps weights totalling that amount were unhooked from one of the piles hanging underneath. The same was done for every passenger, suitcase, crate of cargo or member of the crew, weights being taken off when anyone went aboard, and replaced when they stepped off again. The result of this careful balancing was that even when fully loaded up the *Hindenburg* still actually weighed the same amount as before; that is, about a quarter of a ton.

The *Hindenburg* carried about fifty passengers, but her crew was nearly as large, forty-five. When all these people were aboard we were ready to leave the hangar, and a tractor towed the trolley, to which the ship's belly was clamped, very slowly out along rails until she was well clear of the hangar. Hundreds of men held ropes attached to the nose and other parts of the ship to steady her in case a gust of wind should happen to catch her enormous bulk. She was then unhitched from the trolley, light as a fairy, held down by her own insignificant weight and steadied by the ropes.

We sat there, motionless in the heat of the late summer afternoon. There was not a breeze to taughten the stay-ropes. A hush fell over the crowd watching from only yards away. Dr Eckener, the grand old man of airships, leaned out of the window of the control cabin and waved his hand. The foreman of the ground blew his whistle, the ropes fell away from the sides and half a ton of water cascaded to the ground from the ballast tanks. Then all was quiet again, but the people on the ground began very slowly to get smaller as the eight giant hydrogen bags inside the hull began to lift us clear. I leaned out of one of the windows – something one can never do on a modern passenger aircraft – and watched as the faces beneath us became more upturned. There was no furious rush down a concrete runway, nothing but an absolutely silent rising. The engines had not even been started up.

Soon we were rising even faster. Friends of crew members waved up from straight below as we continued to rise like a giant bubble in the cooling evening air. At 2,000 feet a little hydrogen was released to check our upward lift and balance us once more with the air, and as the four great motors roared into life a cheer rose up to us from the crowd below. Dr Eckener stood at the controls and headed off toward the sunset and the Rhine.

In an airplane the passengers are really confined to their seats, partly because there is nowhere else for them to go. But the *Hindenburg* was very different. She had two decks within the hull, with opening windows on the outer side, and the upper deck had the dining saloon on one side of the ship and the lounge on the other, with two hundred feet of promenade deck. Passengers could open the large windows whenever they wished, and I leaned against the window sill, staring down in fascination at the world below as the *Hindenburg* forged ahead over the Rheinland.

Shining from beneath the nose was a bright searchlight which lit up brilliantly a patch of ground perhaps 200 yards across, and I could see woods and fields and vineyards, and occasionally a bend in the great river.

Two hours out from the airfield we were crossing the suburbs of Cologne, and as we passed obliquely over the river the great twin spires of the cathedral rushed across the patch of light below us and disappeared again into the blackness.

I stayed at the window hour after hour, just watching. I saw Rotterdam, with the big ships lying in a haze of smoke against the wharves, then here and there the flash of a Dutch light vessel amid the faint silvery gleam of the North Sea. Eventually we reached the English coast over the flames of the blast furnaces of Middlesborough and headed out across the wild moorlands of the Pennines. The dawn was faintly announcing its presence as the sands of the Solway Firth shone up at us and we cut the corner of Scotland into the vastness of the Atlantic. When the sun eventually rose behind us there was no land in sight.

It was not until our third day on board that we reached the other side of the Atlantic over Newfoundland, and even then we saw very little as the land was shrouded in thick cloud with only a rare parting to show the forests of fir below. But when we were above the clouds I could tell exactly the height at which we were flying, just by looking at my watch. The airship had an echo-sounder instead of an altimeter based on air pressure, and every minute or so a loud squeak like the pip of a radio time signal was shot down toward the earth, slightly ahead. Striking the sea or the ground, the sound bounced back again into the air at such an angle that it would strike the airship, and the interval that passed before the sound returned enabled the height to be registered automatically in the control cabin. Knowing that the sound was travelling at approximately 1,100 feet per second, and that it had to make the round trip down to the ground and back again, I was myself able to make the calculation. The longest interval I recorded on my watch was twenty-two seconds, which showed that we were at a height just then of about 12,000 feet.

An airship had its special problem of balance. While an airplane is flying on its course it continually uses up fuel and becomes lighter. This is all to the good, as the plane then needs less power to keep it flying. But an airship had to keep as near as possible to its exact balance with the air around it, as otherwise it would tend to rise too high. Any loss of weight from using up the fuel had somehow to be made good. The most obvious means would be to release some of the buoyant gas to bring the ship into balance again, but this had certain disadvantages. It decreased the margin of safety, and the ship would have to fill up again with gas when taking on a fresh load of fuel for the return trip. So some other means of making up lost weight had to be found.

The *Hindenburg*'s system was to take water out of the clouds and run it into tanks inside the hull. As the droplets condensed on the outer skin they ran into little runnels, and so to the tanks. If the ship passed through one cloud every few hours quite enough water could be caught to make up for the loss of fuel weight. Of course there would perhaps be rare occasions when no clouds could be found on the flight course and there was no alternative but to reduce the hydrogen in the bags, but on this flight we were never too far away from clouds – and on one occasion we went twenty miles off course to catch a good cloud and milk it.

On our third night aboard we passed down the coast of North America and just before dawn came right in over the Statue of Liberty and looked out across New York harbour at the dense mass of skyscrapers crowded on Manhattan Island. Then we turned southward, slowly losing height, until the huge airfield of Lakehurst came into view with its sturdy mast to which the *Hindenburg*'s nose was to be moored. Dr Eckener brought the ship into the wind and cut the speed of the motors until we were hovering over the field at a height of about 1,000 feet. When we were quite still, some gas was released and the great ship began to fall, slowly at first but then faster as the 200 men of the ground crew raced across the grass to grab the guide ropes dropped from the nose. Only when we were thirty feet above the ground was the fall checked by dropping a shower of water, and we landed on the single wheel below the gondola with no more than a gentle bump. The ground crew hauled us toward the mast, and the ship was shackled to it. We had arrived.

The people on the airfield congratulated the captain on having created a new record for the crossing.

On the *Hindenburg*'s next flight to America Dr Eckener knocked another nine hours off his record by taking her right up over Greenland and Baffin Land to get a full gale blowing on her tail. But the great ship was only to make half a dozen trips. Not many months later she fell in flames over the same airfield in one of the greatest of air disasters.

When I heard the news I felt I had lost a real friend. And I knew, too, that it was not just the end of the *Hindenburg* but of all of her kind, for ever. The next generation would never cross the Atlantic in that same wonderful way. Nor would those on the ground ever see the gigantic shape in the sky, or hear the curious squeak of an echo-sounder from far above the clouds or watch the great pencil-shaft of her searchlight moving surely across the countryside. It was the end of the age of a great technical achievement. The world would belong to the heavier-than-air transport, from then on.

TO CLIMB BY NIGHT

I was probably lucky to go up to Cambridge in an era when only three qualifications were needed to enter a college. The first was a reasonable but not necessarily brilliant academic record at school. The second, a knowledge that the parents would be able to come up with the fees; and third, an indication that there were no special habits or circumstances which might offend the proprieties of life in the college. Even then, it was possible for a student to have special treatment if there should be some slight misunderstanding, as when, in my days at Magdalene, a young gentleman from a Far Eastern country arrived with seven wives because, as he pointed out to the astonished tutor upon his arrival, there was nothing in the leaflet of college regulations that indicated in any way that over half a dozen wives was unacceptable. The college very sensibly allowed him to rent a house for them in the Chesterton Road.

I went over from Rugby by train for the entry examination. I had never been to Cambridge before, so the impression it made upon me was immediate and enormous. I was shown to a sumptuous suite of undergraduate rooms in the new building designed by Lutyens, and I had only just unpacked my bag when there was a knock on the outer door and a large, friendly, humorous man with reddish hair presented himself and asked if I had everything that I needed. He introduced himself as one of the tutors, Frank Salter, who happened also to be a first cousin of my father.

The entrance exam would be next morning. There would be a short written paper – which I believe was only to provide a possible excuse for rejecting a candidate – and then there would be an interview. The Master of the college would then ask me a number of questions, Salter said.

'Like this; Do you play chess? To that the answer should be No, or the Master will run through the first fifteen moves for both players and then say it's your move next.'

Salter laughed at his own joke, obviously intended to put me thoroughly at ease. 'Yes. And then it's do you play bridge? The answer should be No, as likewise the Master will deal four hands out of his head and ask for your lead.'

'I see,' I said laughing politely at his little joke.

'Then, do you like music? No, I'm not asking you; that is the Master's next question. You say Yes, rather! And your favourite composer? That must be Sullivan. The Master is cracked about Gilbert and Sullivan, and likes translating it into Latin. The final question is: if you are admitted, will you row? Say Yes, as the College boat club is pretty well down the drain. It won't be binding, of course.'

I thought it was rather charming of Salter to come and spin this yarn just to amuse me and set me at ease. Next morning I went over to the college hall for the written paper. It set the tone of the Magdalene of those days, rich in wealthy Old Etonians, by its essay subject:– *Describe the workings of a soda water syphon.*

Then came the interview, upstairs in the Combination Room. I wondered what the four dons present would ask me, but in fact it was only the Master who did the interviewing. And to my great surprise it was exactly as Frank Salter had said. Chess? Bridge? Music? Yes, Sullivan. I would love to row. I answered properly, and was in.

Once installed after my return from Germany I very quickly discovered as an undergraduate that there were interesting activities at Cambridge quite apart from the Natural Sciences Tripos and rowing. Climbing, for example.

For a long time this activity, much of it centred on Cambridge, was secret, but eventually the beginnings of a specialised literature appeared. First was *The Roof Climber's Guide to Trinity* published anonymously and consisting of just what its title suggested. It was an instruction manual for initiates. Some of its directions, such as to use a crossbow to fire a string from one roof to another so that a rope could be hauled across, seem improbable, but the guide was in use by night-climbers – for the occupation was always practised in the dark – around 1930.

Then in 1937 came the remarkable work *The Night Climbers of Cambridge*, a book reprinted in 1952, when it seems to have been greatly in demand. The author, 'Whipplesnaith', apparently wrote for those who had not yet taken up climbing seriously, because he exhorted his readers to test their suitability by sitting on a narrow window-ledge thirty feet above the ground and looking down – those who failed this simple test being dealt with free of charge by the recently established National Health Service. But he also provided good photographs of the most sacred arêtes and traverses, with difficult routes picked out in dotted lines to assist beginners. Many of these illustrations showed climbers actually in the process of scaling statuary, or apparently featureless walls.

Early college architects provided just what a climber required, both in the general shape and design and also in the materials used for building. Long chimneys capped with an exacting but not quite impossible overhang were often incorporated and King's Chapel is a particularly inspired example of this interesting though functionally useless arrangement. Great attention was also paid to providing a surface which would afford a grip for the seat of the hose or trousers. Hence the great use of deposits from the Middle and Upper Jurassic beds and particularly of Oolitic stone, the hard coarse grains of which provide a surface which is practically non-slip in all weathers.

Later however, university architecture became debased and functionalism was abandoned for concentration upon meaningless form, as in the case of the Fitzwilliam Museum. In this building of curiously decadent design a vertical pillar set out from the wall provides an excellent piece of chimney climbing, but the chimney itself is closed at the top with a mass of masonry so poorly shaped as to be quite insurmountable. The carvings above would be useful, but it proves impossible to reach them and what might so well have been an attractive ascent is marred by inept construction.

The secrecy so necessary to the climber has unfortunately meant that few have written in detail of their remarkable exploits, but what might be veiled references can be found in literature extending back over centuries. Raleigh – an Oxford man – wrote the line 'Fain would I climb, yet fear I to fall' – which suggests that he would not have passed the window-ledge test; but Collins, another Oxford poet, described the spires of the university as 'dim-discovered', an epithet which must have stirred the imagination of climbers of his day. Macaulay on the other hand was a Cambridge man, and he used the term 'reeling' in connection with spires in the university, which suggests that he must have made the ascent of the Divinity Schools, across the street from his college, for on that building the steeple was notorious – as Whipplesnaith pointed out from his own experience – for its habit of swaying but not quite collapsing, like an Irishman after whiskey.

It was just twenty-five years after going up to Magdalene that I happened to cross the familiar market place in Cambridge and was struck with the awful realisation that something had changed. Over the years I had become accustomed to averting my eyes when passing the gaunt mass of the Caius New Building at one end or the new Guildhall at the other, but I was unprepared for the shock when I discovered that Hobson's Conduit had disappeared. This pleasant Gothic-style structure had been taken down, I was informed, because it was in a dangerous condition – the usual excuse of those who want to sweep away things of nostalgic beauty.

I was sad that it had gone, because the conduit's tendency to crumble was its most important asset. Nobody drank from its water, but generations of undergraduates had used the fountain for the particular purpose for which it was so admirably suited, and many of the best night-climbers must have gained their first experiences of overhanging pitches of crumbling stone upon its Gothic columns before graduating to more difficult ascents. Far from being dangerous, the fact that the masonry of the conduit was liable to come away in sizeable chunks was of the utmost educational value and must have saved the life of many a night climber who, without previous experience on the humble conduit, might well have plunged to his death from the crumbling cornices of Trinity Hall or the deceptively solid-looking turrets of that greatest of all climbs, King's College Chapel.

Everest can hardly compare in interest with King's Chapel. The latter could only be climbed at night and the ascent had to be carried out without the assistance of a whole cavalcade of sherpas. Success in reaching the summit was more likely to earn rustication than a knighthood, and for this reason alone the greatest secrecy had to be preserved not only during the ascent but also afterwards.

The precincts themselves had to be entered by stealth, usually by way of the pass over the western gates. Once inside, there were wide lawns and broad expanses of crunchy gravel to be crossed before the dark shadow of the north-west chimney was reached and the attack on the main face could be launched. Porters on the whole sleep deeply, but Fellows of colleges are notoriously light sleepers, tossing and turning in fitful slumber as the horrors of Linguistic philosophy or the behaviour of the University Grants Committee haunt their troubled minds, or the combination room port robs their stomachs of much needed rest. The whispering brush of jeans against the statue of a benefactor, or even the mere cracking of a knee-joint might easily be enough to rouse a leader of intellectual life and bring him to his window in a condition that borders on the neurotic. For this reason the more experienced climber usually carried a small cobble-stone in his pocket and in case of danger he flung it quickly toward one of the other buildings, making good his escape while the hue and cry was concentrated around the area over which the broken glass lay scattered.

When a Himalayan climber encounters a section of the mountain which is not entirely to his liking he callously takes up his pick-axe and alters it, sending hundredweights of ice thundering down the slope to the valley below. But no night-climber would ever treat a building in this impatient manner. If the pitch is a difficult one – and few mountains can boast vertical chimneys half the length of those on King's Chapel – he accepts the fact as a challenge to his skill and overcomes the obstacle by determination alone.

If anybody was inclined to 'tax the royal Saint with vain expense, with ill-matched aims the architect who planned . . . this immense and glorious work of fine intelligence' as Wordsworth suggested, it was certainly not a climber, for a more challenging and fascinating ascent could hardly be devised.

So far as is known, the building has only once been climbed from the ground to the topmost pinnacle without a helpful rope or other safety device, and that was in 1936. Strangely enough the climb was not planned in advance but was accomplished on a sudden impulse. A Magdalene undergraduate was awakened long after midnight by his tutor blundering into his bedroom in error. After the apologetic don had retired the climber suddenly realised that he had the most cast-iron of alibis. Had not the tutor seen him in bed and asleep at one-thirty? Five minutes later he was dressed, out of the window, and away round the Backs taking nothing with him but a tiny flag to tie to the summit to encourage others, an emblem which lasted for more than a year before it was finally shredded by the wind.

The chapel climb was extremely exacting, but the college prevented a repetition by inserting chock-stones armed with spikes in the 'chimneys' which ran from the ground to the roof in one exhausting pitch. Above that was the corner turret with two overhangs, before at last the climber could have the splendid view of the peaceful university area asleep beneath the stars.

I happened once to be showing a continental guest round Cambridge, and noticing the chock-stones at the corner of King's College chapel, he asked me what they were for. I explained to him that they blocked the route by which a person could reach the roof. He thereupon asked me the typically foolish question of the foreigner, 'Is there then no staircase inside?'

After swallowing my natural irritation I proceeded to explain to him the reasons why, I thought, climbing held such an attraction for a fair number of undergraduates in every generation. (Whipplesnaith had no difficulty in raising nearly a score of assistants to perform the climbs he wanted to describe in his book.) First, it was a forbidden activity. Disobedience to rules has always been a strong trait in the British, I pointed out. Then there was no doubt the satisfaction of having achieved the apparently impossible, and the ready acceptance of a severe climb as a challenge to one's skill. But mercenary motives such as selling the story to a tabloid newspaper were never involved, as that could lead to rustication and unwelcome interference with studies. And the desire to be alone, and to achieve something without the aid of others was perhaps also a factor. I put these points to Whipplesnaith when I had his book sent to me for review by *The Spectator*. He was inclined to agree, but he thought that first and foremost the thing about night-climbing was that it was fun.

Whipplesnaith's book would have been called a 'definitive work' if it had but been concerned with the artistic side of the statuary encountered during the climbs – for his excellent plates showed climbers spread-eagled on the facade of Clare, crouched in the Lion Chimney of the Fitzwilliam Museum, scaling the main gate of St John's, the Trinity Library and other famous arêtes. The routes were described in remarkable practical detail, too.

'Laying the left forearm flat on the lower ledge to the left, and holding the upper ledge with the right hand, pull with the right hand and push up with the left. Fortunately, all the stonework except the gargoyles on this building [the south face of Gonville and Caius] *is in excellent condition.'* And climbers should have steady nerves, he stressed, ready for the unexpected. *'As you step to the parapet, a flurry of pigeons may disturb you. Numbers of them sleep inside the parapet. You may even, as has been done before, put your foot actually on to a bird. The surprise will be mutual, but don't step back and raise your hands . . .'*

Whipplesnaith's work was for sale on the tables of Bowes and Bowes and Heffers, so colleges with the best climbs described in it saw themselves threatened by possible hordes of novices scaling their statuary and scrambling over the sacred edifices of their royal patrons. Some inspected and reinforced their spiky defences. King's first attempted to deter newcomers by suggesting that parts of their buildings were so decayed that to put a hand or foot upon the stonework was to risk immediate death. In fact no increase in the number of climbers was experienced. Climbers were, and always would be, a highly enterprising few.

During the year before the publication of *The Night Climbers* the frequent exploits of an unidentified climber and his assistants had the colleges guessing. But unsuccessfully. A sudden bright flash in a college court in the darkness of the small hours was enough to show that something was afoot, but to discover the whereabouts of the climber was by no means easy. Occasionally an unusually wakeful or vigilant porter would identify the source of the flash as being in a particular corner and would rush to intercept the photographer. But Whipplesnaith had anticipated this event. At the sound of an approaching enemy a figure with a camera would break cover and run off, just not too fast to be overtaken and caught. He then turned out to be a member of the college concerned, and the most the porter could do was to demand the camera, tear out the film and bid the protesting owner a surly Goodnight. And while the dummy photographer was thus occupying the guardians of the night in the porters' lodge the real photographer quietly made his escape, bearing the successful pictures with him.

To what college did this man belong who so brazenly climbed on one or two nights every week, with photographers in attendance? Every gate-list (for at that time all comings in after ten o'clock were carefully recorded) was closely scrutinized and in some cases staircases were checked during the night hours in an effort to pin down the leader of the endless series of mountaineering expeditions on the faces of the sacred college buildings. What none guessed was that he was not an undergraduate in residence at all. He was a graduate, and he lived in Market Harborough. He would drive over to Cambridge with his photographers, walk in through a college gate before ten o'clock, and after performing the ascents on his list he would stay in the rooms of an undergraduate or a benevolent don and walk out again next morning unchallenged.

So now quite suddenly, when I saw that the conduit had been taken away, it seemed to me that real danger threatened one of the essential facets of Cambridge life. If the fountain had been frivolously swept away, could there be any guarantee that a similar fate might not overtake the gateway arête of St John's, the second pitch of Cloister Court, the south traverse of Caius, even the revered pinnacles of King's itself? It seemed that the gathering winds of materialism might threaten to reduce the two greatest universities of the world to a state in which they would no longer be centres of high night-time endeavour but merely places of earth-bound study and technical training alone.

THE BYWAYS CLUB

It was an old friend from my schooldays at Rugby who introduced me to the Byways Club, and so to Walks. A few months earlier, a London businessman who was 'Something in the City' – and Something in a large way – had become so appalled at the conditions into which some people were born, and in which they lived the whole of their lives until death mercifully took them away, that he was moved by an intelligent curiosity, or compassion, or more probably the silent but ingenious planning of the Holy Spirit, to live for several months in a slum lodging-house in darkest Soho, in which two other rooms were occupied by working prostitutes. His intention was not to reprove or convert, but to understand the root causes of what went on in the world, and in this ingenious way he came to know far more than many social workers about the darker aspects of slum life in the years of the depression in which Britain then found itself, the Great Depression of the thirties.

C.C. Walkinshaw, or 'Walks' as we called him, eventually moved from his lodgings and became warden of the Mary Ward Settlement. In those days the all-sheltering umbrella of Social Security had not been designed, let alone unfurled, and it fell to voluntary effort to provide whatever was possible for the less fortunate and underprivileged in what would now be known as Inner City areas. A settlement had nothing to do with a housing estate; it was an institution supported and run by volunteers, to provide an anchor for those lost in the dismal semi-slum areas of – in this case – London. A settlement would probably have a boys' club, maybe a girls' club, facilities for pensioners, the chance of a decent meal, access to sports facilities and maybe a gymnasium as well as medical counselling and a whole host of ancillary services for those who felt lost and yet had the initiative to focus their lives at least in part around the settlement.

Settlements were naturally to be found in areas such as Dockland and King's Cross, and the Mary Ward was situated off the Euston Road, where it had a useful catchment area to the north. Walks, who was extremely well-off, lived simply and comfortably in the Mary Ward, where he kept open house for young people in general and members of Byways in particular. He looked more like a teddy bear than a financial wizard, but he was well-known in the City. Once when short of ready cash in London, I went into a Westminster Bank in the City to try to cash a cheque. It was quite clear that the clerk did not believe that I had an account at the Westminster in Cambridge (there were no bank cards in those days), and he summoned an assistant manager to explain to me that without a telephone call at my expense to check with the Cambridge branch, to cash even a small cheque for me was unthinkable. He had just said his familiar piece when Walks happened to come into the bank. He nodded to me with a friendly 'Hallo, Roger,' and went on his way. At once the odour-of-bad-fish expression vanished from the face of the assistant manager, who rushed to open the door for Walks before hurrying back again to apologise for having so much as asked about my financial standing and if at any time the bank could oblige . . .

The idea which Walks conceived was simple, but brilliant. He realised that an enormous impact upon inequality and suffering under bad conditions could be made by Cambridge graduates, provided that their eyes had been opened while they were at the university. He decided to form a sort of *Corps d'Elite* of young men who might afterwards be ordained, or who would join the civil service or enter one of the professions. It did not matter what their ultimate personal goal might be, for whatever line they should decide to follow their influence, Walks thought, would be felt. So he founded the

Byways. It was a most unusual society. It had no rules, no membership fee, no premises, no club tie, not even so much as an entrance ceremony or initiation. If a member knew somebody that he thought would be suitable as a member of Byways, he merely invited him to the next meeting, and that was that.

Those Byways meetings were as informal as could be. There was no secretary, and no minute-book. Nothing was recorded. Once every term Walks would be invited to come down to Cambridge and he took the members out to a snack lunch. There were no speeches, no initial grace to start the meal. Members simply chatted to Walks, and he to them. Maybe in the evening there would be beer in the rooms of one of the post-graduate members such as Alan Leeke, who had become chaplain of Clare College and so had sufficient space at his disposal. Now and again a guest would be invited to such a meeting, a figure from the world of boys' clubs, anyone who had something useful to say about the social services – or, more correctly, the lack of them. The guest met members in an easy and informal environment – and made an impact upon them.

One could always spend a night at the Mary Ward if up in London for a show, using it as a free hotel. During the vacations it was usual for members of Byways to spend a few days in London helping out at the Mary Ward's boys' club, or doing whatever they could to be useful in a practical way at one of the settlements run (as some still are) by the public schools or Oxbridge colleges. The idea worked extremely well, and somehow there was never the least sensation or realisation that one was in fact a trainee, nor was there any conscious social or class barrier between oneself and the clientele of the social clubs. After a few years one could find Byways men in the Probation Service, in Youth Clubs, in the Church, in the Home Office, and even among the District Commissioners in such places as Kenya and Uganda, or as officials in the Punjab.

There was no register of members present or past, and no attempt to keep young men on as members after they had left Cambridge. The object of Byways was quite simply to stimulate a social awareness, with no political preconceptions, in the kind of young men whom Walks wanted to see at work in the world with their eyes open. And it certainly succeeded.

Inevitably, Byways became a victim of the war, passing unnoticed as its members were scattered. Probably nothing quite like it exists today, for much of what was achieved by the settlements of those days has for better or worse been taken over by government agencies or has become the province of paid, trained, certificated, and sometimes unimaginative social workers. Besides, undergraduates nowadays have their noses pressed hard on the academic grindstone, and have less time to look at the world around them.

And times have changed, too. Whatever poverty still exists, by the standards of the depression of the 1930s the poor nowadays are not all that poor. Social Security, if only up to a point, has come to stay. Medical services are free, even if there may be a frustrating wait before treatment is possible. And much of what has been achieved in these directions is undoubtedly due to the influence of men who first began to awaken during those happy, informal lunches when Walks invited them to join him in a pub, or was their overnight host at the Mary Ward.

During the Long Vacation there was one special activity in which Byways members became greatly involved, and to such an extent that they generally outnumbered the others who gave their time and energies to this unusual enterprise.

In the middle 1930s Britain was still in the grip of one of its periodical Great Depressions. There was high unemployment, wages were low, Social Security had not yet been introduced as a pillow for the heads of the less fortunate, and the Dole was remarkably meagre. In the case of a single man it was seventeen shillings a week (85p).

There was near starvation – except for the enterprising – and there was a degree of hopelessness and debility which it is hard for people nearing the twenty-first century to imagine. The hunger-marchers who came down from Jarrow to Westminster to present the facts of their destitution to the assembled Members actually marched. They did not go in air-conditioned buses, or drive their own cars. The poverty was real.

One of the facts that came to the notice of Byways members and others who had their ears to the ground and their eyes open, was that even as the recession was lifting, many of the unemployed were in fact so weak and enfeebled through the years of want that when they were offered a job they could not take it. That is, they took the job, and probably within the first week they collapsed from exhaustion, aided by malnutrition. It was this state of affairs that led to the formation of the Unemployed Camps, staffed by undergraduates.

The idea was fairly simple. Enough cash would be raised to hire for a month or more a complete camp with tents, kitchen equipment, tables and benches and everything needed from a specialist firm in Liverpool which would deliver the whole consignment and dump it on the ground at the chosen spot. We also picked up an unemployed ship's cook and an assistant, and these men were paid for the job. We did not think that undergraduate cooking could be relied upon to cater for such large numbers. We had a properly thought out catering programme too, which was far ahead of Byways beer and sausage.

The chosen spot. That was not so easy to find. We wanted clean air, exhilarating surroundings, and a place where the men could work hard for the whole of the morning every day, up until lunch time. It was this last point that was difficult, because it meant finding an estate or other place where something could be done which would occupy the combined efforts of 120 men (100 unemployed and 20 undergraduates) for the whole month, but could never be said to be taking the bread out of the mouths of other workers. There was, then as now, a strong anti-charity feeling among some of the most rabid socialist borough councils. We had a typical example of this in Wales, where we discovered a small mining town that could very well do with a municipal swimming pool, there being no such facility there.

A camp was organised in the countryside nearby, and the men got to work. Altogether some 12,000 man-hours of work went into the job, and the result was a splendid swimming-pool. When finished, it was solemnly handed over to the council, amid applause and rejoicings. But the moment the camp left, the council brought up equipment and filled in the swimming-pool. Why? Just because it had not been constructed by union labour. What was achieved by this action was not easy to imagine.

I went on two of these camps, both of them at Chillingham in Northumberland, the home of the sole surviving herd of wild cattle which, to judge from the drawing on the front of the Lindisfarne Gospels, has remained virtually unchanged for twelve hundred years.

The estate and the cattle belonged to the impecunious Earl of Tankerville, and the extensive woodlands upon his lands were in need of clearance. This was a job to which nobody could possibly take exception, especially as the splendid Norman castle itself had been unoccupied for some years. The countryside was beautiful, there was bathing in a river, and unlimited scope for walking in the Cheviots – except that the scope was somewhat limited by the unemployed men never having walked except to the pithead, and becoming worn out after half an hour.

We had to have the camp, we had to have food, and we had the funds with which to buy it. I was in charge of the catering, and I took the opportunity to obtain wonderful fresh butter from a nearby farm. But after the first breakfast there was a deputation of complaint. What was this stuff? Butter? They had never had it.

We also needed to have a hundred unemployed men, and to find these we had the help of the Tyneside office of the National Council of Social Service. The men were offered a month's holiday, but they had to pay. Not much, and only about half their Dole, but it was a sensible principle that they had to sacrifice something in return for the enormous benefit they received. And that benefit was, in brief, that they were so well fed and so amply exercised that every single one of them could be guaranteed a job upon leaving; and would not only have a job but be fit enough to keep it. Altogether the camps were a great success.

One day we were faced with disaster in the kitchen, because the delivery of meat had failed to arrive at the butcher's five miles away. (We had no refrigeration, so we had to live from one day to the next where perishable foods were concerned.) I mentioned the problem to a couple of the men, and they said there was no problem at all. We would go sticking and stoning.

Now I had no idea what sticking and stoning might be, but I sometimes have wondered since then whether it might not be an activity introduced at the time of the Viking raids upon the Northeast. These men knew well enough how to stick and stone, as they indulged in this activity to help fill their own empty larders back home.

We went up to the moorland of Ross Hill, overlooking the domains of the Earl and the cattle park surrounded by a wall several miles in length. We climbed over the wall, and like the others I selected a stick and a stone the size of a small cobble. We then spread out in a straight line, about a dozen of us, each several yards from the next. Then we advanced.

We had not gone more than fifty yards when a rabbit started. Immediately there was a hail of a dozen sticks and a dozen cobbles, but the rabbit escaped into a patch of nettles. But chased rabbits, it was explained to me, do not dart into burrows, they merely lie low. However, the rabbit had no chance to lie for long. Gathering up their sticks and stones the mob rushed the patch of undergrowth and the rabbit started again. It was not long before it was hit, despatched, and put in the bag.

The chase went ahead, and soon we were approaching the famous herd of cattle. These creatures, I knew, had peculiar habits of their own, one of which was to form a phalanx when threatened. The chief bull was in the middle of the front row, which was composed entirely of bulls. There were more and younger bulls down each flank, and the cows and youngsters were packed into the square led and flanked by these three lines of warriors. When I saw the cattle taking up this formation I was somewhat ill at ease, and far from leading my excited troops I looked around for a tree which I could climb in case of emergency.

Just then another rabbit started, and racing toward the cattle ran straight through the first line of bulls and disappeared. The men were racing after it, and it was in vain that I yelled to them to stop. Shouting and waving their sticks they ran on toward the herd, with myself lagging behind. The bulls began to roar, the leader pawed the ground. There followed a tremendous trumpeting, and then . . . And then, the whole herd turned tail and fled as though the devil were after them.

We bagged thirty rabbits, which was sufficient for the dinner.

PRONE TO ACCIDENT

I had grown up without having any great interest in psychology, and the wonder first stirred in me when a friend of mine elected to spend six months travelling from London to Edinburgh and back in first class sleepers twice every week, in order to have himself analysed. In the fifth month he went off his head, but as there was a waiting list for sleepers on that route he did not have to pay for failing to give forty-eight hours' notice of cancellation to the railway.

The sudden conclusion to his course of therapy aroused my interest in psychology, and when I heard that it was a Freudian analysis I wanted to know more. So I began to delve into the works of Sigmund Freud and discovered some startling things. It was Freud who made me realise that a writer did exactly the same as a child at play – that is, he creates a world of his own and then re-arranges it in a way that happens to please him better. Freud also taught me why people were afraid of falling out of windows – previously I had thought they just didn't like the idea of falling out – and it was Freud also who cleared up the mystery of why people like scratching their names on ancient monuments. There is evidently much more in this habit than meets the eye, though it is not something I like to talk about at mealtimes or mention in polite company – and no doubt the great Viennese could have told me why I have these particular irrational hesitations.

Shortly after that I watched a psychologist selecting from the common herd of soldiery those who were suitable for commissions. He fixed them with a stare and asked each of them the same question, 'Which is the larger, an elephant or a flea?' The men assumed that there was a draft in the wind to some place where accurate knowledge on such matters would be important, and as none of them wished to be sent out East, they all replied 'Flea, Sir,' except for a lance-corporal who asked whether he was referring to any particular stage in the embryonic development. Up until the fifth day the flea was larger, he said, but after that the elephant won easily. The lance-corporal was given a commission in the Army Educational Corps and the psychologist changed to asking about Nelson's Column and a matchstick instead.

It was on that occasion that I came to realise that psychology must have peculiar insights of its own, and so I attended a course on Industrial Psychology in London, which turned out to be much the same as any other brand only less sordid but more grimy. And there I learned some surprising things – for instance that Jung had a dream of Basel cathedral covered in horse shit, something which proved a turning point in his life, as I am sure it would have been in mine. And I also learned that some individuals are accident-prone.

I doubted this for a while, and then I remembered Baldry, who had been my kitchen assistant at the unemployed camp where I was in charge of catering. He was about forty, and he wore gym shoes with a Sunday suit and a cap. He had been out of work for several months before the camp started. Originally this was the result of getting out of the wrong side of the train in Newcastle station, but the day he left hospital and went up to the Labour Exchange to tell them he was fit again he walked through the glass door but forgot to open it first. Some people might have thought he was absent-minded, but not a bit of it. Things just happened to him. He was no W.B. Yeats standing in the roadway; he kept to the pavements gray – as Yeats did sometimes apparently – but it had not saved him from being buried in a load of celery when a tyre burst on a lorry bound for the wholesale market.

When Baldry had got over the door incident he was sent away by the council's casework officer for a rest, and that was how he got washed up in our camp. Along with ninety-nine others he arrived for our special lumber therapy. It was not really his idea of a rest, but he was happy at hauling away at logs. Then on his second day the head flew off somebody's axe and struck him blunt side first on the back of the head.

The camp medical officer was keen on psychology too, and particularly what he called 'suggestion'. When Baldry recovered consciousness and felt the back of his head and asked what had happened the doctor suggested he had just eaten too much porridge for breakfast. Baldry was nonplussed for a while – he never ate porridge – but the doctor stuck to his story and when one of the other men later asked Baldry what it felt like to be felled with an axe-head Baldry thought the man was fooling him, and as he did not like to be fooled he tried to kick him. The man side-stepped just in time, and the doctor (who was only a second-year medical undergraduate) had to go to Berwick-on-Tweed and find out how to fix a dislocated knee.

Baldry was a helpful fellow and when I let him work the bread-slicer it never occurred to me to tell him that he ought to stop when he reached the end of the loaf. Fortunately he was not a concert pianist and it was only his left hand. He got a useful disability pension, and was able to take a job waving red and green flags at motorists where the County Council was re-surfacing a stretch of the main road.

I never actually saw him again, but when a year or two later I was flicking through the Registrar General's mortality returns I noticed a new column in the sub-section headed 'By crushing'. No name was given to the solitary case, but I thought I recognised the entry as Baldry's only memorial. There was no footnote to say whether the road-roller was driven by steam or internal combustion.

MR WENDON

Easter holidays gradually became a time of working at revision for impending examinations, and there could be no more suitable place than Windy Gap in which to settle down to study without interference. There among the pine woods near Ainsdale I would retire for a week or two with a couple of friends from Cambridge, to work from after breakfast until midday without even a break for elevenses. Such a 'reading party' was at that time quite common – Magdalene ran three under the aegis of various Fellows – and it was an excellent way of studying without interference.

The only human contact any of us had in that private wilderness was Clarke, the morose gamekeeper of the surrounding woodlands. He kept the key to Windy Gap, but otherwise he had very little to do with us. He never appeared to smile, and it was not often that he spoke to any of the family either. But one day he told my parents about the previous owner, a Mr Wendon.

'He was a strange man,' said Clarke darkly. 'He never did want as anyone should ever live here after him. It was him as made this place, and he said he would never leave it. Not even after he was dead, he said. "You mark my words, Clarke," he said to me, "I don't want any man ever to have this place when I'm gone. And if they do, I'll come back and show them that I may be dead, but I'm not gone, and I'm going to come back to what by rights is mine." Yes, he was a peculiar man, but he was never one to tell lies. And he said as how he had put a curse upon the house itself.'

Months passed without our ever recalling Clarke's lugubrious talk, and nothing happened to remind us of it until shortly after the arrival of the Reverend Robinson.

This individual was actually a grandfather clock, and it took its name from the fact that when my father first saw it in a shop in Liverpool the assistant said to him, 'I don't think you can have that one Sir. It's the Reverend Robinson.' But the assistant discovered that the cleric in question had changed his mind, so the clock was indeed available, and shortly afterward it arrived at Windy Gap. It was fully seven feet high, and stood in the corner of the living-room, ticking away serenely with the assurance that we should wind it up every week, and stop it when we left.

One evening when we were at supper, the footsteps began. The bungalow was of wooden construction, and three steps led up to the back door from the sandy yard at the back. The footsteps began faintly, then grew gradually louder as they progressed deliberately along the passage and came to a halt, apparently just outside the living-room door.

'That must be Clarke,' said my father. 'Go and see what he wants.'

I opened the door. There was nobody there, and I said so. My mother looked at my father with a nod of her head which seemed to say 'Mr Wendon', but neither of them said anything.

Next evening the footsteps came again. Once more I went to the door and flung it open quickly. The passage was empty.

Little by little we became used to the visits of Mr Wendon. He never did us any harm, and there were no tangible results of the curse of which Clarke had told us. We got used to his visits, and perhaps we became a little proud of having a cottage that was actually haunted by the previous owner. After a few months we were so accustomed to him that we would have missed him if he had forgotten to come. We liked him.

But some people did not. My parents used to lend the place freely to others, and once it was occupied by a dozen ministers from churches in the St Helens area who wanted to have a retreat. The effect of Mr Wendon's nightly visits did not lead them to try any kind of exorcism, but it worried them so much that two of the clerics could not stand it any longer, and left after Mr Wendon's second visit. When the others mentioned the footsteps to Clarke, he confirmed their suspicions that they were supernatural.

'That'll be Mr Wendon's ghost,' he said in a matter-of-fact way. 'He's been coming here this last year or two, regular like.'

The Easter vacation reading-party with my two friends from Magdalene gave the three of us the opportunity to hear Mr Wendon's arrival each evening. Promptly at twenty-two minutes past seven we would hear the first faint tread on the wooden steps, then the sound growing louder and closer until it stopped abruptly. We were so used to it that soon we never bothered to open the door to see who was not there.

One evening one of us was sitting in the corner of the room, leaning back in his chair just in front of the Reverend Robinson. At the sound of the steps he jumped up, opened the front of the clock and peered inside.

The pendulum was just striking against the clock-case, giving the sound of a step once every two seconds.

We examined the clock carefully during the next day or two and discovered that one of the cogwheels in the movement, which was all cut by hand, was slightly eccentric, with the result that the pendulum swung a little wide of centre, which meant that once every twelve hours the fourteen mysterious knockings or steps were repeated. Mr Wendon's ghost was laid, and we were somewhat disappointed to find that his hauntings had a rational explanation. Experimentally we altered slightly the stance of the Reverend Robinson, and when we did so no ghost came to visit us at twenty-two minutes past seven or at any other time. But when the day came for us to leave we carefully restored the clock to its original position. And we never told anyone of our discovery.

It was a year or two later that my father had a letter of thanks from a family to whom the bungalow had been lent for a week.

'Did you know the bungalow was haunted? You must have done, but I suppose you did not mention it in case we were put off. Not a bit, I can assure you. It's thrilling! Every evening the ghost comes along the back passage at soon after twenty past seven, and once we heard him in the morning, too. Old Clarke says it is the ghost of a Mr Wendon, who used to live here before you bought the place. It seems he put a curse on the place, although his ghost doesn't seem to do anybody any harm. But it really is most exciting!'

Then, after more news of their stay, there was a postscript.

'By the way, your grandfather clock was run down when we arrived. I thought it best not to wind it up, because I know how sensitive these old clocks can be.'

FATHER OF CHEMISTRY

$$P \times V = C$$

This famous equation, which is concerned with the relationship between the volume occupied by a gas and the pressure exerted upon it, cannot by any stretch of imagination be called exciting. Even when I learned at school that its discoverer was Father of Chemistry and son of the Earl of Cork the knowledge did not greatly intrigue me. Boyle's Law was no doubt useful to those who wondered about gas pressures, but beyond that it did not fire the imagination. And so it remained buried in my memory circuits until the day when I went into the Cambridge Corn Exchange to see whether there were any interesting books for sale in the auction of the library of a Cambridge professor. I saw six enormous leather-bound volumes of the collected works of Robert Boyle in the edition of 1772. There was little competition for them when the bidding began, and I bought them in easily and cheaply, and purely out of curiosity.

Little by little as I dipped into them I became fascinated by the versatility of a man who, though known only for this one formula, could write upon *A Discovery of the Admirable Rarefaction of the Air*, and could also reflect *Upon the Sight of a Fair Milk-maid Singing to Her Cow*. Above all, he tackled what to me was the most essential matter of all in *The Christian Virtuoso*. This, one of his major works, was subtitled 'Shewing that by being addicted to Experimental Philosophy a Man is rather assisted than indisposed to be a good Christian.' In this work Boyle faced precisely the same problems as any modern research worker may do, and he wrote about them to great effect.

I quickly became fascinated by Robert Boyle, and he became a great source of inspiration. He was a founder member of the Royal Society – the 'Invisibles' as they were then called – and he was a great and careful experimenter. He was convinced that to study nature in terms of cause and effect would certainly reveal many facts which could be very useful when applied to human life and welfare. All the same, this was really of secondary importance to him, for first and foremost he was seeking the truth, not just to catalogue new discoveries but because he was convinced that by studying nature he would come to a greater understanding of the ways by which God operated. So, whether he was researching into matter, or the nature of a flame, or the compression of air, he was always striving to find an interpretation which harmonised with his own personal experience of God's providence in love. For him, discovery went hand in hand with religious awareness and he was convinced that the wisdom and ingenuity of a loving God would be further revealed through the telescope and the microscope – both of them comparatively recently invented. Nature was God's other Bible. There were two chief ways of discovering the attributes of God, he wrote; the study of his word in the Bible, and of his works in nature. Boyle never believed that man represented the whole of the ultimate purpose of God, yet clearly mankind was far above the rest of the creatures.

Christian tradition, the Bible itself and personal experience were the foundations of the faith of the scientist Robert Boyle, and after my own musings and attempts to sort out the relationship between science and faith I found it stimulating to discover that much the same conclusions had been arrived at three centuries earlier by a great thinker.

Robert Boyle had no doubts whatsoever about the loving nature of God. In this he was very much more than a child of his time, for he thought and wrote a great deal on that subject. Man could reject the freely offered love of God, and very often did so, but that made no difference at all. It was, Boyle wrote, just like a lunatic rushing headlong into a wall, dashing out his brains but leaving the wall unshaken. Well, maybe; but I doubt if this simile was really suitable, for the wall was not in a position to be sad about the incident, whereas anyone – even God, as far as I could hope to understand him – would surely suffer the pain of rejection, even if he freely forgave the one who rejected him.

Boyle saw the will, the inherent desire to love God, as a gift from God himself, and the love given by God was constant, unchanging, reaching from the beginning to the end of time and allowing mankind to live in a state of permanent spiritual ecstasy. So far so good; but how, he wondered, could this love allow the awful sufferings with which so many humans were afflicted? He thought of the wretched captives chained to the oars of galleys, of those with disease or gangrenous injuries and tormented with pain, living only in suffering as one part after another was amputated, so that they witnessed their own slow dismemberment and death. *Copious showers of tears everywhere water if not overflow the vale of human misery*, he wrote, as he strove to find an explanation which would allow a God of love to permit such a situation.

This question of how to reconcile human anguish with a loving God has of course worried thinkers from Job to modern times. And it would be surprising if this were not so. Boyle began by accepting the traditional view that pain was either a warning (which it sometimes obviously is) or a punishment inflicted as a retribution for sin. He actually regarded his own stammering as a punishment, probably for pride, but as time went on he became much too familiar with the immediate causes of suffering in sickness to accept that either warning or divine punishment could possibly be involved in every case. Yet having reached that point he could only go on to say that we as humans were hamstrung by being forced to look at things from a very earth-bound or parochial situation, one might say a worm's-eye view, and he trusted confidently that in heaven the mystery would be solved. *'There, I hope, we shall have clearly expounded to us those riddles of providence which have only too often tempted good men to question God's conduct in the government of the world.'* Meanwhile, he thought, we were like people who had dropped into the theatre in the middle of a play and had to leave after seeing no more than a couple of scenes.

Perhaps today we can see some of these matters a little more clearly, because we know very well that our own life has been built up through the billions of years of evolution. This long and successful climb was achieved through two basic mechanisms:– aggression, and pain. But if the aggressor, the predator, were always to succeed there would be no chance for other creatures – and even the predator would then starve to death and become extinct. The balance in nature which made the great advances possible was brought about by protective mechanisms based squarely on pain. At the simplest, pain is the trigger of a reflex reaction. Touch a hot saucepan, and the pain sends messages up the sensory nerves and down to the muscles which contract in a fraction of a second to pull back the hand, even before the pain has been registered in the mind. Pain of this kind, Boyle's 'warning' was for long ages the guardian of the survival of the individual organism. There was genetic selection for efficient sensitivity, for the pain that protected.

Yet even in animals there was a more subtle, a more refined pain. An animal would not survive if it waited to be activated by actual physical pain when the sharp teeth of a predator closed upon it. The danger had to be anticipated, evaded if possible before it could strike. And this was achieved by another mechanism, fear.

Fear starts a reaction to avoid physical pain, a pain which can be seen approaching. The fear may not be less unpleasant than the pain it forestalls but it will, with a bit of luck, have a chance of saving the creature. An animal may shriek with fear at the sight of an approaching enemy, and so may a person. Probably the shriek will have little or no effect in deterring the predator, but the real shaking, all-pervading pain that is fear may save the creature by causing it to flee for its life, bolt down a hole, leap for safety, or climb a tree.

These reactions, as we now know, are indeed genetically determined, selected, passed on across the ages of evolution. That being so, I think it follows that the very real pain and terror which exist throughout the creation are in no way the dirty work of some medieval devil. They are the very stuff of mankind's own gestation and birth. Had Robert Boyle been able to have some of the facts of the evolution of life unfolded before him he would surely have come to the same conclusion.

Quite apart from the suffering and pain which he considered might be warning or protective, Boyle noted two other categories which contributed to the *'downpour in the vale of human misery'*. One was the suffering deliberately caused by other men, as in the case of the galley-slaves, but what to him was less easily explained was the sort of catastrophe which theologians used to term 'natural evil' – a rather unfortunate term surely because in reality evil is always something done, whereas the things in question are not done by anyone or anything. 'Natural evils' are just there as part of the fabric of the world we live in, dark spots on the shining silk of the creation.

These causes of unmerited suffering include epidemics, floods, earthquakes, volcanic eruptions. These things are more than just unpleasant. They are not obviously the works of man, and their mere existence seems to reflect upon God's concern for humanity, or upon his love, or even his ability as a competent creator. Could not God have fixed the construction of the cooling crust of the Earth so that there was no need for Vesuvius to blow its top off? Did he just not know enough physics?

Natural disasters and their like there definitely are; but they are disasters to *us*. We would all of us rather have the world safe, soft and easy. But if we look at the amazing versatility of nature, at the fantastic design of matter which can replicate itself and undergo variation until we can love, laugh and glory in the seagulls diving and soaring on the updraught at the cliff edge, then we need not be too surprised if some of the necessary by-products of this gigantic process are not absolutely to our liking.

These 'natural evils' are all parts of the one enormous and brilliant but vastly complex process that includes the genetic evolution of life, which has led from the merely physical constituents of this world through the thousands of intermediate forms to reach its culmination in man. Man with the remarkable ability to show love and to receive it also.

Some regard these natural disasters as events deliberately designed to be a challenge to mankind, but it is difficult to see what sort of a challenge is provided by the eruption of Mont Pelee or the latest Los Angeles earthquake. If one regards nature as a whole, then with what we know about our present local space-time cabbage-patch I think we can accept that the whole creation is good, even in its uncertainties and pain. That is something which Robert Boyle accepted through his own faith – even if he was forced to conclude that the full explanation would only be given to him in heaven.

The idea that sickness and disease are things which are literally acts of God, or a punishment, or the unavoidable result of human sinfulness, is by no means extinct. There are cases – AIDS-related diseases being the most obvious – where it would not be too difficult to make out a case for divine retribution, particularly if one were to believe God to be more interested in punishing people than forgiving. The connection between sin and disease, not only in humans but in the whole of nature, was a subject which cropped up in conversation when I was travelling with a friend from Liverpool Street to Harwich.

Leonard Griffith was at that time the minister of London's City Temple, a church which was generally regarded as London's foremost preaching pulpit. Many famous preachers had been installed there at one time or another. He was invited to speak at a conference in Rotterdam, and aboard the boat train for the Hook Leonard sat reading a theological tome, and opposite him in the compartment I was reading rather lighter material. The train was somewhere near Manningtree when I glanced out of the window and saw that all the stately elms which edged the Essex fields were dead, or dying.

'Look, Leonard,' I said, tapping him on the knee. 'Look at those trees. They are elms and every one of them is killed by the Dutch Elm Disease.'

Leonard glanced out of the window, and shuddered. 'The effect of human sin,' he said briefly.

'Human sin? But Leonard, it is not human sin at all. It is the beetle which spreads the virus and that kills the elms.'

'It is due to human sin just the same,' Leonard declared confidently.

'Human sin has nothing to do with it,' I objected. 'How do you make out that those trees are being killed by sin?'

By this time the rest of the compartment was very wide awake. Not that anyone wished to intervene in the argument, but a subject of this kind was not what one usually heard bandied across a carriage from one side to the other.

'You can't get away with a statement like that unless you can follow it up with sound reasoning. Come on. Explain how human sin is killing the elms across the Essex countryside.'

'We are probably observing nothing more than the final link in the chain of events,' Leonard replied. 'You see, all across the country there are towns – like Chelmsford twenty minutes ago – which have a lot of industry. Those industries are powered by human greed to make as much money as they can, regardless, yes?'

'I can't necessarily go along with that,' I said. 'But I will grant you that people would not be manufacturing anything unless they were paid wages and salaries, which they may very well need to support their families. It is not necessarily sinful.'

'If it is carried to excess, it certainly is,' he answered.

'All right. Have it your way. But what about the beetles spreading the virus of the Dutch Elm Disease?'

Leonard considered, hardly aware of the eyes of all our fellow travellers in the train, who looked at him with a wild surmise.

'It is probable that what comes out of factory chimneys has some effect upon the trees. Probably reducing the natural resistance of the trees themselves to the virus so that they are wide open to its attack. So, you see, it is sin – greed in this case – which is killing them.'

'I see,' I said, which was not absolutely true.

'All disease, all sickness and death is the direct or indirect result of the fall from grace of humanity. In other words, of human sin,' Leonard declared.

'But Leonard, we know that it is a virus in this case which causes the disease. Do you mean that the virus itself is the product of human sin?'

Leonard considered. 'Probably,' he said. 'After all, we have it in First Corinthians, don't we? *Since by man came death* – Paul knew what he was talking about didn't he? Death came through sin for mankind. And through mankind for the other creatures too, like the trees you pointed out. In a world without sin there would be no disease or death.'

'No disease?'

'Certainly. Take cancer. It will probably turn out to be caused by overindulgence. By greed, that is. Sin.'

I thought for a while. 'Leonard,' I said, 'I want you to do something when you get back to London after the conference. I want you to go to the Wellcome Medical Historical Museum, down around Portman Square, and go and look at the skeleton of the dinosaur. That dinosaur died because it had tuberculosis of its hip-joint – there's no doubt about that whatsoever. And being a heavy animal it just collapsed, poor beast. Its skeleton was eventually dug up, and the damage to its thigh is there for all to see.'

'Well,' said Leonard. 'What of that?'

'That dinosaur lived roughly one hundred and twenty million years ago, millions and millions of years before there were any men around to indulge in their favourite occupation of sinning. Go and look at that skeleton, then tell me how that unfortunate animal was a victim of the effects of human sin, if all diseases have their origin there, as you said they have.'

Soon the train reached Parkestone Quay and we made our way to the ship. We never then, or afterwards, referred to the Essex elm trees, not even when we were back in England and he was continuing at the City Temple. A year or two later he left London and was installed in the Deer Park church in Toronto, in his own country. After that, I lost sight of him.

It was several years later that I saw his familiar writing on a letter addressed to me in London. After giving the news of his family, he returned to the matter we had discussed.

'I really want you to know,' he wrote, 'that our conversation in the train on the way to Harwich marked a turning-point in what I believed then, and now. It made me completely revise my ideas of sin, and realise that sin is one thing, but sickness and diseases have not necessarily got anything to do with it. It was a great revelation!'

Not everyone would have had the humility to say that.

LAB LIFE

It was one day early in September that my wife and I arrived by car in Herefordshire. We had decided to take a week or more of holiday exploring the Wye valley and the Welsh Marches, so we sought a suitable hotel in the little town of Ross-on-Wye. We enquired at one, then at another; but no, it seemed that they were completely booked out. Finally we tried a pleasant hotel from the olden days of coaching.

The receptionist shook her head. 'Sorry, Sir. All the accommodation is already occupied,' she said. 'Every room has already been taken for some weeks past. There is not a place in the whole house.'

'Is there really nothing,' I said, almost in despair. 'Not even a bed in the billiard room or something?'

She smiled. 'No, Sir. Every available room is filled. That is, except for one on the top floor which we never let.'

'Never let? Why not?'

'Well, Sir, there is . . . but people might complain. They might think the hotel was dirty. You see, the ceiling is always covered with flies. Hundreds of them. It is always like that, and we have never been able to stop it.'

This sounded interesting. 'What species?' I asked.

'I've no idea, Sir. But they are all over the plaster.'

'May I have a look, just out of curiosity?'

'Of course, if you wish. But you would not want to stay there, Sir.'

She gave me the key and I went up the stairs to the top floor. The room had two unmade beds, but was pleasant enough. And the ceiling had several hundred small flies walking over it. I took a chair and climbed on it to investigate. A moment later I was running down the stairs two at a time.

'We'll take it!' I exclaimed. 'They're *Drosophila melanogaster*!'

How the ceiling of this one room came to be a happy rendezvous for the fruit fly I could not imagine. Perhaps a building labourer had spilled some cider into the mix when trowelling the ceiling. But there was no doubt about the fact that the *Drosophila* liked it.

As soon as we were installed I acquired some empty milk bottles from the staff and slipped out to buy a sheet of blotting paper, a small bottle of cider, and a packet of cotton wool to provide stoppers for the bottles. Maybe the hotel staff thought that I was off my head, but the fact was that I was researching on the mechanism of certain gene changes in *Drosophila*, and in the zoo lab we were always on the lookout for new mutant stocks, so the bedroom in the hotel at Ross-on-Wye was an exciting discovery. One could have no idea what gold mine of mutant genes might or might not be present in the fly population. It was an easy matter to make a mash of bananas to put in the bottom of each milk bottle, and then to lure the flies with the blotting paper soaked in cider. When I had half a dozen stocks of flies duly established I reckoned that it would be sufficient, and the milk bottles with their dipteran populations travelled with us for the rest of the holiday in the back of the car.

The real excitement would come later. The flies laid their eggs and the grubs hatched out to start gorging themselves. Then they pupated, and two or three weeks from the night in the hotel the next generation was emerging. That was when I had to scrutinise them one fly at a time after giving them a quick whiff of anaesthetic, to search for any obvious differences. After breeding for another two generations to allow more chance for recessives to show themselves I was able to add five new mutant stocks to our bank of flies.

None could say that lab life was dull. But I could well understand that people engaged in research could very occasionally be more concerned with their own reputation and position than with a strict regard for truth.

The first example of such a scientist I came to know of was Gurwitsch. He was professor at Jena, I think, in the nineteen-thirties, and at Freiburg there was plenty of tittle-tattle about him over what would have been a tea-break if they had been able to make a proper pot of tea. Gurwitsch, like most German professors at that time, decided the line of research that everyone in his laboratory was to follow, and the credit would go to him for being the head of such a brilliant school of knowledge.

It seems that Gurwitsch was watching mitosis (cell division) down his binocular microscope, when he noticed that the cells were dividing much faster than usual. Something had doubled the rate of division. He could think of no reason for this, except perhaps some unsuspected outside influence, and looking around the immediate vicinity of his experiment he noticed an onion lying disregarded on the bench – at least, that is the story as we had it from Hans Spemann. In a brilliant flash of intuition he realised that he had stumbled upon something totally new to biological science, and he named that something '*Mitogenetische Strahlen*' (mitogenetic rays). Some strange emanation from the sprouting onion shoot must have affected the rate of cell division in the tissue he was examining. Excitedly Gurwitsch removed the onion and looked again. The rate of cell division had returned to what he would normally have expected.

His epoch-making discovery held the key to a great future. His assistants and the research men throughout the laboratory were immediately told to drop everything and get to work on mitogenetic rays, where and how the emanations occurred, and their remarkable qualities. It transpired through experiments that the rays would pass through several inches of solid lead, but curiously enough were stopped by an ordinary piece of plate glass. They emanated from onions under certain conditions, and also from other living things. But not all. A fever of activity spread throughout the laboratory as Gurwitsch and his school performed one experiment after another, and wrote a whole series of learned papers on the subject. When I looked in the Cambridge University Library to see how many papers had appeared, I was astonished to find that the outpouring from that laboratory measured nearly a whole yard on the shelves.

The fact that other laboratories could not get the same results did not deter the professor. But one day one of the research workers came to him and asked if he might speak to him. He then told the professor that he had examined the matter with great care and he had come to an important conclusion. And that was, quite simply, that mitogenetic rays did not exist.

To his amazement the professor smiled, and merely answered 'Yes. Of course I have known that for quite a time.' He then looked at his colleague and added, very pointedly, 'And what chance do you think you would have of obtaining a lecturership or a professor's chair in another university if you had to admit that you had spent your time working upon and writing up something which did not exist? Get back to your work. Mitogenetic rays are what we are working on. You understand?'

The young man understood all right. Maybe he resigned, but Gurwitsch continued to pump out paper after paper on his pet subject. Yet the trouble with lying in research is that somebody is sure to repeat the experiments elsewhere, and however many papers come pouring out of the original source the deception cannot be kept up for ever. This should have been obvious, but apparently it was not. When the end came, the Jena laboratory was the laughing-stock of the biological world, and I rather doubt if any of the staff who had been forced to continue falsifying their results easily found promotion to posts in other universities.

The Gurwitsch case was merely one of pride, and refusal at whatever cost to admit that one had made a mistake. Much the same was true of Kammerer, though he did not involve so many people in his deception.

Kammerer was a convinced Lamarckian – that is, he thought evolution had proceeded through the inheritance in successive generations of acquired characteristics. The usual illustration is that because giraffes had to stretch higher and higher to eat the leaves on which they fed, their necks grew just a tiny bit longer (though still containing only seven vertebrae), and this tendency to longer necks was inherited. So giraffes simply grew taller and taller, hereditarily.

Kammerer decided to perform experiments that would demonstrate this sort of effect, and he chose the salamander for his work. This engaging creature has a protective colouring of blotches of black and yellow, and it has the ability to change its colour within certain limits, so that it may avoid detection. Kammerer's idea was simple enough. He would bring up salamanders in yellow boxes, or in black ones. He would then mate them to ones similarly brought up, and the offspring, born on a neutral background, would be either more yellow or more black than normal, according to their parentage.

I once had a copy of Kammerer's book *Die Neuvererbung erworbener Eigenschaften* (*The inheritance of Acquired Characteristics*). It was interesting. It showed photographs of the resulting young salamanders, and how the coloured boxes of their parents produced inherited changes in the colour patterns. The only trouble was that somebody went into the darkroom in the laboratory and found the photographic plates being touched up to accord to the theory. Kammerer was disgraced, and his photographer shot himself.

Then of course there was Trofim Denisovich Lysenko, whose case is better known, and was much in the news in the 1940s and 1950s. Lysenko came across a paper which reported that plant growth could be accelerated by short doses of near freezing temperatures. This 'vernalisation' is often true, and it is now a very important technique in the

Dutch bulb industry. Lysenko used the idea to enable crops of cereals to ripen earlier, and he managed to do wonders for the Russian peasants and their harvests in the times of the great famines. But then he went on to say that this acceleration was inherited.

There was a political side to all this. He hoped to show that people could be changed for the better by Marxism, and that this improvement would be inherited. Such a theory would appeal greatly to the uneducated statesmen that Russia was producing, and in 1948 he won the blessing of the Communist party, declared Mendelian genetics to be a load of rubbish, had the leading geneticists of Soviet Russia relieved of their posts and banished, and himself appointed as head of the Institute of Genetics.

Of course Lysenko's experiments were repeated at Harpenden and elsewhere, and were found not to work. Although he had received the Order of Lenin and the Stalin prize for his efforts, the end was not long delayed. When his protector Kruschev was ousted, Lysenko got the sack too, and Russian genetics was able to get back on course again.

By the summer of 1939 a heaviness was felt by everybody in Britain, and those working in laboratories were not exempt from it. The Greater German Reich was expanding continually, country after country was being over-run as a 'definitely last territorial claim' and there was a feeling in the air that it was highly unlikely that war with Germany could be avoided for ever. Work went on very much as usual, even if there was an uneasy sense of futility in it. Nobody could pretend that the structure of the eye-facets of Drosophila, or the correlation between the rate of vibration of the wings of a house-fly and its speed through the air were matters which would shape the course of the world. However, several lines of zoological research had more positive possibilities. Work on undifferentiated tissue and what became of it was of possible application to regrowth of tissue in wounds, and it was towards this that some of us now began to turn our attention.

And then it suddenly dawned upon somebody in high circles that Britain would be in imminent danger if war should actually break out. Not because of German U-boats sinking the Atlantic shipping which was the national life-line, but for a totally unexpected reason. What threatened every man, woman and child was simply starvation at the hands of the terrestrial larvae of a crane-fly. These leathery wire-worms nibbled the roots of crops.

In the event, nothing was done until the outbreak of war, when the Ministry of Agriculture, or Food – I forget precisely which – decreed under emergency regulations that every plot of grass, whether field, tennis court, golf course, bowling green, or lawn, (but not cricket pitch, of course) was to be ploughed up immediately and sown with root crops or cereals. But now it seemed that governmental experts had discovered that an insect larva was widely distributed underneath the national turf in alarming quantities. These tough and leathery little creatures, wire-worms, were insidious enemies which nibbled away at roots. Their population under British grass varied very considerably, and so an omniscient government now decreed that cereals should only be sown on land where the count of wire-worms was lower than some figure which I have also forgotten, but let us suppose one billion per acre. Otherwise their attacks on the roots would cause crops to fail and we should as a nation be still nearer the edge of starvation and defeat. It was therefore necessary to sample the turf in all fields, tennis courts, bowling greens and lawns (but not cricket pitches) from John o'Groats to Land's End, and estimate the density of the wire-worm population. This interesting task was handed to university laboratories, including one adjacent to our zoology lab.

But how was this Herculean task to be accomplished? Professor Welney seized the opportunity. No doubt it was sheer patriotism, but the prize of being the man who could achieve this might perhaps be – well, maybe the Birthday Honours list was not thought of except by those of us who were not involved in the problem.

Professor Welney and one or two of his closest favourites in his laboratory dropped everything to produce a very ingenious machine which could do the job. Something like a gigantic apple-corer was produced, the radius of which was such that the area of turf cut with it was exactly one square foot. The clod of turf was then put in a glass tank, in which a few gallons of water were vigorously stirred and swished around by a kitchen mixer. Within a few minutes all the stones and earth had gone to the bottom of the tank, the roots, grass and wire-worms coming up to the surface of the water.

On top of the water was a layer of an inch or so of toluene, and above that was a layer of yet another fluid which did not mix with the toluene, but floated on it. The ingenuity of all this was that it provided two successive interfaces, and when the floating material rose in the water only the wire-worms came to rest at the boundary between the two upper fluids. Everything else either sank below them or floated to the top.

Running down into the wire-worms-only level was a small conveyer belt, suitably sheltered where it passed through the fluid above. The wire-worms were impelled toward the bottom step of the escalator in currents caused by small strategically placed propellers, driven by belts which connected their axles to a Meccano electric motor. So, as the stirring went on, the wire-worms all floated toward the escalator – which was provided with little stair-like ridges to catch them – were then carried up clear of the tank, dried by rolling down a length of blotting paper, and tipped over the edge to land in a dish which was mounted on a very sensitive balance. The dial of the balance was now very ingeniously calibrated not in grams, but in tens of thousands of wire-worms per acre.

This fantastic piece of engineering virtuosity was naturally an object of great pride to those who had produced it, and so Professor Welney decided to organise a demonstration to show off the invention. A tea-time party was laid on in the laboratory, and many worthy and important people in the university were invited with their ladies to come and admire the device and see it in operation.

We all of us watched spellbound as the earthy mixture in the tank began to be stirred, and the wire-worms sorted themselves out at one of the fluid interfaces, drifting in the current toward their private moving staircase. Up they went, rolled over, and tumbled down into the dish of the balance. As the very last of the larvae tripped down the slope the machine was turned off. Professor Welney read the scale, and we all applauded.

All, that is, except George Fairleigh, a research entomologist. He was looking at his watch.

'Four minutes and thirty-four seconds, I make that,' he exclaimed casually as the applause died away. He turned to Robertson, the chief laboratory assistant. 'Have you got another core handy?'

Robertson passed him a circle of turf on a tray.

'Take my watch,' George said. 'Say GO!'

The chief assistant watched the second-hand as it came up to zero.

'GO!'

George sat down at the bench, pulled the clod to pieces with his bare hands, picked out all the grubs and put them in a little heap. Swiftly he counted them, multiplied by the number of square feet in an acre and gave the answer. 'How long was that?' he asked pleasantly.

'A shade under two minutes, Mr Fairleigh,' said Robertson, hardly able to conceal his delight.

George brushed the earth into a neat little heap, and said nothing. One or two of the biology undergraduates risked a titter. The amusement spread, and some of the guests tactlessly laughed outright. Welney's personal aides looked embarrassed, but the professor was white with suppressed fury.

That was the last we ever saw of the wire-worm counter. It was also very nearly the last we saw of George Fairleigh. His room remained closed, but one morning he came over to the laboratory to say goodbye to myself and one or two others. It had been made very clear to him that his room was needed for other vital purposes, and within a few weeks he had left Cambridge for good to take up a position as lecturer in another and newer university.

THE RIDDLE OF THE SANDS

The other great scientist who always fascinated me was Carl von Linné. His botanical garden was situated at Uppsala in Sweden and I hit on the idea of going there from the Thames by inland waterways. It would be a long voyage but not an impossible one, and quite apart from the visit to the Orangery where the great botanist had laid out plants in their proper order of relationships, the voyage itself across five countries should prove full of interest.

The first stage was to leave the Thames and cross the Channel to Ostend. One could travel across Belgium and Holland and so reach the Ems, then the Weser, and thence arrive at the Elbe, bound for the Kiel Canal and the Baltic. The German information office in London was most helpful and provided me with quantities of information about everything to be seen or done along their part of the route. Or almost everything. The only thing they omitted to tell me, presumably because they did not know, was that the lock at one end of the only link between the Weser and the Elbe had been out of commission for some months already.

The link concerned was the Hadelner canal, a small waterway which crossed the miles of peaty moors of East Frisia. It could not be used by large boats because a railway bridge had thoughtlessly been built across it at a height of only nine feet above the water, but nine feet was enough for me, with two inches to spare. The canal began at the head of the tideway of the Geeste, a small tributary of the Weser, into which it flowed at Bremerhaven, and it ended at Otterndorf, a hamlet at the southern side of the Elbe, not very far from the entrance to the Kiel Canal on the further shore. This small waterway would provide a safe and sheltered passage across the corner of Germany, bypassing the area of sands so well described by Erskine Childers in the best spy thriller ever written.

It was the *Wasserschutzpolizei* in Bremerhaven who broke the news about the canal being closed when they had come aboard for a cup of tea. German customs men, water police, and all those to do with the sea invariably took the chance to have a proper cup of tea instead of the faintly coloured, tepid fluid that is served up by German restaurants. The reason for their addiction was that in their youthful days these men had been in the German navy, and so in 1945 they had been rounded up and interned, either in Britain, or in a British-run camp in Germany. While their families back home were finding it hard to put a meal together, they were living on excellent rations and were constantly provided with good, strong, proper tea. They had become used to tea-breaks and to afternoon tea-time. Here at Bremerhaven the *Wasserschutzpolizei* came aboard and asked no questions of us – except that it must surely be tea-time – and so we sat and chatted. They mentioned the closure of the lock at Otterndorf and even phoned the lock-keeper there to see if there were any chance at all of a boat passing, but there was not. After an hour or so one of them looked at his watch and said he must really be going. And he went – to fetch his wife to join the tea-party.

The conversation eventually turned back again to the matter of how we were to reach the Kiel Canal and the Baltic. The lock was going to be out of commission for at least three more months, so it seemed that we had no choice but to run down the estuary of the Weser to the sea and turn back up the mouth of the Elbe. To anyone looking at a map of the north German coast this would not appear to be a very long voyage at all. Bremerhaven was practically on the coast, which then turned northward to the Elbe entrance at Cuxhaven. The whole distance could not be more than twenty miles – three hours voyage perhaps. But this is merely an illusion of the landbound cartographer, for the area between the two river mouths is bounded by sands which extend more than ten miles out to sea and dry out for several feet above the water-line of low tide.

I had read *The Riddle of the Sands* and remembered enough of it to be rather disinclined to try my hand at cutting the corner of this astonishing area which seemed to be as much sand as water. It would of course be possible to follow the main channel of the Bremerhaven shipping right down to the Roter Sand lighthouse, then strike northward for the Elbe No. 1 lightship, where we could turn eastward into the water of the Elbe. But this would mean going thirty miles out to sea (further than crossing the English Channel), turning, and then running back again. Such a voyage was not in any way formidable in good weather, even if perhaps rather boring, but the weather was ominous and I did not want to be caught in a severe storm thirty miles from land.

We were pondering the problem when one of the policemen said he had an idea. *Der alte Peters*. Peters was a shrimp-fisherman of Cuxhaven who had spent his entire life shrimping among the gullies and sands off the coast and had made a speciality of piloting boats, not round the banks but right across them. At exactly the right state of the tide there was time, the policeman explained, to run *über die Watten*. It could be done, definitely, and *der alte Peters* was the man to do it.

I was not enthusiastic. I had the Admiralty charts and a glance at them showed the whole area to be a maze of banks and ditches covered at high water and quite devoid of any buoys or marks. The chart was liberally sprinkled with those sad little signs of the naval hydrographer which consist of the front end of a hull standing atilt, and where there were none of these there were the hardly more encouraging indications such as 'Wrk', 'Masts', 'Numerous remains of wrecks' and so forth. There was also a note added to the effect that no reliance should be placed upon the mapping of the channels, as the sands were continually shifting.

We also had on board a German pilot guide to the area, and this stressed that there were rapid tides, dangerous seas and unexpected shoals and shallows, so that *none but the most exceptionally experienced local navigators should venture anywhere in the vicinity*. But there were two pieces of information to reassure the foolhardy. The first was that on one of the inshore banks was a disused lighthouse provided with a stock of emergency rations to enable shipwrecked mariners to survive, and the other that the uninhabited island of Mellum bore a platform raised on stilts, on which one could survive from one tide to the next.

Our own *North Sea Pilot* described the area below Bremerhaven as 'a wide estuary much encumbered by sands and watts. Many of the sands were quicksands, so that sand was liable to silt up quickly around a stranded vessel', and the water police cheered us up further by saying that we should be careful to keep clear of the Grosser Knechtsand because it was as hard as concrete, and ships running upon it were invariably pounded to pieces. The only other danger was that wrecks in the area were used by the RAF as bombing targets.

It certainly seemed to me to be more prudent to make the long run out to sea and back again, but the *Wasserschutzpolizei* insisted that to take *den alten Peters* would be very much simpler. Besides, it would be a very interesting experience – and that I was only too ready to believe. Eventually I was persuaded by their expertise and judgment, and they obliged by telephoning to Cuxhaven to enquire whether Peters was there. Yes he was. What was more, he was already booked to bring two barges over the sands on the following day and would be arriving in Bremerhaven during the afternoon.

The following afternoon we sat in the sunshine on the Bremerhaven equivalent of Plymouth Hoe, scanning through the binoculars the flow of inward shipping in the

Weser estuary. At length two small family barges of the kind that would otherwise have used the Hadelner canal cut in close to the entrance mole and swung through the narrow entrance of the Geeste. We hurried down to the quay and saw in the wheelhouse of the leading barge a man over seventy, dressed in a broad-checked shirt and blue trousers, drinking a mug of coffee. He had a kaiser-style beard and a moustache shaped like a bow tie, and his thick glasses added to the general impression of a benevolent, short-sighted and slightly pedantic retired professor.

'Herr Peters?'

'*Jawohl!*' He came to stand on the hold cover at the foot of the wall, and peered up at us enquiringly. I explained that we wanted to run *über die Watten*, and he promptly agreed to be there at seven o'clock on the following morning. He would come on his bike if we would be kind enough to ship it along with us. The charge for the day would be forty marks and no extras.

On the stroke of seven next day Herr Peters appeared on the wall by the lock-gate of the Fischereihaven, and we flung him a line so that he could lower aboard the cycle on which he had come all the way from Cuxhaven. When he had climbed down the ladder we gave the required eight-second blast to signal that a ship was coming out of the Geeste mouth, and soon we were in the strong run of tide heading for the blank space of the North Sea. Peters took the wheel and followed the main shipping channel for the first seven miles, but then he left the track and cut off to the right to skirt the Robbenplatte and edge round the Eversand and another wide expanse of exposed golden sand, the Tegeler Platte. Up to this point there had been occasional buoys, and I was beginning to wonder why we needed a pilot at all, but then Peters cut in toward the sandbanks and turned into a deep gulley running south-eastward and in a direction almost directly opposite to the channel down which we had come. An hour later we found ourselves in a maze of sands which stretched in every direction as far as the eye could see. The sun shone lazily overhead and the water around us was yellow with suspended sand. Seals lumbered out of the sea to lie in the sunshine and watch us with slight suspicion as we passed them. Here and there a narrow inlet wound away to disappear between the hills and dales of golden banks but Peters threaded his way between the plates and hillocks with complete assurance.

At length we reached a broad expanse of calm, dead-looking water which overlay the inner side of the Grosser Knechtsand. Although it looked to me to be quite uniform it was far from being so. Peters lit a cigar and stood at the wheel, turning now to the northward, then to the east or the south, but he never looked at the compass. There were no visible marks of any kind whatsoever, just the various yellow mounds of beautifully clean sand, and here and there a piece of stranded driftwood or the rusted remains of one of the 'numerous wrecks'. To our left the ridge of the Knechtsand rose smoothly from the water with the remains of three broken hulks peering over the top from the further side. I remembered the *Dulcibella*.

Peters certainly knew the way. Even if the water looked as though it had a constant depth, the fact that we sometimes passed within thirty or forty yards of black-backed gulls standing on one leg showed how deceptive was the appearance, and I noticed that Peters not only glanced at the contours of the distant banks, but frequently peered over the side of the boat to tell from the behaviour and form of ripples the direction of the channels he was following. Three hours out of Bremerhaven he eased off, and asked me to sound. The boathook showed just four feet of water, and Peters looked at his watch. We should do well to wait half an hour, he said. Here we had a foot of water beneath the keel, but further ahead it would be shallower. It was important not to arrive at the shallowest point too early and run aground. He explained that he never liked to have much less than a foot of water beneath him, and that was a view I easily shared. I dropped the hook in the sand.

Peters began to talk about his trade. He had shrimped the banks for over half a century, and he took more than five thousand pounds worth of shrimps into Cuxhaven every year. That was not all profit as he had to maintain the boat and pay a couple of hands, besides looking after the nets and gear. But it was a profitable business nonetheless, and he had made enough money to buy a new modern shrimper for his son, with all the latest mechanical gear. But one needed more than a good boat. The best boat in the world was no use unless one understood the shrimps themselves and their way of life – and that was why many a man had tried his hand at the business and failed. Sometimes other boats would follow him out from Cuxhaven, he said, drop their nets within a hundred yards of his, but at the end of the day they had not taken a third of the catch that he had. Why? Because they did not grasp that one must *understand the shrimps*. If he were to ask them what a shrimp ate, they would have no idea.

Like any other creatures, shrimps would be found where their food was found. So the important thing was to know in what way the abundance of food would be affected by circumstances. A light wind from the west would build up more sand on this bank to our left, but a stronger one would make the waves break and scoop off the top layer of the sand, stirring up the tiny worms for the shrimps to eat them, and depositing them . . . where? Ah! That was where the knowledge came in. Over in that gulley on the right there would be no shrimps today, but four days earlier they were teeming in their millions. Yes, the sands were continually shifting, and so was the food of the shrimps. It needed years and years of study before one knew for certain where from day to day they would be found in all that maze of sands and creeks.

In due course I sounded again. The water had risen by nearly a foot, so we set off once more and reached the inner edge of the Hohenhörn Bank, close to the spot where the attempt to wreck the *Dulcibella* miscarried through the sheer good fortune of her being swept over a nick in the ridge. Peters now turned due east, threading his way between steep-sided banks, passing some of them so close that one could have leapt ashore from the catwalk.

Soon we saw ahead a twisting line of birch saplings planted by fishermen to mark the channel around the next watt, but the channel had moved so far out of position during recent storms that Peters left some of the marks as much as a hundred yards to one side, and then cut so close to others that the twigs brushed our halyards. Just then the sun began to fade away, and the sea became merged with the sky in a uniform silvery sheen. The air was still, the banks vanished from view, swallowed up in an eerie blankness. Peters looked up at the sky. There was a storm out at sea, he said, and in Helgoland there would already be a gale blowing. As Helgoland was only thirty miles distant I secretly doubted it, but events were to prove that Peters was correct.

Half an hour later we were making our way over greyish water so still that a matchstick dropped overboard would make ripples on the surface. Within our circle of vision there was not a mark or perch to be seen in the unbroken dullness of a steely blue. The sun had disappeared, yet when we offered Peters a compass, he declined it with a smile. He seemed to be looking up at the sky as much as at the water, but he kept on, making up a mile or so and then curving away in a wide arc.

'Soon we shall see Neuwerk,' he said. 'Over there.' And a minute later, 'There it is.' He pointed away over the port beam to where a solid medieval tower loomed faintly out of the dimness.

Neuwerk was a small island lying in the mouth of the Elbe. It was not a particularly hospitable place, but it was a favourite excursion for seaside visitors from the coastal resorts. Nearly four miles from the nearest shore, it could be reached on foot or even by car across a causeway. But there, as on the short crossing to Lindisfarne, unwary landlubbers were often trapped by the returning tide. Through the binoculars I made out the shapes of several wrecks which had once been family cars that had left the return too late.

Peters was cutting a couple of miles inshore of Neuwerk, just outside the Steil sand which abuts onto the coast.

'I picked up a pair of *Engländer* in my boat just here, two years ago,' he said. 'They were standing on the bonnet of their jeep with water up to their knees, shouting and waving like men demented.' And no wonder, for it must have been a decidedly unpleasant experience.

Skirting the invisible coast we came to another long line of perches, the 'Sticker's Gat' of Erskine Childers' story, and at their further end we came into the main stream of the Elbe. With the strong tide behind us another half hour brought us up to the Alte Liebe lighthouse beside the entrance to Cuxhaven. There was already a curious ruffle on the water, and up on the signal semaphore of the Alte Liebe Peters' alleged storm in the Helgoland area was confirmed. Borkum was marked up at Force 6 on the Beaufort Scale, but Helgoland at Force 8. Within half an hour another couple of points were notched up on the Borkum signal, and the waves began to slop through the piles of the jetty to warn of an imminent storm.

It is easy for the visitor to Cuxhaven to believe the story that he may be told about the curious name 'Alte Liebe' for the lighthouse on the point, which stands inshore of a large bank close to the harbour entrance. But the popular story is incorrect, and the true explanation was given to me by Konter-admiral Siegfried Engel, who translated one of my books into German, and whom we invited aboard to steer some of the way down the Elbe when homeward bound from Sweden on another occasion.

Soon after the Prussian-Danish war of 1849, a Danish cargo vessel ran aground off the coast when rounding the point. This was one of those occasions of sand quickly forming up around the vessel, which could not extract itself. But it was literally within a stone's throw of the promenade, and the population indulged in the typical if rather pointless occupation of xenophobia by throwing stones at the wreck, and doing so in such quantity that they eventually created a considerable shoal.

The name of the Danish vessel was *Olivia*. So the shoal was known as the Olivia, and by a simple process of transformation in the mouths of the locals eventually became Olle Lieve, which being interpreted is the Plattdeutsch for Old Love. Hence the story about sailors saying farewell to their old loves as they sailed out into the North Sea. The shoal was marked on the charts as Olle Lieve, and it merely remained for a conscientious cartographer of the Prussian Admiralty to remove the offensive dialect when he revised the chart, giving it the proper Hochdeutsch rendering of Die Alte Liebe.

We had already rounded the Old Love and were lying in the harbour, watching the locals fishing up eels between the piles, when the storm burst upon Cuxhaven in a thundery downpour, but by then Kapitän Otto Peters had already reached home on his cycle and had no doubt handed his wife the prize of a packet of real tea from our stores. As for myself, I could now appreciate what the German guide to the Weser-Ems area meant by 'exceptionally experienced local navigators'.

PRINCEPS BOTANICORUM

It was certainly an interesting voyage, but it took two summer holidays, not one. And that was because of what Boyle would have called a 'natural disaster'. We had only just arrived at Gothenburg when the Göta River was closed by a landslide, but in the following year we crossed Sweden and reached the home at Uppsala of the biologist who wrote of himself:

God has permitted him to see more of his created work than any man before him.
None before him has pursued his profession with greater energy and more listeners.
None before him has been a greater botanist or zoologist.
None before him has become more renowned throughout the world.

Well, there's nothing like self-appreciation. And although Carl von Linné (as he was called after his ennoblement) or Linnaeus, as he is more generally known, was undoubtedly a most able scientist, a pinch of modesty might have been welcome. But that was not in his nature. In the Swedish spring and summer, with all its variety of flowers, he would give peripatetic lectures in the surroundings of Uppsala, attended by two or three hundred students. He was similar in that activity to Professor Asschenheimer of Freiburg in the 1930s. But in other ways he was not at all like the courteous Asschenheimer. He was accompanied by a brass band of trumpets and French horns, and when he wished to make remarks about some curious plant or bird or insect which had come to his notice he would halt and summon the stragglers by the sound of his musicians. Then the students would crowd around him and listen – according to Mr Coxe, a Fellow of King's who was present on one such occasion – in respectful silence while he offered his observations.

Of course Linnaeus is most familiar just as the letter L at the end of many a Latin name of classification of animals or plants. His system was based on studying their reproductive processes. *'The genitalia of plants we regard with delight, of animals with abomination, and of ourselves with strange thoughts,'* he wrote in his *Philosophia Humana*, and his most famous attempt to classify by structure was in a work on the sexuality of plants. In it he wrote with an unlikely sense of beauty and dignity of *'how the petals contribute nothing to generation, serving only as bridal beds which the Creator has so gloriously arranged, adorned with such noble bed curtains and perfumed with so many sweet scents that the bridegroom there may celebrate his nuptials with his bride with all the greater solemnity.'* To him, creatures showed a similarity of structure which indicated a certain relationship, but he went no further than to see the many astonishing patterns of structure as plans which existed in the mind of God before the creation was begun. It was Darwin and Wallace who took his work and built further upon it, and it is true to say even today that the whole of evolutionary theory derives from the work of Linnaeus. It may be equally true to say that once the evolutionary horse had got the bit between its teeth it ran away with the cart, so that the idea of inheritance of random genetic variations upon which natural selection works to produce changes in the species is such a holy doctrine that anyone who dares to point out cases (such as the development of the vertebrate eye) in which such cannot possibly be the whole truth, is regarded as an infidel, a betrayer of the great all-pervading power of evolution.

Linnaeus was conceited and he was also sometimes downright rude. If he disliked colleagues in the University of Uppsala, he would name particularly stinking and obnoxious weeds or fungi after them. And when he gave up attending services at the village church of Danmark near his home, to which he was always accompanied by his dog, he allowed the dog to continue to go to church without him. Unfortunately the dog had the habit of barking during the sermon, and when the long-suffering rector complained to him that the barking disturbed the congregation, Linnaeus merely replied that the rector should have realised that the dog was only barking because it realised that the sermon had gone on far too long already.

Linnaeus was regarded as an authority without equal on living things, whether animals or plants, and when a commission was appointed to undertake the revision of the Swedish version of the Bible, he was invited to be a member so that he could check the terms for biblical animals and plants, particularly in the Old Testament. He was very irregular in his attendances, but one change that he endeavoured (unsuccessfully) to have made was the statement in *2 Kings v*, about conditions during the siege of Samaria. The King James version in England continued the same statement, that an ass's head was sold for eighty pieces of silver, and a quarter of a measure of dove's dung for five pieces of silver. Linnaeus pointed out that nobody could eat pigeon excrement, and that this was an entire error in the translation. The fact was that a plant which grew widely in the Middle East produced glutinous seed-pods that had the appearance of bird droppings, and so would naturally enough be known to the locals at that time as Dove's Dung. Indeed, its current Latin name (supplied probably by himself) was *Ornithogalum*. But the committee was not convinced, and dove's dung it remained. However, much later the editors of the New English Bible followed Linnaeus's suggestion, and instead of the dove's dung they used the term 'locust beans' – whatever they might be.

There are two relics of Linnaeus's time as Professor of Botany at Uppsala. One is the botanical garden in the city itself, and in this the plants are set out according to the classification which Linnaeus developed. Annuals on one side, perennials on the other, the garden can prove a disappointment to anyone familiar with Wisley or the Saville gardens, because it is not there for decorative purposes, and there are more weeds (duly classified) than herbaceous border varieties. Yet it is interesting for demonstrating the very unlikely close relationships which exist in the realm of botany.

The other legacy is Hammarby, the little country house where Linnaeus lived and worked, a beautiful example of an unsophisticated Swedish home, but with the unusual feature that the walls are papered with plates from eighteenth century herbals and botanical works, many of them extremely finely drawn.

But however much Linnaeus may have boasted of being the greatest biologist ever known, his fame apparently did not greatly impress his fellow Swedes. When in 1778 he died, he left his papers and specimens to his widow, who seems to have been a rather niggardly woman but at the same time not devoid of commercial acumen. She was intending to sell the collections piecemeal to foreign collectors, when her son, who had succeeded his father as Professor of Botany, persuaded the executor of his father's will to allow him to retain the collections for his own personal use in exchange for his renouncing his share in the remainder of the family property. But only five years later he died, and his mother immediately asked her husband's executor to dispose of all the collections and library.

This the executor agreed to do. The sale was advertised also in Holland where the advertisement was seen by chance by an English medical student, J. E. Smith. This young man wrote to his father, suggesting that at the executor's quoted price of 1,000 guineas the collections and library might turn out to be a good investment. His father, an East Anglian businessman, agreed, and forwarded the money. Yet even then, Smith had no idea of the scope and value of what he was intending to acquire, but when he received the catalogue of the sale he at once deposited half the purchase price in the executor's account. He lost no time in completing the purchase, and so it came about that some 19,000 sheets of exquisitely mounted plant specimens, several thousand shells, insects and minerals, and a unique library of 2,500 scientific books together with the entire existing correspondence of Linnaeus himself, were all packed up in Sweden and stowed aboard a British merchant ship in Stockholm harbour.

After the ship had sailed out into the Baltic, a belated recognition of the fact that the country's greatest scientific treasure had passed out of their hands led the Swedes to send out a warship from Gothenburg to try to overhaul the ship. But the captain was a canny man, and as soon as he realised that he was being followed he changed course in the dark and threw off the pursuit.

When the cargo arrived in London, Smith could hardly believe his good fortune. But to sort and preserve such an immense collection was beyond the powers of one individual, so he wisely approached some of the leading scientists of the day for help, and the Linnaean Society was formed, with Smith as its first president at the age of only twenty-six.

As soon as he had completed his studies, Smith put all his energies into the work, and devoted his whole life to the task of arranging, cataloguing and storing the amazing treasure which had come his way. And so it came about that thanks to the enterprise of this one young man, the Linnaean Society, which has published the many works of Linnaeus that were not already published before his death, is situated not in Stockholm, but in Burlington Street in London's West End.

If Sweden was at first disappointed that the Linnaeus collections had left the country, there is no doubt that the incident was a fortunate one. Smith himself proved to be an admirable and devoted owner of the material, which was certainly very much better cared for than it would have been in Sweden, where it would have been split up and sold piecemeal. Very soon the Linnaean Society was to achieve the highest of reputations among the great scientific institutions of the world, and it has provided a fine and permanent home for the work of the man who has justly been called the prince of botanists.

FAREWELL TO THE DESERT

Linnaeus was the first traveller to write of his experiences in Lapland. He made a journey to that far northern part of Scandinavia in order to examine the flora and fauna, and his descriptions fascinated me. His diary also contained several sketches showing a people very far removed from the rest of the country in dress and manner of life, and in their housing. So it was from the *Princeps Botanicorum* that I had perhaps a faint idea, but as yet not a resolve, that I might one day try and follow where he had gone.

Fourteen years later the chance came. I had forgotten about Lapland until one day when I was working in London I happened to mention to a Swedish lady that I had been invited to the re-opening of the Strömsholms Canal, and her comment surprised me.

'I know you like walking, so while you are up in Sweden why don't you walk the Kungsleden?' She went on to explain that Kungsleden, the Royal Path, was a track that began far up in the Arctic, at Abisko, in Lapland.

Lapland! Linnaeus's descriptions suddenly came back to me. Yes, I said, I would certainly try to follow Kungsleden. But first I had to make some enquiries.

Greta thought that the facilities along the Arctic section of the Royal Path would be limited. There she was right. Abisko itself was on the railway that ran to Trondhjem in Norway, so it would be the place to start, but after that there would be no settlement of any kind for at least a week of walking, although every here and there the Swedish Tourist Association (STF) had built either a kind of wigwam (*kåta*) in which one could take shelter, or a small hut with a bedstead or two and army blankets – but nothing else. There would be no provisions until I reached another settlement, a long way down the line.

The STF in Stockholm was extremely helpful. The section of path I intended to cover was 25 miles long, they told me – but a Swedish mile was 10 kilometres, so I had to reckon on 156 miles over rough country with no human habitation for the first 100 miles. That meant that I would have to carry all my food with me, and I decided that I would take a margin of two days rations to spare, in case of bad weather or injury of some kind.

The problem of course was weight. Young people seemed to need to carry so much that they were almost doubled up under their loads, but I was already fifty-seven and needed less food – and perhaps had more experience in walking. In the end I decided on an absolute limit of twelve kilos, rucksack included. The load would comprise a camera, two changes of shirt, a change of trousers and socks, pyjamas, toiletries, and a sleeping bag for use in the shelters. I realised that there would be torrents to be waded, so a pair of gym-shoes would be useful for the stony river-beds. I had maps, and a cheap compass bought for six shillings and sixpence at the local ironmongers. I decided against cooking, and as water would be available everywhere I was left with a margin of about four kilos for food. Having looked up the calorific values of almost everything I could think of I established that my supplies should consist of chocolate, Swedish hard-bread and a modest amount of smoked reindeer, which I would buy in Sweden. The only (and very sensible) warning the STF gave me was on no account to wade a stream with a rucksack on my back. The current could be formidable, and if one stumbled and fell, then the rucksack might hold one down with fatal results.

The day after the canal celebrations I boarded the express at Västerås and by nine o'clock next evening the train had reached the limit of the tree line beyond which only an occasional patch of slim birch saplings struggled to eke out an existence. The sun was in the north-west, shining high and bright over the cold blue of a lake several miles across. This was Torneträsk, the huge sheet of water in the north of Swedish Lapland, a wildly beautiful lake then, as unspoiled as the day the receding ice had left it. Across the water the snowy night-caps of the Norwegian mountains cut a jagged alpine outline against the brilliance of the sky, the sun glinting off their snow-fields to be reflected in the direction of Abisko. I found it hard to convince myself that it was almost bedtime by home standards, that the sunshine so late at night was real, no different in quality but only in clock-time from that which flooded southern Sweden with its clear northern light, or bronzed the torsos of bathers on the Mediterranean shores.

I left the train at the Abisko halt. The place, such as it was, lay fast asleep, unreally quiet in the brightness of the sunlight. Here and there among the scrub birches was a patch of snow, and white drifts lay only partly melted on the beach of an island a little way out in the lake. Beyond it the sun now sent a trail of fiery gold across the water, and between my path and the shore the sapling birches trembled ever so slightly, their stems protruding pale and slim from a carpet of red bell-heather. I could not recall a lovelier, more romantic scene, and I rested on an ice-polished rock until long after midnight, wondering at all this astonishing beauty spread out, as it seemed, for myself alone. For of others I saw no sign at all.

Later in the day I set out southward. I reckoned that I could walk for about eight hours, and would need another eight for preparing my humble evening meal and for sleeping. But that accounted for only sixteen hours out of twenty-four in the day, so what was I to do with the rest? The answer was simple – I would re-organise my activity into days which were only sixteen hours in length. This meant that I would walk for twelve Pilk-days in a period of eight conventional days, and so I would cover the ground fairly quickly and not have to worry about the clock at all. I found this worked extremely well, and there was no difficulty in adjusting to a new rhythm when the daylight was there all the time.

Part of the irresistible allure of the wide, semi-barren Arctic waste lay in its silence. The quiet was astonishing, something unimaginable to one who had grown up in industrial Lancashire. It was a silence so intense that one could almost take hold of it. No sound of human origin broke it even for an instant. The nearest automobile might as well have been on the moon. No aircraft flew high overhead. The utterly unspoiled, unruffled serenity of a part of the world existing as it had done for thousands of years was awe-inspiring, fascinating, something which drew me to it and yet made me feel very, very small.

And yet the silence was not absolute. I was sitting on a boulder and pondering the immense noiselessness of the Arctic wasteland when a sound behind me made me start. It was a noise like a squib spluttering and fizzing just before the moment of explosion. I spun round on my seat, but saw nothing.

Soon the noise came again, and this time I turned quickly enough to see a little furry creature, gold and black and very like a hamster. He was watching me with his black eyes, and when I stood up and stepped toward him he flattened himself out at the hind end and raised his front to look important. He blew out his big moustache until it trembled, and showed two long upper teeth. He did not back away, not an inch. Instead he squibbed and fizzed and screamed at me in his comic little voice. I could understand what he was saying, too.

'Go away! Go away! I'm much bigger than you!'

This was the first time I had seen a lemming, and from now to the end of my journey they were to be my constant companions. I was rarely out of sight of lemmings alive or lemmings dead and half eaten, and for more than one-hundred miles I can rarely have taken a footstep without treading on the droppings which often lay drifted in the track like small brown catkins of birch or alder.

I had the company of other creatures too. Now and then I would come upon a dotterel perched on an isolated boulder, breaking the Arctic silence by piping to its mate. There were purple sandpipers too, and a phalarope flying up in rather too much of an obvious hurry showed me where her nest lay with four well-camouflaged eggs. Down below the tree-line the noisy rattle of a ptarmigan split the quiet with a sound like the rattle of a football supporter, but the call which surprised me most of all by its sheer improbability was the beautiful double note of the cuckoo.

The most startling and impressive bird however was not the dotterel or even the snowy owl, but one I had never seen before. Wherever in the stony wilderness I came upon a stretch of moorland with a dark, peaty tarn, a pair of birds would be there, sitting on guard to watch for any danger that might threaten their hidden eggs or young. As I came nearer to their private pond they would begin to call to each other in a single, shrill note, continually more urgent. Then, as they soared up, I noticed the very long forked tail straddling a pair of ribbon-like feathers which trailed behind, vibrating in the air. I stood and watched, and with a shriek one of them came plummeting down, diving straight at me. Only at the last moment did it put out a pair of fin-like air-brakes set at the back of its body and come whistling out of its plunge within a foot or two of my head, merely to wheel away and gather height for another attack while its mate came in to strike in turn. They were long-tailed skuas, and they were quite certain that the world belonged to them. Once again I was made to realise that even if the skuas were uncommon in this part of the world, *Homo sapiens* was infinitely rarer, a species without the least effect upon the ecology of the tussocky land over which I was tramping mile after lonely mile from lake to lake and river to river.

As I walked on across this immense wasteland, the snow-topped hills to either side looked very ancient, rounded and worn, ground and polished by the thousands of years of relentless pressure of the slowly moving ice sheet of the last glaciation. This patient, age-old tiredness of the hill tops made me feel even smaller and more insignificant as I strode along beneath them in a week of just one of the summers of a life-span which, compared with their age, was so short. I felt very much as the writer of the eighth psalm must have done. He was impressed by the staggering immensity of the universe compared with his own tiny, transient being, held in a care which he could trust. My own awareness was of the immense power and slow sureness of the forces which had shaped such beauty, but the dependability of the care for the individual was just as real, even if that individual was a solitary walker following the scattered line of cairns through the desert rather than a poet of Old Testament times.

All the way I was within the sound of water. Trickling under the scrub, dripping over stones and roots, the rustling of a beck hurrying toward the valley, the bumping and tossing of a fast river against the boulders in the torrent bed, these sounds were the only ones to be heard apart from the hiss of lemmings and the rare call of a bird. And the water was clear, cold, clean, as though it had just been formed from brand new molecules of hydrogen and oxygen by command of some mysterious force up in the northern sky beyond the horizon.

It was on a Sunday evening that I came to Saltoluokta, the only settlement on my route. As I lay on a real bed that daylight night, I only regretted that I had arrived too late to attend the service in Saltoluokta's church, for however little the liturgy in Lappska might have meant to me I would indeed have liked to enter that pretty building of turf with its bent wooden frame of spruce and pine, and to have taken my pew by helping myself to a reindeer skin from the pile by the door to lay it on the earth, beaten hard and strewn with birch twigs. I would have liked to, just to give thanks for the wisdom that could allow me to be a part in space and time of the incredible, ingenious beauty of the creation, and to carry home with me a vision of another world, of a country as then unspoiled, beautiful beyond dream or description, a land where nature was very largely untamed and untouched. A place where the sun could shine for twenty-four hours in the clarity of a sky unpolluted, to sparkle in dancing reflection from water that was never still but pure and unclouded by the smallest peck of dirt. A land which was part of our own fine, varied and crowded planet, but one where man was very rare indeed and could only feel very humble.

Three days later I was nearing the end of the trail. One of the great delights of my walk had been to be absolutely free of even the sound of automobiles, but by now I was so used to the silence that when I faintly heard above the all-pervading whine of mosquitoes in the woodland the unmistakable lower-pitched hum of a car in the distance, the sound was as exhilarating as that of a nightingale on the edge of a city. The only possible road was the one that led from the outside world to Kvikkjokk, so I knew that the hamlet could not be far distant.

A sense of excitement made me quicken my pace, breaking into a run as I dodged between the trees and moss-strewn boulders. Soon I was aware of another sound, a thundering roar away to my right, a noise that could only be that of the mighty torrent of the Kamajokk river. Brushing aside the mosquitoes I hastened onward, converging all the while with the sound of untamed waters on my starboard hand.

I came out of the woodland into a clearing with a small red-stained barn and the scent of freshly scythed grass. It was the first outpost of the village of Kvikkjokk, 'the meeting of the waters'. One more marsh to splash through, then a signpost pointing to a gate. I was staggering with sheer excitement as I scrambled up the steps of the hostel perched among the pines on the cliff over the river. With immense power the Kamajokk roared past beneath the windows, the foam tossing and sparkling in the brilliant light of late evening, the spray drifting to lodge on the needles of the pines.

I had arrived at the end of the greatest and most strenuous trek through the wilderness that I would ever make, a trek that made me more aware than ever before of the inherent wonder, and beauty, and brilliance of the world where I was privileged to live my life.

When ten years later I read in a Swedish newspaper that the government had decided to built a motor-road up to Abisko, I could have cried. They have done it, too. And so the last real desert in the western world has gone for ever.

PLUS AND MINUS

On the return voyage from Sweden we found Peters to be already occupied with his shrimps, but he recommended us to the retired skipper of the Cuxhaven lifeboat, a taciturn man of over eighty. He was very willing to take us round the corner from the Elbe to the Weser, but he preferred to do it at high water because he was rather less familiar with the shifting channels through the banks.

It was a thundery day, and for the first time in my life I saw a water-spout. The sea rose up in a column several yards in diameter and then spread out mushroom-fashion to return again as a downpour of salty rain. Although not within half a mile of the spout, we had a little seaweed falling on the deck in the downpour. And a few shrimps. I asked our pilot what would happen if the spout should come right over us.

'*Nicht gut*,' he said, shaking his head. And that I could well believe.

During the storm we had the interesting display of blue tongues of fire flickering about the yard-arm of our short mast. It was a curious sight, and I knew it was what sailors call St Elmo's Fire. But the flickering flames could sit on the halyards without burning them, and one could even reach up and have the flickering transferred to one's finger-tips without the least sensation. The fact that static electricity could behave in this beautiful way without causing any damage made me wonder exactly what it was.

Back home I consulted an encyclopedia, which told me plenty about St Elmo himself being a fourth century Syrian bishop, but dismissed his fire with the bald statement that it was static electricity. But what was that?

Nor was Lenin more helpful. He once wrote that Communism was Soviet Power plus the electrification of the whole country. Even if he apparently meant this not figuratively but engineering-wise, it was not much help. Electricity was just a mystery to me and it only came my way in print in the form of an annual circular from the Electricity Board explaining that from next January electricity would be considerably cheaper and I should be delighted by that, even though at the same time it was highly regrettable that the charges per unit would have to be increased.

Some people think electricity is expensive and the new annual rate exorbitant, but I think the Electricity Boards deserve all they can get. I know that they would get it even if they didn't, but I still think electricity cheap at the price, and I can't reasonably grudge them the extra fraction of a penny per unit, because there must be lots of bits of electricity even in a single unit.

A unit lasts a whole hour, and when I lived in London the LEB had to send the electricity whizzing up the wires all the way from Wandsworth to fly round the house under the floorboards and then back home again, and when the Teddington people time it with a stopwatch and find that it goes 186,281 miles and a few hundred yards not in an hour but in a single second – well, that gives some idea of the number of bits that go galloping through the pantry cupboard in an hour, flicking the little wheel with a red spot on the edge as they go by.

Besides, electricity takes some making. It doesn't just grow like tomatoes or lie around in carboniferous beds like coal. It actually has to be made, more or less out of nothing at all. I believe Thales was the first man to lay it on and he made it by stroking a cat's tail with a piece of amber, but there are other ways if cats are not available. Pets are not allowed in the Science Museum in Kensington, so they make electricity there out of a pile of bits of metal and wet blotting paper inside a glass case. Now and then they have to wet the blotting paper again, but the thing has being going for years and years, and as it is not safe to leave electricity around without anything to do, the Museum people let it ring a bell.

Then there are mechanical methods. I remember once seeing a circular for teachers which said 'Make electricity with a sewing-machine and an old gramophone record (Whimshurst principle)'. This suggested a more elaborate method than cats or blotting paper and maybe this is how they do it commercially, but I think it needs more know-how than the leaflet indicated because I've tried all ways, from long players to compact discs. I can do much better just pulling my shirt quickly over my hair if I haven't oiled it, and if I look in the mirror I can see little blue sparks – though they are not quite the same as LEB electricity because they are roundish, more like St Elmo's fire, and not zig-zaggy like the proper ones the LEB paints pictures of near the bottom of pylons.

I never really understood what electricity actually was until I asked a physicist, who explained that you could put the thing in a nutshell by saying it flowed but was not fluid. At first I did not really grasp this, but he went on to make it clearer by saying that in non-technical language it could most easily be regarded as a series of inconceivably small presences of something which was not really there. These presences hurried along to fill up the gaps left by absences, and these absences were not absences of nothing but absences of definite entities that were not really there either – not because they were absent but because they were never present. Looked at like this, he said, all electrical phenomena were self-evident, and if Einstein had spent a lifetime trying to square them with gravity that was merely because he was concerned with prime causes.

Perhaps electrical phenomena really are self-evident, but I still don't understand why stroking a cat with an amber stroker produced absences – or it may be presences – whereas a wire-haired fox terrier doesn't work although a moleskin waistcoat does, even with sealing-wax.

Actually, the LEB makes two kinds of electricity, the plus kind and the minus kind. They both run in separate wires to the socket on the skirting-board in what my electrician calls a condewit, and the plus kind will only go in brown wires and the minus kind in blue ones – they used to be red ones and black ones until the EEC stuck its oar in. There is actually a third hole in the socket but it is only for show, as I saw the electrician connect it up to the water-pipe when he thought I was not looking.

When the lamp is plugged in it lights. I am not suggesting that this is unusual, but surely it is puzzling that all the pluses and minuses can be turned into a sixty-watt glow. I asked my physicist friend how the change occurred and he said that when I plugged in the lamp it was just that I was joining the bulb to the brown wire and the blue one at once – and so it became excited. I think that must be true enough, because when the electrician was fixing another socket which smoke had been coming out of for a week or two he happened to take hold of the ends of the brown and the blue together, and he became excited too. Very, actually, though I think it may partly have been because he was Irish.

The real problem to me was why the lamp got excited, and when I put this one to the physicist he said it was because there was a very thin wire inside the bulb – so thin that the electricity could not run through it as easily as it could along the main cables. It was all a matter of ohms. I think the truth is that the minuses manage all right because they are slim, but the pluses are awkward and spiky and get their legs jammed in the walls of the tunnel, particularly on the bends.

When electricity has been used it has to go home again to the LEB 'to complete the circuit' and be fettled up for sending round again. Instead of using wires the electricity people sometimes just allow it to find its own way back through the ground by what they call 'earthing'. The strange thing is that not only the LEB but the BBC and the PMG and Mercury and everybody all trust their own electricity to find its way home at breakneck speed without either getting lost in the sewers or heading in the wrong direction. It is as though the Wandsworth pluses know that they belong there and deliberately resist the temptation to pop up in the Mountview telephone exchange or join the throng in the Southern Region's private supply place and take a quick trip down to Brighton along the outer rail.

Textbooks say that electricity does this 'naturally', but it still strikes me as very clever, particularly when one thinks of the tussle there must sometimes be with other electricity going the other way and the possibility of misunderstandings with the French pluses which are allowed to come over for a quick visit to the grid in the busy winter season.

But as a matter of fact even electricity can make mistakes occasionally. I know, because once when making a trunk call I decided to lean back and sit on the radiator while they were trying to connect me. Exciting wasn't the word for it. I was shocked.

ARNO PIECHOROWSKI

On the way back to London from the home of Linnaeus by boat, I decided to take what appeared to be a short cut by entering the series of small canals which led from the Dortmund-Ems Canal through into one of the major waterways of Holland. The first cut in this curious series of waterways off the Ems led dead straight for ten miles across a heath, between high banks topped with pines. Arriving in the evening at the little town of Nordhorn I was informed that the bridge would be swung next morning at six, and that the key was kept by a woman in the furniture shop. And that proved correct. So shortly after seven in the morning we came to a small stone lock under a bridge, and on a tree beside the lock a faded board proclaimed *'Deutsch-Niederländische Grenze. Übertritt verboten!'* But there was no barrier, no customs house, none of the usual trappings of officialdom at a frontier.

A farmer came out of a steading close to the lock and stared. Then he fetched a heavy steel crank and began to wind at the sluices. We were the first boat in the last eight months, he said, and next week the canal was to be closed for good. But a British boat, coming from Stockholm and bound for London, raised problems which were too great for him to solve, so he directed us to enquire at a red-tiled building under the trees beyond the canal.

It was the school, and the first thing that caught my eye was a canoe standing on its end against the wall by the doorway. Its owner was the young headmaster, Arno Piechorowski, a canal enthusiast who had paddled his own canoe through the length of Norway's only considerable inland waterway, the Telemark Canal, all the way from Bandak in the middle of the country to the coastal town of Skien, where the skis come from.

151

While we waited for the frontier officials from Nordhorn to arrive to deal with the formalities Arno Piechorowski showed me round his school. Arno was also second master, he was head of the languages department, bursar, chief of mathematics and in charge of singing and sport. In fact this young man with his wife Edda managed the whole place and taught everything to the twenty-five pupils from the farms around the hamlet of Frensdorferhaar. There were eight classes grouped around separate tables in one classroom of his happy single-teacher school. Class 1 had two members seated at a low table, and the chairs gradually increased in size up to Class 8, but as yet none of the pupils had quite reached that dizzy eminence.

The school had a good house for the headmaster and his wife, and there were two classrooms, one of which was used entirely for handicrafts. Dutch was taught as a foreign language rather than English, as it was more use in that out-of-the-way corner of Lower Saxony, but German also had to be taught as a foreign language to many of the pupils who, strangely enough, spoke Saxon.

Arno excused himself when the customs men arrived – ostensibly to see the passports but in reality so that they could have the chance of a good pot of tea – and we had just finished the passport inspection on board when I was aware of a shuffling and whispering from the direction of the bridge above. Going on deck I discovered that the first lesson of the day for all the pupils was to come and inspect the unlikely ship that had come a thousand miles to beside the frontier tree at Frensdorferhaar. The children beamed to us from above, and while the farmer struggled with the rusty machinery of the paddle-gear we talked of England, and Sweden, and Lower Saxony, and their beloved Frensdorferhaar. When at last the lock was emptied and ready for us to leave, Arno turned to his pupils with a smile.

'And now, how about a *Ständchen, ja?*'

The children formed into the rows of a choir, with the youngest in front. The passport officers stood on the lockside, the farmer leaned on his windlass, and only the rooks in the elm above us continued their chatter as Arno stood at the centre of the bridge and set the tempo with beats of his hand. One, two, three, and the choir broke into their melody, singing with all the gaiety and purity of tone which German children seem so easily to bring to their music.

Ach! Bootsmann. Ach! Bootsmann, Wann fahren wir auf See? The lovely, rolling, surging song of a sea the singers had never even seen rang out to drift along the canal, and as the children waved their farewell to us we never imagined that the postman would bring us at Christmas their letters, telling us of how they were preparing for the festival in their own happy family at Frensdorferhaar.

Their own happy family. Yes, for it was really one great family, ruled over by the kind, loving couple, Arno and Edda. And then quite suddenly two years later that happy atmosphere was cut off, by decree of the government. It happened this way. Children and young adults in Germany were beginning to ask questions; what they heard about the events in the Third Reich prompted worries in their minds. Was it really true that these frightful things had happened? If so, how could it have occurred? And so on. In fact the teaching of history in postwar Germany was fraught with difficulties, and I knew of a girl of sixteen in Marburg whose class was cautiously told about the frightful treatment meted out to the Jews. Of course, yes, it was most regrettable, but it had to be admitted that they were rounded up and starved, or gassed, or murdered. That was part of history, see? Everyone was naturally ashamed of it, but there was no point in concealing it. At the end of the morning lessons this girl went home, opened the front door, stood just inside it and called for her parents. She then related what she had been taught that morning at school. 'Is it true?' she asked.

Well yes, it was. It was a terrible blot on the history of the country, and . . .

She cut them off. 'And what did you do about it?'

The parents began to explain that it wasn't as easy as all that. Raise a finger, and you probably joined the number of those sent to the slaughter. Of course one didn't condone such things, but . . .

'And you mean to say that you, my parents whom I have loved, knew that this was going on, and you said nothing, did nothing, nothing whatsoever about it? I shall never speak to you again.' The girl left the house, slamming the door behind her. The parents never saw her again, or even knew where she had gone.

I am relating this because it highlights the difficulties which confronted the government and schools in dealing with information about the recent past. And it was partly because of this difficulty that the German government had now decided that a proper investigation must be made into precisely what went on in some small community where there was, in 1939, a modest, average sprinkling of Jews in the population. They selected the small town of Nordhorn.

Arno received a letter telling him that he had been seconded to carry out this investigation, the results of which would be published under government auspices. Arno was a sensible choice because he himself had fled as a refugee from the East, he had no special contacts or friends or relations in the area, he was an intelligent man and could be relied upon to do a job well.

When the letter arrived, Arno was horrified. He wrote to Bonn and assured them that no good would be achieved by muck-raking in the past, that if dogs were buried they were best left buried, that the atmosphere of trust and hope which had been growing up as a tender shoot during the last fifteen years could be much better fostered in other ways. But to mount a sort of Inquisition – no, that was something he would not do.

His honest refusal was, I think, sensible. He wanted to teach his happy family, and develop attitudes in them that might prevent such horrors from happening again. But the German government was not prepared to take No for an answer. He was an employee of the Lower Saxony education authority, and the government had obtained their permission for his assignment to the task. That was that. There was to be no discussion.

Arno protested that the authorities of Lower Saxony might not be any too pleased with what he would discover and put in his report, but his objections were brushed aside. State employees did what they were told. He was given two years for the investigation, with official authorisation to ask any questions he liked of anybody he wished.

So, with the greatest reluctance, Arno began to look into the happenings in Nordhorn during the years of the Third Reich. The report was duly published at the end of that time, and Arno sent me a copy. I began to read it, and it nearly made me sick. As he had foretold, there was almost nobody in the little town of Nordhorn whose hands were clean. The whole awful story was set out clearly. The first notices *'Jüdisches Geschäft'* posted on the windows of some of the shops, then the occasional smashed plate-glass window, the refusal of continued membership of local clubs and societies, allegations that Jews had eaten large meals on the so-called 'Self-denial days', the turning of blind eyes by the police, the indifference of the mayor and the councillors to what was going on. Arno described in moving simplicity the funeral of one of the town's most stalwart and beloved citizens, who was Jewish. Everyone knew and respected him, and yet when he died there were only two old men out of the whole population of Nordhorn who had the bravery to walk bare-headed behind his coffin.

That was only the beginning. Little by little night closed in upon the very ordinary members of a very ordinary small town community who happened to be Jewish or have Jewish ancestors. When the last little group of men and women and children were escorted to the train that was to take them to their death, none uttered a word of protest. They had no use for their fellow citizens if they were Jewish. But their homes, their belongings, their businesses – well, that was a different matter.

Even before he sent in his report, Arno knew that he and Edda would have to leave their happy home and large family in the school at Frensdorferhaar. The government could see that too. Far too many of the guilty, of those who had sent their fellows to their death, were still alive and flourishing, and occupying positions of respect and importance in the community. Arno and Edda were transferred to another state within Germany, to Baden-Württemberg, where a school was found for them about as far distant from Nordhorn as possible in a hamlet buried in the depths of the Black Forest.

It was a while before Arno sent me the address, but I was determined to visit him in his new location. The hamlet lay deep within the sombre pinewoods at the end of a very minor road. It was somewhat difficult to find, but I took with me the skis which I had used many years before and started to follow the trail of the heights from above Baden-Baden. The scenery was beautiful in the extreme, the dark forest decked out in a mantle of snow that glistened in the clear winter sunlight. I found the hamlet, a mere handful of scattered farms and smallholdings, but the families that lived there had enough children to supply that most excellent of educational institutions, the single-teacher school.

I had perhaps expected Arno and Edda to be depressed, but no. Deservedly, they had found their feet in just the situation that suited them. The children loved them, and the schoolhouse had that wonderful and indefinable scent, not just of pine and wood smoke, but of that very special and natural happiness that cannot be manufactured artificially.

We sat up far into the night, talking of Frensdorferhaar, and of the hamlet where they now lived. We did not mention the Piechorowski report. And then I fell asleep on a mattress laid out for me near the warmth of the *Kackelofen*. With the winter cold, the warmth of the room and the delight in finding how these two young people had weathered the storm I slept so soundly that I was only just in time to remove my bedding before the first of the children arrived, happy, red-faced with the winter cold, but obviously at home as they hung up their jackets and took their accustomed places in the areas allocated around the room to forms 1 to 7.

FRITZ THE FORESTER

It was a succession of random chances that led me to make the acquaintance of Fritz Hockenjos. Wanting to have breathing space from the run of lectures, committees, and dealing with publishers on the one hand and shipyards on the other, I decided to take a break of a week or two.

Winter was not really the most sensible time to go aboard a boat to sit and think, so one Saturday night I packed a bag and took the bus out to London Airport instead. I had not thought about a destination, but from the indicator board I saw that the first outward flight that carried a cheap night fare was a Swissair plane, so I bought a ticket. In the small hours the aircraft arrived at Basle, and I took the bus to the terminus at the Schweizerbahnhof. A train was standing in the northbound platform, its carriage roofs iced like big sugar buns with powdered snow. Its first stop was to be Freiburg, familiar to me from thirty-five years earlier, and so that was where I got out.

Freiburg's station had not changed. It even had the same indefinable smell of the nearby woodland. At the coach station the first post bus was bound for St Märgen, so I took it, and it was not yet nine o'clock when the bus drew up outside the post office in that small Black Forest village.

I trudged through the brilliant new snow toward the church, a mighty twin-towered baroque building in red sandstone. Leaning my bag against the wall, I pushed open the door and went in. Fortunately I had chosen the starboard side, as I saw at once that this was a church in which the males and females were still placed on opposite sides, presumably to discourage Pepysian straying of the thoughts, and I had arrived in the male wing, right in the middle of the Mass. After the service I saw a notice pinned to the outside of the door. *Protestant service in this church at six o'clock tonight.* A more unlikely announcement it was hard to imagine, so at six o'clock I was there.

The service was a straightforward Lutheran affair, with no nonsense. A pastor had come up from somewhere down in the Höllental valley to conduct it, and the organ was played by a Catholic nun from the remnant of the convent of which the great church was a part. Ahead of me sat a somewhat weather-beaten man in the dull greenish jacket and strong corduroy breeches of a man of the forest. He had his wife with him, and after the service was over he asked me if I would like to drop into the *Forsthaus* for a glass of wine.

Fritz Hockenjos was in fact the chief forester of the Black Forest, kingpin of the nature conservancy of the whole area. He and his family were also the mainspring of the Protestant community of St Märgen, and as we sat looking down over the snowy meadows to the silvery woodlands and across to the distant hump of the Feldberg he explained to me how it had all happened.

The flight of people from the conquering hordes of the Russian army as it rolled over Eastern Germany had brought many refugees to St Märgen, strangers who needed housing, jobs and all the other things which displacement demanded. Some of them were Protestants, but there was no church of that inclination in St Märgen, for the Black Forest was a solidly Catholic area, as most country districts at that time were. But the occupying power was France, and the French were extremely friendly. They had taken over one of the village hotels as an amenity for their troops, and they had invited the Protestants to make use of the saloon bar for an hour or so on Sunday mornings as a makeshift church.

As time went by, a few more Protestant families were added to the membership, and eventually the congregation was strong enough to decide that the time had come to erect a small building of their own, where they could feel more at home than in the morning-after-the-night-before aroma of the hotel bar. There was also an added incentive, the French were soon to be clearing out altogether and the hotel would then revert to its normal use. So the congregation started an appeal for funds among themselves, and began to draw up plans for the new church building.

News of this soon came to the ears of the Roman Catholic priest. He at once came round to see Fritz in his *Forsthaus*, and asked if it were really true that they were collecting funds for a new church. Fritz replied that Yes, that was so, and their people were supporting the idea enthusiastically.

'Crazy,' said the Father with a smile. 'Absolutely mad! With the world in the state that it is, to scrape your money together and use it for a new church building – what an absurd idea! What is wrong with our church? Put your money to some better purpose and use our church instead. Why not?'

My friendship with the Hockenjos family was to deepen over the years. Any weekend one was likely to meet others of great interest in their home – a prison governor, a theologian, a naturalist concerned with the eroding of the resources of the woodlands. Like myself, Fritz had been at the Albert Ludwig's University in Freiburg, and at about the same time. His work now involved the care of the huge area of forested hills, and he was as knowledgable as he was observant of nature. In some ways he was a second Asschenheimer, but without the cloak and hat and spotless serviette. He was a prolific writer, too, and I learned from him an endless variety of curious facts – why they made cheese in the Vosges but butter in the Black Forest, how the slope of the land masses affected the agriculture in the uplands, and why North America could boast at least ten times as many species of trees as Europe.

Fritz Hockenjos was a man who loved his Black Forest down to its roots. And so, with much lesser knowledge, did I.

If the forest was beautiful in winter, the summer drew me even more. The scent of the hay in the upland meadows, hung over wooden posts to dry, the sharper aroma of the resin from the pines, or of fresh cut logs where the lumbermen were working. The long shadows of the tall straight stems, the whisper of small birds far overhead or the scatter of twigs as a deer bounded away through a thicket – the great forest lured me ever deeper. I heard the buzz of insects, saw the fluttering streak of the butterflies alighting on the moss at the edge of a tiny brook to drink. And the villages themselves seemed so secure, the hay-wains passing through the massive doorways of the farmsteads as they had done for centuries, the fat gingham-covered duvets airing in the upper windows, the roofs coming down almost to the ground to keep away the winter snow. I felt a strange kind of holiness about that great tract of country and, like Fritz, I hoped it would always stay that way.

I only had one point of accepted disagreement with Fritz. I longed to see the Rhine opened up along the southern edge of the Black Forest so that shipping could penetrate beyond Rheinfelden and reach the Lake of Constance. I wanted to voyage up there myself. Fritz on the other hand was determined that no propellers should ever churn the water of those wild and lovely river reaches. Although all the powerful shipping and governmental interests were on my side, and the Austrians were pushing hard for a shipping-route open to the Ruhr, Rotterdam and the North Sea, it was Fritz and the conservationists who won. I am glad they did, for they were right in thinking that to make the Upper Rhine navigable would have ruined it, whatever the Austrians might say. Ships inevitably bring a sheen of oil, a smell of diesel, and dirt from the ceaseless pumping of bilges. More serious still, the barrages and locks would alter the water table, reduce the rate of flow, and play havoc with the fish and the birds. Besides, with the rest of the Rhine already stinking with phenol and all the other great streams either barraged or polluted or both, only the Upper Weser and Upper Rhine remained swift, sweet, free, clean and canoeable.

Fritz and his associates won their victory in an ingenious way. They gave all-out support to a move by a group of Swiss naturalists to press their government to have a certain small area of the country designated for all time as a nature reserve in which no mechanically propelled boats of any kind would be allowed. This tract of country was on the Rhine, upstream of Waldshut, and by a peculiar quirk of medieval boundary fixing there was a section where the river made a loop, but the boundary-line was drawn more or less straight. The result was that Switzerland had a considerable enclave of land on the Black Forest side of the river. The effect of this was that the Rhine was, for a moderate distance, Swiss from shore to shore – whereas elsewhere the national boundary ran down the centre of the stream. As soon as this area was made into a nature reserve, the dreams of shipping contractors and small-boat yachtsmen went up in smoke. And the birds remained undisturbed.

It was a year or two later that I arrived at St Märgen on skis, in the middle of the winter. I had hardly had time to unpack my rucksack before Fritz arrived to tell me that one or two of the local men wanted to have a word with me, and so did the two burgomasters, that of St Märgen and the one from the neighbouring and rather larger village of St Peter. We were to meet at the *Stammtisch* in the *zum Hirschen*, that evening. More than that he did not say.

After dinner I found some seven or eight village elders gathered round the table in the corner of the saloon, some from St Märgen, but others from St Peter, and the small hamlet of Thurner was represented by a farmer. We talked of nothing in particular for a while and drank quarter litre *schoppen* of the favourite wine of the neighbourhood, the excellent Glottertäler from the western slopes of the Kandel. It was clear to me that something was going to happen after these preliminaries, but I could not guess what. Fritz had given me no indication at all.

The burgomaster of St Peter called for another round of Glottertäler, and when the glasses had been brought he began carefully to set out the matter which was worrying them all. The Bonn government, he explained, had persuaded the Land of Baden-Württemberg that a six-lane motorway should be constructed across the southern part of the Black Forest, with no other object than to cut twenty miles off the road distance between Paris and Vienna. No doubt this would save twenty minutes or so of time for Parisians heading for the delights of Viennese opera, and twenty minutes for Viennese on their way to the Folies Bergères, but for the locals it would be sheer disaster. To construct such a motorway it would be necessary to widen the entire valley where it passed through a bottle-neck in the neighbourhood of St Peter, but the government seemed confident that with sufficient quantities of dynamite the landscape could be blasted away. The forest could easily be felled where necessary, and the traffic route could then sweep through the meadows behind St Märgen and turn south-eastward, past Thurner. The whole scheme had been carefully worked out, and the majestic new roadway was due shortly to come off the drawing-board and be put out to contractors.

The mere idea of the roar of traffic day and night on a six-lane highway had something of a nightmare quality about it, and none was anxious to have the drift of oil-laden and stinking air which had been through thousands of radiators and cylinder-blocks flowing over their villages. They had made protests, they had sent deputations to make representations to the central and also the Land government, with just the success I might have expected – none at all. All their attempts to have the motorway halted had been brushed aside, so the village fathers had decided to turn to me.

Me? But why should officialdom pay any attention to me, I objected. If the Fremdenverkehrsamt and the Schwarzwaldverein and the local councils had failed, how could I possibly alter the government's brazen intentions?

'We do not know,' the mayor said, with a shake of his head, signing to the landlord that we could well do with a third *schoppen* of Glottertäler.

'We think your voice might help. They might listen to you.'

'But . . .' I began.

'Think about it,' said Fritz. 'You could write to the President or somebody. You can think of something. They probably regard us as just a lot of peasants.'

Next morning I walked out and saw the village lying serenely in the snow, unaware of the din and stink which would so soon be descending upon it. The air smelled deliciously of resin, and wood smoke, the sun glinted on the red sandstone of the great church. I could have cried that some official in a transport ministry could plan a fate so fearful for the people, but I very much doubted that I could do anything to avert it. And then later that day as the post bus took me down toward Freiburg and the way home, I had an idea. As soon as I reached London I sat down and wrote a letter addressed to the Federal Minister of Transport.

I explained to the Minister that I had heard about the motorway, and thought it a most excellent idea, a worthy and even a necessary improvement to the transport network. But I had a personal worry, I said, about which I was taking the liberty of asking his advice. I had written in some of the most reputable papers, I explained, extolling the charms of St Peter and St Märgen as places in which those in need of rest and relaxation could be sure of peace and quiet. St Märgen was in fact advertised as a *Hohenluftkurort*, a place of pure and healthy air where the visitor, as I had myself written, would find only the soft murmuring of the breeze in the pines, the pure-scented air, the beauty of an undisturbed night beneath the stars, a peace that could go far to restore health to the tired or run down. But now, if readers should take me at my word and actually go there, only to find the countryside scoured by dumper trucks and the air heavy with the diesel fumes of giant excavating machines, would my reliability not be in question? Readers might even sue me for the cost of their holidays, I suggested. What was I to do? Should I now ask the same papers to accept another article from me in which I should apologise for the error and warn their readers on no account to risk a Black Forest holiday?

This letter brought an acknowledgement and an assurance that the Minister was considering the matter very carefully. Which was evidently true, because three weeks later I had a further reply, the gist of which was such that I even went to the unusual extent of putting in an international telephone call to take the good news from Highgate to St Märgen. The writer was instructed to inform me that I need not worry, nor retract anything I had said in print. The Minister had weighed the various alternatives very carefully, and had come to the conclusion that the motorway through the valley of St Peter and St Märgen should not be constructed. An alternative route through an industrial area near Basel might prove to be suitable, but whether that were feasible or not I might rest assured that the original proposed route was definitely and finally abandoned.

And so it was. I have been back to St Märgen several times since then, and the tall, graceful woodlands are still at peace.

THE GOLDEN RAVEN

Das Wandern ist des Müllers Lust, das Wa . . . a . . . a . . . a . . . andern. But it is not absolutely necessary to be a miller, nor to be besotted with Schubert to find that walking can be a wonderful revelation. And it was Fritz Hockenjos who told me of another long-distance walk, longer than my trek in the Arctic.

There were three well-marked paths which traversed the whole of the Black Forest from north to south. The most westerly of them, which kept as far as it could to the tops of the hills which fell away to the Rhine plain, was the Westweg. He suggested that I should walk it from end to end, and then write up my adventure for the journal of the Black Forest Association, which would be interested to know what a foreigner thought of it.

So it came about that early one morning I found myself in the hall of the railway station at Pforzheim, a town which occupied itself with making clocks of every kind. In the railway hall I was walking up and down like Christian Morgenstern's hen*, but I did not screech 'Where, where is the station master', as his representative of the poultry did. Instead, I was examining the walls, the doors, the window-ledges, the seats, everything. A railway official was watching me anxiously, and in the end he came over to me.

'Are you looking for something?'

---

* *In der Bahnhofhalle, nicht für es gebaut,*
geht ein Huhn, hin un her,
'Wo, wo ist der Herr Stationsvorsteher?'
   Christian Morgenstern, *Galgenlieder*.

'Yes,' I said. 'I am looking for a lozenge.' The main long-distance paths were all marked with lozenge-shaped signs in various colours.

'A *lozenge?*'

'Yes indeed. A red one,' I answered.

I could see the thoughts flying through his mind. This animal is dangerous! Do not attempt to feed it! Avoid all sudden movements. He stepped back cautiously, smiling nervously, then turned quickly round and hurried away.

I eventually found the marking at the edge of the town and set out on the trek of 200 miles.

It was about three o'clock when I came to the hamlet of Dobel, where the threshing floor was being prepared for a barn dance with the local band. I would willingly have stayed for that, but I had by now only covered thirteen miles, and I had to average twenty if I was to reach Basel on time to catch my Swissair flight to London.

'I'll walk for another hour,' I said to myself. 'That should be enough for today. I could do with a good meal, after a night of travelling, so I shall find a pleasant inn and turn in.'

I walked another hour, and saw thousands and thousands of tall pines. I walked on for another hour, and then a third. I never saw another soul, but soon after six I came upon a hut. The windows were boarded up, the door locked. It was not until shortly before seven that the path came out to a road, and in a clearing a man was engaged in trying to pack his wife, a grown-up daughter, a table and three chairs and a collection of pots and pans into his car. He pleasantly informed me that Yes, only a quarter of an hour further ahead I would come to the Hohloh Tower, and if I dropped steeply down to the left from that point I should come to Kaltenbronn. There I would find a *Kurhaus*. A Sanatorium, a Cure-house? I was alarmed. 'But I am not even ill,' I explained. All the same, twenty-five miles out from Pforzheim I would willingly have rolled my eyes, let my tongue hang out, and imitated all manner of symptoms of mental or physical ill-health in order to receive a night's shelter.

'You don't need to be ill,' said the motorist with a laugh. Kaltenbronn was only a so-called *Hohenluftkurort*. It was once upon a time the hunting-lodge of the Grossherzog of Baden, but now it was a hotel.

A better and more comfortable hotel I have never discovered. I had an excellent dinner and slept like a log. When I awoke next morning I saw that it was raining heavily, but having been born and bred in England this did not deter me. I have always maintained that nobody in England should make their plans dependent on the weather, for in that case one would merely stay at home until one died of old age. Either the weather forecast is bad (but incorrect) or it is good (and also incorrect). So, either in the radio weather forecasts or in reality it is continually raining. Much the best under these circumstances is neither to listen to the radio, nor to look anxiously up into the sky, but to carry on with whatever was planned. The result is that the depression or wet front or whatever it is supposed to be realises that one is not to be intimidated, so it moves off and tries its luck elsewhere. So I decided, even with neither anorak nor macintosh, to set out again at once after breakfast, and by then there was no more than a damp cloud which clothed the woodland in mysterious beauty.

I met very few walkers, and most of those I encountered were young ones, not grandfathers like myself. Most people who walked over the Black Forest tended to do so earlier in the year, before it was too hot and whilst enough of the magical beauty of spring remained. All the same, it was with some astonishment that I noted from the visitors' book at Alexanderschanze that 273 walkers down the western path had overnighted there ahead of me that year. I spent the night there too, for on the fourth day it would be necessary to cover thirty-five kilometres at a single stretch, without an inn, a hamlet, a shop, or any opportunity to find food and with only three springs of water in that whole distance. Nevertheless, one could pick unbelievable quantities of bilberries, and what with those and the ripe raspberries and strawberries which grew over all the clearings even the most fastidious gourmet should have been satisfied.

On the seventh day I decided to make a detour, quitting the path and making over a little to the west in order to visit Fritz at St Märgen. And in so doing I happened to pass the Brend Tower. Then I knew precisely where I was, and I hurried down the meadows to the Golden Raven, an inn I recalled from many many years before. It had not changed, except that the former landlord was no longer there.

'Where is Herr Ehrath?' I asked.

'I am Herr Ehrath,' the young man said from behind the bar. 'Perhaps you mean my father, who died some years ago.'

We dug out the visitors' book of a quarter century past, and I pointed to my name. Then I told him about the night of the snow.

It was just after Christmas, and the Golden Raven had plenty of guests staying for a week or more of modest skiing, the kind of reasonable, gentle skiing with no ski-lifts or other expensive accessories involved. But then a thaw set in which melted almost the whole of the covering of snow, and a drizzling rain fell over the tops of the hills. The hotel guests were depressed, because there was no other entertainment at the Brend. There was no other house for that matter, and the nearest village of Furtwangen was about one hour's walk distant. The only activity among the German families was to play cards and drink beer. We all knew that by next morning the little snow remaining on the north-facing slopes would have gone. Herr Ehrath tried everything he could think of to cheer up the guests, but the gloom persisted.

Seated alone at a table in the corner of the saloon was a weather-beaten old man in a grey felt cloak and corduroy breeches. He arrived every evening at about six o'clock and began his way through a whole bottle of Schnapps. A remarkable blunderbuss stood in the corner beside him, and once every hour or so he would look at his watch and exclaim portentously if somewhat muzzily '*Ja, ja.* After midnight he will come. He will run across the meadow.' Then he would take another glass of his liquor and wait; and each night Herr Ehrath would advance upon the huntsman shortly after midnight and announce briefly 'He will be coming now.' I suspect this was merely to get the huntsman out of the premises while he could still just manage to walk.

The one of whom they spoke was a fox, and when the landlord had said his habitual piece the huntsman would rise unsteadily and perform a curious old-fashioned loading operation, pouring gunpowder down the muzzle of his gun. Then he would hold the muzzle to his eye and peer down the darkness of the barrel. I thought it a wonder that he had never shot himself, but Herr Ehrath asked me one evening if I had not noticed that the man lacked several fingers on one hand. He was repeatedly shooting himself, it seemed. Only a week or two earlier he had called in for a final drink after shooting at a fox, and on his way home afterwards he noticed a trail of blood in the snow. Clearly he must have wounded the fox, so he carefully followed the red trace across the snow-covered meadows. To his surprise the trail led round in a wide curve toward the inn, passed straight through the door, and ran directly to the chair where he had been sitting.

The hunter's midnight departure was usually the signal for apprehensive silence. Each night we waited for the bang, but still more anxiously to hear him fumble for the door latch again. On this night he rose as usual, loaded his gun and staggered to the door. As he opened it he let out a terrific cry.

'*Schnee!*'

The snow was already half a metre deep and still falling so fast that one could almost see it piling up. We all rushed out into the moonlight, gathering armfuls and flinging the snow over ourselves in exuberance. We shouted like children, and soon everyone was engaged in a snowball battle, a struggle which slowly moved from the snow outside to the warm comfort of the saloon. Even the huntsman slung his gun over his shoulder and joined in.

One of the guests was a rather portly businessman, a jovial fellow from Stuttgart. Compacting a solid ball of snow in the doorway he took deliberate aim at Herr Ehrath where he stood behind the bar polishing a glass, and then flung with all his might. He scored a bull's eye, but not on the intended target. He had aimed too high and the shot passed well above the landlord's head to strike straight between the eyes the portrait of the *Führer* which glowered down upon us disapprovingly from over the further doorway. As the snow squashed out to cover the whole of Hitler's nose and temples there was a roar of delight. But it lasted only for an instant before being frozen into an embarrassed silence.

It was just then that the huntsman appeared round the outer door, brandishing his blunderbuss. Sensing the strained atmosphere he looked at the others and then in the direction in which all eyes were turned. When he saw Adolf the Great's face obliterated by the snowball he let out a roar of approval and in front of the horrified gathering he raised the gun to his shoulders, swaying unsteadily from side to side.

'I'll finish the bugger for good and all,' he roared. He came to something like a steady stance and took aim.

The man who had flung the snowball happened to be a party member, and this sacrilege was too much for him. He snatched at the blunderbuss and wrenched it away from the man.

The huntsman was bewildered by the pained silence around him, and after looking blearily round the room he shrugged his shoulders and turned to stagger out into the snow, leaving the gun behind.

As the door closed after him there was a slight easing of the tension. The snow was beginning to melt on the picture and the *Führer* appeared to be weeping at the shortcomings of frail humanity.

Herr Ehrath picked up a dishcloth, looked at it and put it down again. Then he drew out a very fine silk handkerchief, and climbing on a chair he mopped off the snow with all the delicacy of a midwife cleaning up the tender skin of a newborn child. Filled with emotion, we watched him in silence.

Somebody, I thought, should pronounce the blessing, and in a way that was just what Herr Ehrath did. He laid the cloth down gently and swept his hand over the congregation with a curious reverence.

'*So*,' he said soberly. '*So, so. So!*' He paused for a moment or two, like a priest waiting for the congregation to say 'Amen'. Just for an instant I caught his eye, and as our glances met I saw his lips tremble, and I quickly looked away. It had been a matter of touch and go whether or not he could carry off his scene. I knew instinctively that if the guests had not been present Herr Ehrath would have seized the huntsman's gun himself and blown the picture to pieces.

MASTER MATHIS

It was in the summer of 1930 that we set out on foot as a family across the Bavarian mountains toward Oberammergau. We were bound for a performance of the famous Passion Play, which was staged once every ten years, with additional performances at centenaries and half-centenaries of its original coming into being in 1634. The play started as a vow, a kind of thank-offering perhaps, for the deliverance of the village from the worst ravages of the Black Death which was then sweeping so fearfully over much of Europe. We arrived in the evening, found our way to our lodgings with a member of the cast (there were in fact very few villagers who were not involved in a production which could put seven hundred people on the stage at once) and awaited the morning.

Promptly at a quarter to nine the somewhat mournful signal began which summoned us to take our seats, and at nine o'clock the chorus filed in from both sides of the stage and the prologue began.

I was not, I remember, greatly impressed. At least, not spiritually. The staging of the drama, and in particular that of the Old Testament still tableaux, was certainly brilliant enough to arouse a mild admiration in a fifteen-year old, but seven hours on a hard seat (with a welcome break for lunch) was somewhat too long for my enthusiasm. Though not bored, I was definitely not overwhelmed. Perhaps that was in part because I had not at that time reached any great proficiency in German, but in the main it must have been that I had been adversely conditioned by the Ormskirk Street Chapel at St Helens, to which we walked every Sunday morning, to hear the preaching of the worthy minister John Grant. I did not like Mr Grant, and when he came to dinner and our airedale bit him in the leg underneath the dining-room table I was secretly delighted.

No, the Oberammergau Passion Play made no special impact upon me. Not then. But when I went again four years later the effect was one that was to stay with me for ever. Twice since then – four times altogether – I have been to the village in the year of the Passion, and each time it was to be the same. I was left speechless. It was not just the haunting music, nor the spectacular staging of the Old Testament tableaux which were to remain with me. It was the sheer reality. Never again was I able to hear the ponderous prose of the King James version of the New Testament echoing down a cathedral nave, nor read to myself a more modern and perhaps more moving version such as that of J.B. Phillips, without seeing before me the incidents precisely as they were acted out upon the Oberammergau stage against a backdrop of mountains that represented the real, tangible world. It was the feeling that one was actually there, sitting on a seat at the side of the market-place in Jerusalem, watching the mad, exultant, pitiless crowd that came thronging through the alleys to be worked up to scream hatred toward the one who had come to show them what God was really like. I had a terrifying sensation of cowardice, of failure to leap onto the stage and scream that this was sheer folly, wickedness rampant. It was a heart-rending feeling that one knew exactly what was going to happen if none should raise a finger in protest, and that one was too cowardly to do so.

When Judas, by no means the simple sort of betrayer as he is so often portrayed, discovers that the Kingdom of God is going to involve sacrifice, the renunciation of ambition and of power politics, and a deliberate exposure of himself to persecution, to mockery, and the contemptuous disdain of his fellow men, he decides comparatively easily that this is not for him. *'Ich nicht! Ich nicht!'* 'Not for me!' With cold, calm and terrible realism Judas speaks not only for himself but for millions of us across the ages.

Desperately one tries to comfort oneself with the thought that we are much more civilised now, and that if the mission of Jesus were to occur in our own day he would not be crucified, nailed to a cross. And of course he would not. He would be given a three minute interview on the television and maybe half a column in one or two Sunday newspapers, and then he would be written off as a well-meaning crank, pleasant in a curious way, but unfortunately far too influenced by radical theology. Give him a soap-box at Speakers' Corner in Hyde Park so that he can let off some of his steam – the police can be relied upon to keep a good-humoured and watchful eye upon him so that there will be no risk of a breach of the peace. And if there should be any kind of trouble, incitement to disobedience or the like, the stipendiary magistrate is a thoroughly reliable man. He can be relied upon. He is used to dealing with odd-bods. He will refer the man in the kindliest possible way to a psychiatrist for a background report before there is any question of sentencing him to a reasonable number of hours of Community Service.

In the twentieth century we are just as accomplished at executing people, but we do it more subtly and far less messily than did the Romans at the time of Pontius Pilate. But the pain of the crucifixion is none the less real. Perhaps it strikes even more cruelly than that inflicted by the old-fashioned, solid hardware of hammer and nails.

On later visits, the effect was perhaps even more intense. The wonder of the universe was there in the backdrop of the pine-clad rocky hills, just as it had been before, but to that was added an insight, something like the sudden realisation that overwhelmed the Roman officer, a man who was thoroughly accustomed to the on-goings of Jewish cranks and fools and criminals, but who in a flash realised the truth about that central figure on the cross. It was no longer for me just a matter of awe at the glory of the beauty of the physical world or the sheer ingenuity of the mechanism of life itself, but a blinding light of understanding that – Yes, that was the truth. That was what God was really like; a magnificent creator, certainly, but also a very real individual who was crucified not just by misguided Palestinian Jews long ago but by myself and others, every day, year in and year out, in this twentieth century of repetition.

Oberammergau has of course been partly taken over by the tourist industry; that is, the Passion Play has become for many people just one stop in a package tour that includes a whole set of castles built by the eccentric Ludwig II of Bavaria; so it has just become something to regard as an entertainment. Personally I could not take such a tour. The impact of the performance was such that my wife and I just had to go up into the surrounding hills for a few days and leave the souvenirs and the rest of the trappings to others, while we savoured the astounding truth of what was so beautifully and fearfully portrayed.

I had been to Oberammergau three times before something happened to make me recall those words of the professor who sought to instruct foreign students in suitably adapted German history.

'And so, *meine Herren*, you will see that beyond any doubt the honour of having been the first National Socialist must be accorded to Matthias Grünewald.'

It was more than a quarter of a century since Professor Felsentraeger had thus concluded the second of his talks designed to convince foreign students that long before Adolf the Great had come upon the stage, National Socialism had had a highly respectable parentage with connections in all the right places in history.

The reason why I recalled his words was that I was planning to take the Canal du Rhone au Rhin from Strasbourg southward, and turning up the waterway in my *Guide de la Navigation* I followed its course parallel to the Rhine and came to where a branch led off to the right. It was a dead end branch only a few kilometres long, but when I saw the name *Embranchement de Colmar* I remembered Felsentraeger, and what he had said about the

Grünewald pictures being in Colmar. I decided immediately that my old admiral's barge *Commodore* would that summer turn her nose into that cut and take us to see the pictures which the first great Nazi had painted.

The canal was unspectacular, running straight as an arrow across the Alsatian plain. But it was pleasant, the home of ducks and coots, of anglers, and occasionally storks. Kingfishers and dragonflies swept past us as we chugged along the seven miles of cut to reach at last a muddy and stagnant basin where half a dozen vessels from France and the Netherlands were unloading hardboard and fertilisers. But once out of the dock gates, we found ourselves in a city of astonishing beauty, a place of narrow, winding streets and timber-framed houses and roofs with tiles glazed in brilliant, shiny colours, and the Unterlinden museum which, until the Revolution, had been a Dominican community. And there, among many other treasures, were the panels of the polyptych which Master Mathis, or Matthias Grünewald, had painted for the monastery of the Antonites at Isenheim.

All the piety, all the grandeur of the intimate knowledge of God of the late Middle Ages poured down upon me from Grünewald's huge canvasses of the Concert of Angels, the Annunciation, the Crucifixion, and the Burial of Christ. But there was much more than piety and grandeur. There was a restlessness of the spirit, a frustration with the orderly conventions of the time and a desire to sweep away all sentiment and see the world as it really was, horribly cruel and bestial, yet filled with transcendent love and eternal hope. If I was grateful to Felsentraeger for having implanted in me the wish to see the altarpiece for myself, any connection between the visionary Master Mathis and National Socialism was obviously nonsense and could be forgotten. All that I could now be aware of was the blanched face of Mary swooning into the arms of the grief-stricken beloved disciple, standing behind the anguished Magdalene at the feet of Christ.

No picture that I have ever seen before or after has remained so indelibly fixed in my mind as Grünewald's crucifixion. It is no gentlemanly crucifixion of the centuries before him, nor was the Christ figure the sickly sugar-candy individual of a Holman Hunt. He was a Christ whose face was distorted with sorrow, whose hands clawed to the sky and whose feet were twisted where the viciousness of the nailing had driven apart the tendons and turned the bent toes in upon each other. The mouth hung open, the rough-hewn crossbar of the cross was bent under the sheer weight of the suffering, and already in the feet the muscles had gone into rigor and the blood beneath the toenails was blue with the coagulation of approaching death.

Against this astonishing picture were set the Annunciation and the Nativity, with their angels who might have been peasant girls from the artist's native Frankenland, and a simple village Madonna; but in contrast to the soothing peace of these and of the canvas of St Antony conversing with St Paul the Hermit in the wilderness, are two other great figures of amazing power. In the Resurrection, the armed soldiers tumble over each other in the blinding light of the blond, brown-eyed Christ whose very features and hair seem to evaporate into the gold of the halo which encircles his body and outstretched arms. The light from the halo flows outward through all the ordered colours of the rainbow to disappear finally, merged in the deep blue of the starry sky of the universe. And if the risen Christ here invites trust as well as wonder and awe, and proclaims the victory over the horror and pain of the crucifixion scene on the panel's reverse side, the depths of purely human suffering and pain are reached once again in the Temptations of St Antony. The kindly, bearded hermit is being attacked by the most extraordinary creatures that the mind of man could ever conceive – and which the mind of God in evolution did not. In a wild confusion of claws and clubs, beaks and teeth, pincers and squinting fiery eyes, these beasts of hell fling themselves upon St Antony, who shields his face with his hand as one of the beasts grabs him by the hair, another snatches at his cloak and dresses up in it with fiendish glee. A third bites at the fingers which clutch the rosary, and something like a giant parrot raises a knobbed stick to bring it down upon his skull.

Yet it is not upon St Antony or the fiends that the eye comes to rest. One notices a figure in the corner of the picture, a human form clad only in a cowl and with the body so racked with sores and disease that of the feet nothing is left but the rotted bones, and one arm is no more than a twisted stump, cut short at the wrist by gangrene. Is it this mutilated, oozing remnant of human shape that has let fall from the bundle of his books wrapped in a ragged cloth the slip of paper which reposes among stinking fungi? It bears the words *Ubi eras Jhesu bone, ubi eras, quare non affuisti ut sanares vulnera mea?* Where wert thou, good Jesus, and why comest thou not to heal my wounds?

No text-book of medicine with all its three-colour printing of medical sores and gangrenous wounds has ever come near to the startling realism of Master Mathis in depicting corruption and decay, and pain; and the secret of the thought behind his Isenheim paintings and the ghastly realism of their execution lies in the fact that they were painted for the monastery of the Antonites, a self-sacrificing order founded to tend those suffering from the fearful *Antoniusfeuer* which swept across Europe in the tenth century to claim vast numbers of victims, and which survived in sporadic outbreaks until at least the sixteenth century.

Grünewald's racked and swollen body of the sufferer in the Temptations of St Antony must certainly have been painted from life, and the livid, gangrenous colours of the tortured and dying Christ on the cross are certainly those which he had seen for himself in the sick-ward of the monastery. In the predella – which portrays the burial of Christ – the same anguished tension of the limbs and the wasted muscles of the livid and blood-spotted body could be taken as a true, realistic representation of some of the features of the dread disease, a sickness which most fortunately is no longer with us.

It was for the sufferers from that terrible plague, and for those that tended them, that Master Mathis painted that picture, with the assurance that the pain is shared and the tortured cry of the stricken sufferer does not go unheard. And not only for them, but just as much for myself and others four and a half centuries later.

Grünewald's message was there in front of me as I stood there in the Unterlinden. It was something never to be forgotten – the certainty that although man might heap the most unspeakable pain and torture upon his God, the same deity has the individual in his constant love and care. For there, in the distance of the sky, beyond the creatures which scrabble and claw at St Antony, the cloud of angels is speeding to the rescue, and on the ruined walls and rafters the attack has already begun.

THE NIGHT MAIL

I was pleasantly surprised after moving to London to find that even if it had not the calm of Cambridge and the beauty of the bleak Fenland, the great city had many compensations. For instance, there was the night mail.

Having written a letter which I wanted delivered by first post next morning somewhere in North Wales, I made my way after supper by Underground to Euston Station, to seek out the mail train, which was due to leave at twenty minutes past nine. It was a train which carried nothing but mail, together with the limited accommodation for the men who sorted mail all the way from London to Glasgow.

I found the train standing at platform two, and on one of the coaches near the rear there was an ordinary letter-box let into the side. I posted the letter ten minutes before the train left, and at half-past-seven on the following morning a postman knocked on the door of the addressee in North Wales, and pushed my letter through the slit. This magnificent service went on, week in and week out, all year round. And not only to North Wales. The train served other areas too – Coventry, Liverpool, Manchester, Cumberland, Glasgow and other destinations. It was, I think, one of the unsung wonders of communication, and in days when it sometimes takes three days for a letter to travel twenty miles, it seems astonishing that such efficiency could have existed. I hope it still does.

I did not wait to see the train depart, but already the row of lights along its side were turned on, making it resemble some huge hawk-moth caterpillar with segmental breathing-holes. But I met the train on another occasion, and that was just south of Bletchley junction.

The Grand Union Canal passes closes to Bletchley, and when voyaging up that waterway the thought occurred to me to see if one might view the mail train at full speed in the middle of the night. So, seeing a postman step out of his van to deliver a parcel I asked him if it were possible.

'Sure,' he said. 'You know where the embankment is, where the branch line from Oxford meets the main line? Right, you'll find a cinder track running up the embankment, just by the bridge. Meet you there tonight, quarter to ten.'

So the last of the failing light saw me waiting at the cinder track as arranged. I had not been there long when I saw the lights of the mail van bumping along the lane below. The van drew up, and two postmen got out, taking their laden bags from the van. They were genial and friendly souls as postmen usually are – for who else could walk about in the English rain and still remain happy – and one of them was my acquaintance of the morning. They seemed to be both surprised and flattered that anyone should really be interested to see them about their nightly work. Picking up their bags and swinging them over their shoulders they hurried up the ash-track on the side of the embankment until we came to a little hut beside the main line.

They had four bags with them, and these had to be got ready for the mail train, which was expected within perhaps a quarter of an hour. Each bag was wrapped in a heavy sort of satchel made of thick cow-hide, and was strapped tightly both fore-and-aft and around. At one end of the satchel was a heavy steel ring, and the bags were hung in pairs on steel fingers which projected from the ends of arms which could be swung out from their posts to beside the track. These two gibbets were thirty or forty yards apart, and the bags were suspended so that they were a foot or so clear of the side of any train that might come by. Each satchel had a light string attached to the bottom corners and tied to the gibbet post, to prevent it from swinging in the draught of a train.

One of the postmen placed an oil lamp to shine on a board on the London side of the first gibbet, to indicate to the train crew that the arm had been swung out. With everything now ready, we crouched down low, with our heads only a couple of feet or so from the rail. I was on no account to raise myself, the postmen instructed.

The minutes ticked away until we heard in the distance the roar of an approaching train. 'That's not him,' said one of my companions. 'You can tell, as he's no lights along the side like ours. More like an express goods, but don't move just the same.'

The experience of lying under the stars and within an arm's length of the rails on which a train was to pass at high speed was electrifying. The noise grew louder, the rail metal sang, and with a tremendous rush and thunder and shaking the locomotive bore down upon us. They were still using steam locomotives as well as diesels at that time, and as the great giant swished past my head I was engulfed in a roar of triple-expansion and a cloud of hot steam, with that indefinable but exciting smell of hot oil. The smoke billowed out overhead, tinged red with the glow of the furnace, then faded to a bluish white. It was astonishingly beautiful.

There followed the clanking of fifty or more wagons, and then an extraordinary calm as the sound faded away toward Bletchley junction. We peered down the track. 'Ah, he's late again,' said one of the men. 'I've known him to be an hour late, but never you mind. He'll turn up.'

The mail train ran from Euston to Glasgow with only a single stop at Crewe. Pick-up of mailbags hanging from gibbets began at Berkhamsted, and was done at full speed. Dropping of mail started at Rugby, and from there onwards mail was both collected and dropped without a break. At Crewe the train panted for breath while the mail for Ireland, Liverpool, Manchester and other destinations was unloaded to the platform. Then the mail would make Glasgow in a single breathless run, collecting and dropping all the way. The train itself was composed entirely of mail wagons, sorting vans and dropping and collecting wagons. Its row of caterpillar lights was essential for the collecting gear projected far from the side and could easily scoop up some unwary railwayman standing at what would normally be a safe distance from the track. But neither the catching-nets nor the dropping hooks projected continually from the coaches because they would otherwise strike the bridges and the signal standards. They had to be put out at exactly the right moment, and immediately hauled in again. This was the business of the mail-men on the train, and they did it by eye and ear. In the case of the catch that we were awaiting, the postal sorter in one of the coaches would wait until he was abreast of the chimneys of the brickworks down the line from the junction, listen to hear the train flash through a bridge, count three, push out the net, pull it in to tip out the bags, and push it out again in time to catch the second pair of bags a moment later. It was always a matter of split-second timing, and remembering the marks. Sometimes the clue was the sound of the changed rhythm as the coach passed a cross-over of rails, or a points, then counting a particular number of tum-ti-ti-tum rail joints before pushing out the catcher. Dropping was done in similar fashion, and at the right moment the bags were swung out to slide off the arm and fall on a special slip-way at the side of the track, ending in a stout funnel-shaped net at ground level. In our case this was beyond the further end of the platform at Bletchley.

We had been there an hour before we could see that the next visitor had a row of lights dotted along the side. I lay down on the ballast beside the track, and the postmen crouched very low beside me. Two of the bags were right above my head.

The moment was impressive, and at the same time terrifying. The mail train had left late and was making up time, and on this stretch of line it could travel at eighty miles an hour. As the wheels of the locomotive roared past I stared up, unblinking. The ballast was jittering with anxiety at the approach of the monster, the singing of the rails grew to a crescendo, and the flickering oil lamp cast fleeting patches of light on the swiftly flashing connecting rods of the approaching locomotive.

'Don't move!'

I could not have moved if I had wanted to. I was frozen with expectation, my scalp tingling with a sensation that was half fright, half relief. I dared not blink as I stared at the bags hanging from the gibbet above me. They swung a little in the draught, but they were held clear of the train. Unconsciously I counted the coaches.

One . . . two . . . three . . . four . . . they thundered past my head with the lights shining out into the dark countryside. Had they forgotten to put out the net? Six . . . Seven . . . bang! The bags were gone, and turning my head I saw the net retract and tip into the coach with smooth, unhurried precision, and then be out again and ready to snatch the load from the next post only a couple of seconds up the line. Another heavy thud as the satchels struck the catching net, and then it was all over. Two more coaches, and the red light was disappearing down the track as the engine whooped to any waiting on Bletchley platform to stand back while the Royal Mail roared past on its way to the North.

The silence afterwards seemed so intense that it was almost irreverent to break it. I picked myself up from the ballast, thanked the postmen for allowing me to share their thrilling nightly adventure, and made my way back to the canal with the clatter of the wheels over the rail joints still running its urgent rhythm through my head.

THE VILLE

I had never given a thought to what went on within the fortress walls of a prison until an editor friend invited me to go with him to the Christmastime dramatic presentation at Wormwood Scrubs, which was a prison for first offenders. He was a Visitor there. Realising that Highgate was not too far from the Ville I applied for permission to be a visitor at that institution.

The Ville was the name given by the inmates to Her Majesty's Prison Pentonville, where once a week I was to present myself at the gate to be let in to sign the register. It was a gigantic, gaunt and forbidding fortress of a place set in a dismal area of North London off the Caledonian Road, and yet only fifteen minutes distant from the middle-class respectability of Hampstead Heath and Highgate.

An inmate was allowed to ask for a Visitor, if he so wished. Visitors were not forced upon the residents and relatively few of the prisoners wanted one, but for those who wished to have a private confidant and a contact (within limits) with the outside world, the system of Prison Visitors was a humane one and an excellent idea. The Visitor served as a link with the more normal world, to help a convict prepare for the day of release, a day which was bound to be fraught with problems.

So much is written about overcrowding and the general iniquities of the prison system that the difficulties of release rarely catch attention. But the fact is that however unpalatable it may be to some to be restricted in their freedom, life in prison solved many problems. One never needed to make a decision of any sort. Time to get up, time to feed, time to wash up or sweep the floor, time for exercise – the whole day was regulated from dawn to evening lock-up hour. One needed never to take any thought for the day – indeed it was impossible to do so. No thought need be taken for the morrow, either. To a person of any enterprise this was the most frustrating and repellent feature of prison life, but to the habitual small-time thief it was one of the most comforting.

No, no thought was required. The menu for the meals of the day was determined from above. Tolerably good food was served in ample supply, there was work, washing, exercise and sleep. Money in small amounts was provided for such luxuries as cigarettes. One had no worries about whether one was going to get the sack because the concern was closing down. There was no need to consider whether the housekeeping money would stretch out for the whole week until the next pay-day. If one was an avid reader – as very few were – any book on any subject under the sun would be procured free of charge from the public library. Any who liked to watch television might – if well behaved – watch the television. A billiards enthusiast might – if well behaved – have a chance to play billiards. The view from the barred windows was perhaps not such that one would have personally chosen, but those inclined to sit at their windows and revel in the glory or the romance of the view were not, on the whole, likely to come from the social layer from which the prison population was generally drawn.

With release, all the practical problems of daily life were thrust upon a man the moment the great gate closed behind him. He had to earn his living. He had to arrange his own life, he had to think. Clearly a man of intelligence and real determination would be so delighted to be released from confinement that he would face these practical problems and solve them, however great – and understandable – the reluctance of prospective employers might be to take on an ex-convict if any alternative applicant were available with the same qualifications. But not many of the inmates of the Ville were men of high intelligence. Very many were 'recidivists', returning again and again to prison. This was not because prison life had destroyed their character, but simply because that was an easy way of life to which they were used. They simply could not face life outside, with all its problems, for more than a few weeks at the most. Life in the free world was too difficult and insecure. That was why several of those I encountered had had only a week or two of difficult freedom before they went through the motions of stealing something at a street market or in a shop when they could be reasonably sure that a policeman would see them. Plead guilty to the bench, the appalling record of minor past offences would be read out to the magistrates, and for another year he would be safely back among his old friends and acquaintances, lags and screws alike, and with luck once more in the familiar Ville.

Habitual residents obviously had no real need of a Visitor, because they had no intention at all of adjusting to the world outside. Yet my first invitation was to just such a man. He had probably applied for a visitor for some light relief and expected some Dickensian churchwarden type who would preach to him about morals and would wince at four-letter words. For some Visitors were indeed of that kind.

At five minutes to six on Wednesdays I would ring the bell at the great front gate and a warder would peep through a squint before letting me in. There were several more gates and much jangling of keys before I was admitted to the cell blocks. These were exactly like those seen in the movies, a fact which curiously enough surprised me. Railed galleries, tier upon tier, ran round a central space and were connected with each other by cast-iron spiral staircases. On the outer side of each gallery were the cells, with massive bolts and huge locks on the thick steel doors, and in each door there was a small shuttered peep-hole so that the inmate could be observed at any time. The colour of the decor was mainly grey and dark green, and greyish men in greyish clothes were wandering about with grey metal dishes on their way to having them filled with a greyish soup. It was depressing in the extreme, and yet there was good humour in the air too, and I got the impression that the screws or warders were on easy and familiar terms with their charges.

By six o'clock I had penetrated all the barriers and found the correct numbered cell. I knocked on the door – because at that time of day the cells were not locked. Perhaps I had expected to find some sad individual who wished to unburden himself of problems concerning his home and family, but I was greeted in a very natural way by a cheerful individual, a small-time professional thief named Harry. Quite soon I took a liking to him.

Harry had no problems at all that I could discover, and if he had had any he could hardly have shared them with me in private, for he occupied a cell with two other men who made it clear immediately that they had not the least intention of asking for anything so foolish as a Visitor, whom they expected to be not only thoroughly wet and easily shocked, but in all probability a copper's nark to boot. Yet after half an hour we were all getting on splendidly, and I found them to be amenable, courteous in a friendly way, and really very good company.

Every Wednesday evening we had a very pleasant private party in that cell. Much the ablest of the three was a charming and cool-headed thief who was locked away for shooting at the police when they came to arrest him for robbery. Luckily he did not hit anybody, or it might have been worse. He did not really like being in prison, but regarded jail somewhat philosophically, as a necessary risk in his occupation. It would have taken him five years, he said, to make as much money, tax paid, as he had collected in a single night of well planned housebreaking, and he thought a couple of years in prison was no more than a reasonable price to pay. It was bad luck that he had been caught, but that was fair enough. A great thing about armed robbery was that you did not have to pay back the money, or the proceeds of the items you had sold through a good fence to some place such as the London Silver Vaults. So now he had no expenses, his proceeds of robberies were well invested on the advice of his bank, and when he came out he would have a good sum at his fingertips, and instead of slaving away in a factory he could happily live on the proceeds. He thought the law was arranged in a very convenient way, and he held no grudges against anybody.

Yet this well-organised man, in common with most of the others I met in the Ville, lived partly in a world of fantasy. It seemed to be necessary for almost every prisoner to invent certain signs of status, so that he was at least on a par with his fellows, if not superior to them. At that time the Jaguar motorcar was the sign of flashy wealth, and many of the inmates of the Ville would boast about their Jaguars to each other. It was a kind of accepted game, for each of them must have known very well that if he had ever owned a vehicle of any kind at all it would not have been more than a run-down, fifth-hand van.

I visited Harry until he was released. I doubt if I did anything for him beyond providing one hour a week when a breath of the outside world penetrated the cell. He did not need me as a bridge, as he fully intended to come back inside at the first opportunity, but I think that he and his pleasant companions quite simply enjoyed the opportunity of chatting about something, anything other than the affairs of the Ville – that subject being absolutely barred to Visitors.

I had already been visiting at the Ville for a year or two when I moved to Jersey, but at that time the flights between London and the island were so cheap that I had no difficulty in keeping up my mainland interests as well as adopting more local ones. I thought it might be a good idea to become a Visitor at the Jersey prison also.

A relic of earlier prison days was still preserved in the Jersey museum in the form of a long, barrel-shaped treadmill in which half a dozen men could take their daily exercise, their combined kinetic energy being expended in turning an ordinary small coffee-grinder which prepared freshly ground coffee for the governor's breakfast. Although this was no longer in use, there was still something rather old-worldly about the prison itself (now pulled down and replaced) which was a pleasant little granite building within a courtyard of stone, approached through an iron gate. One day I presented myself there, and rang the bell.

The governor invited me in, and I sat in an armchair opposite his desk. What could he do for me, he asked.

'I thought perhaps you were in need of a Prison Visitor,' I said. 'I have been one for a year or two at Pentonville, so I know what is involved.'

A look of curiosity spread across the governor's face. 'A Prison Visitor? And what precisely is that?'

'Well, the general idea is that after months or even longer in prison a man may have considerable difficulties when he is released. He has no work, he is unfamiliar with the state of affairs in employment and so forth. It can be a very difficult time for him, and if he has a Visitor that means that he has a contact in the ordinary world outside, somebody who can advise him before release on such things as will help him to settle down . . .'

'Settle down?' the governor said. 'My dear chap, we don't want them to settle down. It's down to the harbour and deported on the first mail boat to come in, as far as we're concerned.'

So that was the end of my idea of being a local Visitor in Jersey. But the Ville could still provide surprises.

Harry was replaced on my rota by another petty crook, who had an extremely good brain in one particular direction. It was the system that prisoners were given some sort of work to keep them occupied, and in fiction this was usually sewing mail-bags. In fact at the Ville the work consisted of dismantling out-of-date electronic equipment from the Post Office, and this gave Keegan his chance. He requested a book on radio construction, and from this he extracted a list of all the component items that he needed in order to build a small transistor radio. His friends were instructed to keep their eyes open for the requisite parts, and eventually he had assembled everything he needed, a complete free kit.

The real beauty of Keegan's radio was that with great ingenuity he had made it up to be completely flexible, and he had inserted all the components into the hem which ran round the four sides of an ordinary handkerchief. If he laid it out flat, he could just hear the programme, but at the slightest whiff of danger he could crumple the handkerchief and push it into his pocket.

It astonished me that a man with Keegan's ability should be confined in the Ville instead of being employed by MI5; but in fact it was the only bright area in an otherwise unbalanced nature.

I doubt if my visits were of any practical use to Keegan, any more than were my weekly visits to Harry. We just had pleasant conversations. Having a Visitor just made a change. And when I heard that an inmate in his block had been caught in possession of a file, with the result that all prisoners in the area were made to strip right down to their bare skins for a rummage of everything in their cells, and his radio had been found and taken away, I was genuinely sad. But I appreciated the fact that he had had the confidence to show it to me, and knew very well that I would never have given him away.

JOHN POYNTER

The one man who really appreciated my visits in a much deeper way was John Poynter, and I kept up my weekly calls to him right to the happy ending of his time in prison. Poynter was a highly qualified male nurse and by the time I came across him he was virtually running the prison hospital, and so far as I could make out he was running the doctors too. He had his hands full, what with ordinary sickness, occasional accidents and injuries, and drug addicts being compulsorily dried out, so he was by no means frustrated. He was serving a sentence for a reason which was legally impeccable but which struck me as trivial in the extreme, and I was surprised that he showed no resentment.

Poynter was a keen driver, and he had twice been ticketed for speeding on the road down to Southampton. His licence was endorsed, and on the third occasion that he was caught he was, of course, disqualified and deprived of his licence for a year. That did not greatly matter to him, because his elder son was already seventeen and capable of driving the whole family down to the seaside.

All went well until Christmas Day, when they were in the middle of the family dinner. There was a knock on the door, and a neighbour burst in, in a state of hysteria. Her baby had just been taken violently ill – it turned out later that she had stuffed it too full of plum pudding.

The woman was so obviously scared that something was seriously wrong with the child, that when she asked John if he could rush her to the hospital he left the table without giving a thought to the fact that he had no licence. He told the family to carry on, jumped into the car and sped toward the hospital as fast as he could. He happened to cross a traffic light just after it had turned red, and a police patrol lurking in a side street spotted him.

To drive when disqualified was naturally a serious offence, and it automatically carried a prison sentence with no possibility of pleading extenuating circumstances. John pleaded guilty, and the bench put him down for nine months. After a few days in the Ville he asked to have a Visitor, and I was lucky enough to have him allocated to my list. I visited John every week in the prison hospital, where he was entirely in charge but still had time for a chat. Unlike many prisoners, he had no fears about what might happen to him when his time was up. The hospital authority for whom he had worked took the unusual line of suspending him on half salary, which of course ensured that they would get him back again at the end of his sentence. A month before his release they restored him to full pay with leave of absence, a remarkably generous and sensible step. So John had no economic problems at all, and he was happy in his work, coping with the sick and injured, and the junkies.

He had a remarkable family. His wife Margaret came up to visit him each week, and her more or less grown-up children took it in turns to come up to the Ville too. They all adored him, and this in itself was unusual, for the wives or girl-friends of most prisoners dropped them like a red-hot brick as soon as they were in prison. But Margaret Poynter did not. She was devoted to her husband.

Their relationship was a curious one. Margaret had originally been married to a man who had beaten her savagely and then gone off, leaving her with three children below the age of six. Eventually she applied for a divorce, but at that time the law was such that she could not obtain one unless the husband could be found, whether alive or dead. And he had simply vanished into thin air. Meanwhile, she met John, and set up house with him and the three children, to whom he in turn was utterly devoted. She could not risk becoming formally married without incurring the risk of bigamy, so she was happy to remain a 'common law' wife. But she took the name of Poynter, and the family lived in happiness for fourteen years, when John's patient badgering of the authorities to allow a divorce on the assumption of desertion for more than seven years was at last successful.

However, by that time John had just been taken into the Ville. The news that he could now regularise the position of himself and his wife and her three children was of course a delight to him. Under normal circumstances prisoners were not allowed to marry whilst serving a term, but there was one exception. If the fiancée were having a baby, the governor had it in his power to authorise a marriage out of prison, as the Commissioners did not wish to be open to the charge of enforcing bastardy. Margaret happened to be pregnant at the time, so John was delighted. He applied to the governor of the Ville, who was only too happy to give his assent and his blessing. Everything was arranged for the wedding to take place at the Finsbury registry office.

And then Margaret had a miscarriage. The necessary certificate of pregnancy could no longer be upheld, and so the governor withdrew the permission to marry. Naturally John was heartbroken about the miscarriage, as Margaret's age meant that the chance of having their own child might never come again; but he also felt that to stop the marriage was unjust, particularly toward his wife.

I went to see the governor about the case. He was a man whom I always found sensible, and genuinely sympathetic and concerned for the men under his care. But there were limits to his powers, and he had not the authority to authorise the marriage of a woman who was not actually in process of having a child. However, he referred the matter to the Home Office, which of course turned down immediately any idea of making an exception in Poynter's case.

John was resigned, but I could see that he had taken the decision very hard. I tried to console him, and told him that he would just have to wait until the day his sentence ran out; but without telling him or asking his permission I wrote a personal letter to the Home Secretary, who at that time was Jim Callaghan. I set out carefully the circumstances, and pointed out that under the regulations as they existed the reason for allowing the marriage in the first place had vanished. But at the same time it seemed to me that the rules bore very hard upon the woman in this particular instance. They had the result of penalising her severely for having a miscarriage. As Home Secretary he had the last word in everything that concerned prisons, and I wondered if he could not find some way of letting the original permission for the wedding stand.

I was not very hopeful, but within a week I had a letter from Callaghan himself, which stated briefly that he had given the matter his sympathetic consideration and had written to the governor of Pentonville to instruct him to arrange for Poynter's marriage. It was an extremely humane and sensible action.

John asked me to be best man, and I was delighted. I was at the registry office to see John and his wife arrive in a smart chauffeur-driven limousine with white ribbons streaming from the radiator cap. No bystander could ever have guessed that this was an official car which the governor had somehow obtained, presumably from the Home Office.

This was the first time that I had actually met Margaret Poynter, although I had heard so much about her from John. She was a kind, motherly woman, good looking, confident and calm. The registrar conducted the brief ceremony. Not many were present, but beside myself and the three young people who had been small children when John first appeared in their lives, there were two friends of the bridegroom in immaculate dark suits and wearing carnations. None would have known that they were not only friends, but two screws from the Ville. Along with myself, one of them signed the register.

After the ceremony, John was trusted to take his wife and family out for a meal.

'Hop it,' said one of the screws with a friendly wink. 'And don't forget to be back by eight o'clock.'

THIRTY-NINETY-EIGHT

I am still not sure what it had 30 or 98 of, or perhaps 3,098, but I bought the car. I just liked the look of it. It had style. Added to that, there was the fact that it had enough clearance over the ground to ensure that if I ran anybody down I could drive right over them without knocking them about with the undercarriage.

When the salesman in the double-breasted suit brought out the log book I noted that the car had been licensed for more than half a century, and I reckoned that if anything could possibly go wrong with the mechanism it would have done so by now, and so I could assume complete reliability. The controls were not like those of any car I had owned previously, but more like the levers of a railway junction signal-box and there were two handles which one could move in arcs around the centre of the steering-wheel, rather like what one could find in a tram. The man in the double-breasted suit worked out which levers to pull, and I drove away cautiously but in style.

To me the car was just one that was refreshingly different, a shade unorthodox. It had a hood which one could put up in case of rain, but it had no door on either side at the front. One just had to climb in, as though getting into a boat when standing in the river. I liked the car immediately, but I had no idea when I drove away from the garage that I was much in the position of a man who is franking his letters with some old twopenny blues which he happened to find down the back of a bureau. Not until a day or two later, when I had mastered the controls and ventured to drive into town. It was at the traffic lights at Regent's Park that a man drew up alongside in an expensive saloon, the kind used by developers.

He leaned out of the side and nodded respectfully. 'Lucky man,' he said. 'I would give ten of these for one like yours . . .' Just then the lights changed to green and he roared away before I had time to strike a deal. I suppose it was fortunate really, as I don't know I could have found garage space for the nine I would not be using.

A day or two later I had just climbed out over the side of the car when an elderly gentleman with a heavy moustache stopped on the pavement and looked admiringly at the car.

'Is it?' he asked. 'Is it really? It is! It's a thirty-ninety-eight, by Gad. Or is it the Twenty-three-sixty, Sir?'

I realised that it was the car, not myself that merited the 'Sir'. Frankly I had no idea, but I could not stand beside my own recently acquired vintage model and admit that I did not know what it was. 'It's the thirty-eight-ninety,' I said. 'I mean, the thirty-ninety-eight.'

He seemed satisfied, and after a last admiring look he lifted his hat and went on his way. But almost immediately another questioner came across the road. He walked right round the car, then dropped on all fours in the roadway.

'I thought it was!' he exclaimed. 'And then I thought it couldn't be. But it is!'

'Yes, it is,' I agreed, though I was not at all sure what.

'It is O.H. isn't it? Or is it S?'

'Yes.'

'I mean which is it? It looks to me like O.H.'

'Oh yes . . . that.' I tried to look knowledgeable. 'It's O.H.'

'Mind if I lift the bonnet?'

My luck held. He lifted the bonnet and purred. 'Just as I thought. It's O.H. all right.' He peered around for a while at the works, and then gently closed the lid again. 'Good of you to tell me all about it, old man.'

I soon got used to it, and by pretending to be rather hard of hearing I came to know quite a lot about my car, even if I could not actually have pointed out the various bits that I could name so convincingly to every fresh enthusiast who asked to be allowed to examine it.

'It's got the old fudge-box in front,' I would repeat confidently. 'And it's got a couple of SUs. The old AV has been changed, as you can see.'

I would be accosted by everything up to generals. One of them said he had a photo in the family album of his father driving about in Palestine with Allenby, in exactly the same model. I thought this interesting enough to go to the library and check up in a History of the Great War. I found that the man was wrong. Allenby used one right enough, but it was a slightly earlier model, though I expect it had the old fudge-box in front, just the same. It was probably the Twenty-three-sixty.

Sometimes I found it rather trying to have to sit impatiently in my car while complete strangers walked round it with their hands in their pockets and kicked the tyres in that strange way that automobile fanciers have. Yet in spite of all the wasted time I decided to keep the car, because it was a wonderful money saver. Not on petrol – not by a long way. But on incidentals.

Previously I had owned a modern car, a sort of half-Japanese thing, and the moment I had managed to squeeze myself out of it and walked away round the corner a policeman would appear and note its number for causing an obstruction. I had become so used to the indulgent smiles of magistrates as they patiently let me ask what I was obstructing and then announced the fine without even bothering to answer my question, that I had come to regard fines as a piece of indirect taxation levied automatically on motorists at intervals of a week or so.

Yet the moment I changed to my thirty-ninety-eight, everything changed. At once. Traffic wardens would not even bother to read the overdue figure on the meter alongside, and if policemen appeared as usual and wrote down the numbers of all the cars along the street they only recorded the others. Never mine. Instead they would often pat the radiator cap gently and pass on. I would sometimes peep round the corner of a side street to watch. There must have been a sub-paragraph or something in one of the Road Traffic Acts about immunity being granted to thirty-ninety-eights. I wondered whether Peel had had one.

(*The prototype of the Vauxhall 30/98 was designed by L.H. Pomeroy for J. Higginson of Stockport in 1913. The car was produced by Vauxhall Motors, with various minor modifications in later years, until 1927. It has been described in Clutton and Stanford's 'The Vintage Motor Car' as one of the greatest cars of all time.*)

NO WAITING

When my thirty-ninety-eight sailed away over the Atlantic to a museum, I had to have a more modern car, and of course I was immediately fined for parking. But that was a good lesson to me. Not a lesson in the sense that it prevented me from parking in future, but because it made me realise how needlessly I had had to fork out good money. Needlessly, because the whole matter of stopping even for a split second in a London street is a matter of a battle of wits, and I had been caught napping.

There was some excuse, though. I naively imagined that if the streets with NO WAITING signs were ones where no waiting was allowed, then as a corollary waiting was allowed in streets which had no NO WAITING signs and where the lamp posts had no yellow belts round their middles. It was certainly imprudent of me to think so because they can even get you for obstruction in the middle of Salisbury Plain, and that is precisely what they did – not on Salisbury Plain but in Islington.

The system is just to get in ahead of the traffic warden or policeman before they can start making a report or issuing a ticket to stick under the wiper, and after my experience in Islington I have always managed to do so. That is why I have never been fined again, even when parking the car for hours on end right beside a POSITIVELY NO WAITING LOADING OR UNLOADING OR EVEN SLOWING DOWN notice.

There are plenty of stratagems. One of the commonest is to buy a couple of CD plates, darken the skin slightly with fake tan and mutter in Welsh or back-slang, meeting the warden's hesitant enquiries with a shake of the head and a good deal of hand-waving. Egyptian cigarettes help, too. This ruse has however become something less than a certainty since an MP blew the gaff on it in Question Time. It's all very well for MPs, with the Palace Yard available and nothing to pay, but ordinary folk just have to do the best they can.

I've never tried the CD method, because I have a British car, not an American one, and this would give the game away. Instead I usually adopt the Harley Street plan and I have never known it fail yet. The scheme is to park deliberately in a NO WAITING street close to a hospital. Just trusting to luck is not absolutely safe however, and it is best to supply a certain amount of corroborative detail. A bone saw on the back seat is convincing, but these things are expensive. It costs much less to furnish a copy of *The Lancet*, with a couple of empty medicine bottles to complete the picture.

Though this is usually successful, there is always the chance that some young traffic wardress with her eye on promotion may think it her duty to intercept the driver when he returns to his car and warn him, or even issue a ticket. This is where prompt action can save the day. The car should be started up immediately and driven off quickly with a smile and a courteous but firm 'I'm sorry, madam, but I cannot stop just now.'

One snag is the poor distribution of hospitals, and there are sizeable areas of both the West End and the City where the busy specialist technique is ruled out for that reason alone. Fortunately there are alternatives, and one is the role of champion of worthy causes. I have never adopted this myself, because I do not like fooling people through their emotions, but for those without scruples quite a range of possibilities is opened up.

It would not be prudent to mention them all, but one of the more obvious is to buy a back number of the evening paper which had the headline 'Traffic Wardens Seek Big Pay Increase' and write legibly in red ink in the margin 'Hear Hear. Write to MP' or some such comment. Left on the front seat, this can save pounds which would otherwise have to be paid to a cleared site car park attendant, or perhaps charged to the firm's expenses.

Frankly I think this verges on the dishonest unless one actually does write to one's MP at intervals about traffic wardens' or policemen's pay to square one's own conscience. My own system is less questionable, and it is copied directly from London buses. I just take out a floorboard and lean it casually against the rear offside wheel, and in fine weather I leave the bonnet open too. No dishonesty is involved, for I do not actually say that the car has broken down; I just leave that as a matter of inference. There is, however, the danger that the official is a motor enthusiast and will want to stand and watch the repairs, but quick action can avert trouble here, too.

'Good evening, officer. I don't really like to ask you, but could you possibly sit in the front seat and press the starter when I say "Now"?'

Natural charm and courtesy, reinforced in the case of the police by the recollection of what Sir Robert Peel said about responsibility to the public, invariably leads the man to do as suggested. I bend down for a few moments deep into the bonnet, then raise a hand and shout 'Now!'

The engine starts and I listen gravely. 'Sounds perfectly right to me. Just accelerate a little will you please. Thanks. Yes, she sounds perfect now. I'm very much obliged to you.' Not an untrue word, it may be noted.

'Don't mention it, Sir.'

'I had better be going, hadn't I? This is a restricted street.'

'Well, I shouldn't worry too much about that, Sir. One can't help these things, you know.'

'Goodbye, officer.'

'Don't forget the floorboard, Sir.'

'Oh, thanks.'

And that's all there is to it, or so I believed until one day when the car was standing in its familiar narrow City street, with the floorboard out and the bonnet up as usual. When I arrived on the scene after tea there was a constable looking at the car in an absent-minded way.

'Broken down again I see, sir. This model appears to give a lot of trouble, I notice. Rotten luck on such a busy man, Sir.'

'Yes, isn't it.'

'I'll try and start her for you, Sir.'

Before I could dive into the bonnet the man had turned on the ignition with my key, and the starter was whirring. But the engine only fired once or twice and then came to a halt. At first I was vastly relieved, but as he continued to churn away with the starter my elation quickly evaporated. The car really had broken down, just where it was.

'Ignition trouble, Sir. It nearly always is. Better have the plugs out.'

I had the plugs out but they were perfectly clean, though my shirtcuffs and jacket sleeve were not.

'Must be the distributor then, Sir.' He pointed down to a sort of pineapple thing with a black top from which a lot of wires sprouted. 'I should take it off, and check the points.'

It was hopeless to plead ignorance, for the kindly officer was standing at my elbow, telling me which bolts and nuts to remove and pointing out the appropriate spanners in the tool kit. For a four pound fifty bill at the dry cleaners I eventually got the distributor loose and opened it up on the roof of the car.

'Nothing wrong with that, Sir, I should say.' The policeman glanced at it professionally. 'Tell you how we can find out, though. You just hold this wire in your hand, and I'll spin the drive.'

He did so. The shock I received was fortunately not enough to kill me. For a moment I thought I saw him smile but I must have made a mistake, for he shook his head sadly.

'Ignition seems OK, Sir. Perhaps the timing has slipped. Was she running all right when you brought her here?'

'Well, er . . . up till then . . . she was,' I said, choosing my words carefully so as not to say anything that was untrue.

The policeman stroked his chin. 'Very strange, Sir. And you've plenty of petrol?'

'Yes, I filled up only this morning, on the way in.'

'Very puzzling, Sir.' He looked at his watch. 'Sorry I can't stay, Sir. If I were you I would put the distributor back and try again. Cheerio, Sir.'

'Cheerio.'

I don't know why manufacturers place the distributor where they do, but I suspect that it is to keep the repairs within the trade and discourage amateurs. However, I at last got it back again, though I tore my jacket in doing so and made rather a mess of my trousers wriggling under the car to retrieve a nut. I tried again with the starter, and only when there was too little current left to turn the engine did I trail off to a telephone box and have a garage truck down to sort things out.

I was an hour late for dinner by this time, but the mechanic quickly discovered that there was no petrol reaching the engine. He discovered why, too. Somebody had cut the wire leading to the petrol pump.

'Whoever would want to do a trick like that?' he remarked as I filled out the cheque on the roof of the car.

I thought I knew, but I didn't say. After all, it was fair enough, really. But I didn't park in that neighbourhood again.

FLOATING VOTER

There's nothing I like more than a by-election. I envy those people who are so certain which of the candidates they want to send to Westminster that they are simply straining to get to the poll the moment it opens. Personally I would ignore the whole business if it were not that I once heard an Archbishop on the steam radio saying that it was the duty of every citizen to go to the polls – and who am I to contradict even an ordinary Bishop let alone an Arch? I accept his judgment and go. More than that, I do my utmost to see that everyone else goes too, by offering my services as a registered driver.

I choose which side I drive for according to the range of cars they offer me. One Party can put up a three-litre Bentley with a blower and I'm theirs for the asking. I find that I can nearly always persuade people to attend the ballot if I undertake to make a small detour by the cake-shop over the back of the hill, or maybe the Hornblower's Arms.

I'm not suggesting that driving between the patisserie and the polling station would see me clear with the Primate, for I realise only too well that he meant that it was the business of the citizen actually to cast a vote. But, with the greatest respect, I can't help wondering whether he would think so if he lived in the same division as myself where there are certain difficulties, not the least of which is the haunting fear that if I vote for one of the candidates he may actually be elected. Somebody once tried to convince me that this was the idea of the thing anyway, but he turned out to be a member of the dance committee of one of the local Party organizations and so he may well have been biassed or even misinformed. Certainly the people I drive to the polls take no such radical view; they don't vote to put a man into Parliament but only to keep the other ones out – at least that's what they tell me when we are on the way to the Hornblower's.

But I really like the five weeks before the actual contest, because that is the time when the big names from the Parties deign to grace our locality and come bowing and scraping and ready almost to kiss one's shoes, let alone babies in prams in marginal seats.

Yes, hallowed and gracious is the time, at least for a while, and if we are marginal we can view the aspirants on the telly in all their cathode-ray beauty, but just in case we can't they make up for it by sending their portraits with a note to say that the others are the most unmentionable skunks who actually call people nasty names and have no regard for truth at all, whereas they themselves are pledged to keep it all frightfully clean and would not dream of saying anything horrid about anybody, not even those deceiving sharks who would skin me alive, sweat me, and put me in a strait-jacket and goodness knows what else if only they were given my X.

I can see that in some ways it all depends on me, and that is not often the case in this precious stone set in as much of the silver sea as the Spanish fishermen are going to let us keep. It's up to me, they say, actually to choose, for better for worse, for richer for poorer, though oddly enough it usually turns out to be the latter as far as I am concerned, and I have it on the authority of those who are in the queue for Westminster that how I vote will determine all sorts of things which are far too difficult for me to understand.

It would be easier not to vote at all, but this would be a betrayal not only of the wishes of the Primate but of the lives and labours of all those who fought and died and chained themselves to statues so that we would all have to suffer so much suffrage. So of course I could vote, responsibly and thoughtfully. And think hard I would certainly have to, because I know that if I were to see those four names set out one under the other I would never remember which one is which, nor what it was they said they really honestly would see to if they were elected. So, Primate or no, it is really far too difficult for me.

Of course one of the candidates will be elected even if I don't vote for him. But I don't want him to be, and yet it's no good going into the polling booth just to vote for one of the other fellows instead, because there's always the chance that my vote will be the casting one and I should have the dreadful responsibility of having kept one of the men out merely to have another one sent to Westminster. Frankly I would like to see them all somewhere, but Westminster is not the destination I have in mind. I just don't think any one of them is worth that huge salary and free postage on their Christmas cards.

This is not a hasty judgment; I always give the candidates a chance to show originality of thought, and as soon as the nominations are in and the deposits have been handed over I write them a letter. To save time I do it on my w/p and so I can run off a copy for all of them, including the Communist candidate, who doesn't really count but is one of those picturesque additions to the English scene like the Vintners sweeping Upper Thames Street once a year, although the Corporation cleaners have just been through with a brush lorry half an hour before. The letter is, I think, courteous to the extent of buttery and it expresses my delight to learn from the Party newssheet just delivered at my house that the candidate will, if elected, constantly bear the wishes of the electors in mind – a characteristic in which, I point out, he differs admirably from other members of his Party, who appear to vote only as instructed by the Whips. I then ask him (or her) what his views are on the Aylesbury branch of the Grand Union Canal and I enclose a stamped postcard for a reply.

I don't always ask about the Aylesbury canal. It may be the population of avocets nesting on Havergate Island, or the effect of laundry waste on elvers migrating up the Severn. But the main Party replies are always the same: 'I *most certainly agree that the Aylesbury Branch of the Grand Union Canal (or the population of avocets, or the effect of detergents on elvers) is a matter of very considerable national importance and I can assure you that, if elected, I will support with vigour the energetic policy of my Party that, having regard to all the weighty and complex factors involved in the present situation, the matter is one that may well need further consideration in the light of which we would not shrink from taking whatever action, if any, might be deemed most suitable in the public interest.'*

The Communist answer is different, for it dispenses with the regard and the consideration to assert boldly that the problem would never have arisen at all if the country had had a Communist government. I think this may be true, though I am not so certain about the annual fluctuations in nesting avocets.

By their replies the two main candidates at once disqualify themselves, because if a man has no views about a narrow canal in Buckinghamshire, he is not likely to be much use on the problems of Britain's declining docks and ports; and a blind patch on elvers and detergents augurs badly for constructive thought on Strontium 90. Nor is a man who has nothing to say off the cuff about Havergate Island likely to throw up anything original about the state of affairs in Belize, or whatever part of our far-flung heritage is next on the list for flinging even further. I recognize that the Communist has something, but I doubt if the rest of us would if he and his pals got to Westminster, and so my referendum only confirms my original conviction that none of the candidates should be voted in – not even by non-voting the others out.

If the prelate did not haunt my conscience I would leave it at that and merely spend the day driving willing sheep to the polling slaughter; but he does – and so I feel in duty bound to take the paper thrust at me. I put a cross against every candidate, Communist and all, because theoretically this records one vote for each and two or more against him, so that I am chalking them all down one point net, which accords well enough with my feelings. There's only one drawback. The totters-up toss my votes to one side, on a heap labelled 'spoilt papers'. I've seen them do it, at the Town Hall. It's quite a large heap too, because there seem to be a lot of voters in our division who work things out just the way I do.

A waste of a vote? Not at all. The candidates are there at the Town Hall to watch the draw, so at least they can see that there are plenty of people who would rather be floating than have any hand in putting them into Parliament. And whichever one is elected, we floaters have the smug satisfaction of knowing that it isn't us who are sending him to Westminster, even if we have failed to keep him out.

HARVEY FLACK

One day in 1953 the telephone rang, and a voice asked whether I would have lunch with Dr Harvey Flack. The lunch would be in a small Greek restaurant near Euston Road which produced the kind of food he liked, and could offer some quite drinkable wines. In fact that lunch was the planning session at which Harvey discussed with his assistant, Joyce Ward, and myself the contents of the forthcoming first issue of the magazine *Family Doctor*.

The British Medical Association had decided to launch a popular monthly designed to inform the general public about themselves, their health, and medical matters in general. It was not intended to bolster the confidence of hypochondriacs, nor to provide a puff to show how enormously clever and self-sacrificing general practitioners were. It was a sensible and much needed attempt to encourage the idea of a medically informed public, and so to take off the family medical man some of the absurd and unnecessary weight which had been dumped on his shoulders by the relatively new National Health Service, which by virtue of its organisation and its method of financing implied to the simpler-minded and thrifty citizen that he had not had his money's worth until, in the absence of some genuine sickness, he had troubled his doctor with some absurd or imaginary complaint.

Harvey Flack had been selected as editor. He was an Irishman who had been a general practitioner in Lancashire, but whose real interest and bent lay in journalism. The choice was an excellent one, and under his able hand *Family Doctor* became a reputable and extremely readable magazine. It did not pander to sensationalism, but was a highly professional production. From the start, it sold widely.

At this first lunch Harvey explained that the magazine was not to be limited to arthritis and mumps, but was to range widely into the subjects around the fringes of medicine which were of importance to parents and families. These would include such things as human genetics, child behaviour, education, falling in love and marriage. It was to be on my shoulders that he intended many of these to fall.

By the time we had reached the cheese we were discussing a possible series tracing the origin of a baby from the moment of conception and determination of sex, up to the stage immediately before and awaiting birth. Even Spemann and his newts could have a mention, because they illustrated the organisation processes at work in the early human embryo.

A particular advantage to Harvey was that I was not 'a proper doctor' – that is, a medical practitioner – and so my material could appear over my own name. This was something forbidden by dodsonfoggery to medical practitioners, as it was classed as advertising. So most of the contributors to *Family Doctor* had to masquerade under assumed names which could not be turned up in the Medical Directory, but I could be myself, because none could say that I was soliciting patients.

I wrote for *Family Doctor* for thirteen years, and probably ate one Greek lunch per article. It fell to me to tackle racialism, and the responsibility for the education of children. I wrote on twins, hereditary intelligence, on relationships with others, on adolescence, and on a whole range of matters that were not strictly medical but were very much concerned with the matter of living.

So successful was *Family Doctor* that after the first fruitful years Harvey launched a new venture under the same umbrella. This was to be an annual called *Getting Married*. Its sales ran into hundreds of thousands, and it tried to cover everything that engaged couples might want to know, from budgeting to the first night in bed – and later nights also – though of course with the delicacy which was still not extinct at that time. It fell to me to tackle subjects such as mutual trust and understanding, and how to behave in a civilised way toward in-laws, however repellent and hostile they might appear at first meeting. A bishop gave his views on marriage in church, a lawyer dealt with house-buying and mortgages. It was an honest and straightforward attempt to help young people at a vital and often bewildering moment in their lives.

All went well until after another lunch in the Greek restaurant, when Harvey said that he was going to devote the issue of that year to attacking hypocrisy and humbug about sex, and the tendency to hide facts about what was then known as 'beating the gun', or in more professional circles as pre-marital intercourse. Harvey did not wish to do this for sensational reasons, but simply because most of the teaching about marriage assumed a sexual innocence and purity which had long since passed away. He wanted to extend the help given by *Getting Married* to embrace those who were forcibly pushed into marriage, or simply had not been as fortunate or efficient as others in their methods of contraception.

My assignment, to which I agreed most readily, was to start from the Registrar General's latest figures, which demonstrated beyond all doubt that one bride in eight was already pregnant at her wedding (as estimated by the birth of a baby within six months), and that among brides up to eighteen the figure was as high as one in three. It was left to me to decide the line I would take in trying to say something constructive to these couples, most of whom had either been driven into a shot-gun marriage, or at least had to marry with a sense of guilt and were often forced to suffer rejection when they particularly needed understanding, help, love and compassion. The article was to be called 'Marrying with a Baby on the Way'. There was to be an article by Dr Eustace Chesser on whether chastity was outmoded, and one by Dr de Kok suggesting that a wife was no longer expected to obey blindly her husband as though he were a master. How wrong she was, soon appeared. But the real storm broke over the articles by myself and Chesser.

The booklet, sold in over a quarter of a million copies, was shot at from several sides. Of course the weekend press loved anything to do with sex, so that they could adopt the familiar role of guardian of public morals. That was to be expected. But the immediate reaction of church leaders was surprising, to say the least. To try to advise young people marrying with a baby on the way to keep calm, think it out, to try to tend their love, heal the mistrust and forgive, so that there could be the kind of love in their home on which a baby would thrive – that, thundered Dr Nevile Davidson in Glasgow cathedral, was 'deplorable, revolutionary and unjustifiable'. I thought of poor old Socrates, but I was not inclined to drink hemlock.

The *Church Times* and the *Sunday Graphic* also produced clerics to condemn such ideas. Nor were the doctors necessarily on our side. Such an attack was mounted on what one of them called 'a group of cranks and literary dunces propounding their eccentric views under the official auspices of the BMA', that that august body trembled, and then actually caved in and stopped the sale – though not until more than 200,000 copies had gone out – so that advertisers could not start wanting their money back.

Soon, of course, the tide turned. *The Economist* and other papers took up the fight on the side of reason. Doctors began to resign from the BMA in protest against its absurd attitude. Clergy who had had to deal with the tragedy forced upon young engaged couples began to join in.

Contrary to what my postman expected, amid all the fuss I only had three letters from the public. One was a warm, congratulatory letter from a lady of eighty-one. Another thought that we needed much better teaching on contraception. The third was from a 'Wee Free' minister in Scotland.

'*Every night for the coming month I shall fall upon my knees and pray my maker that you may be struck dead,*' he wrote. That was all.

I waited for six weeks, then sent him a picture postcard from the seaside. The message was still briefer than his: '*Still alive! R.P.*'

After the BMA ban Harvey was never allowed to be outspoken again. I went on writing for the magazine until 1966, when its end was very near. Harvey had been made seriously ill by the attack upon his efforts, and in the end it killed him.

The corpse of *Family Doctor* could then be trampled upon, and the magazine itself closed.

LADY RHONDDA

When the invitation to lunch with Lady Rhondda came, I was not exactly frightened, but perhaps rather more awestruck. For I had never so much as met her, and did not at that time even know who she was. But her note-heading mentioned the journal *Time and Tide*, and at least I was aware that that weekly paper was (in the 1950s) the undisputed crème de la crème.

Lady Rhondda lived in a flat to the south of the Ritz, and she lived there with her great personal life-long friend Veronica, who was formidably clever and academic. So for that matter was Margaret Rhondda. She was also unusual in that she was a Lady by special Act of Parliament introduced (and voted through) in the House of Lords, because there was no male heir to the family title, which otherwise would have become extinct.

Margaret Rhondda (though nobody would have dared to call her Margaret to her face) was one of those small, tough, genteel and forbidding Englishwomen (though more accurately Welsh, in her case) who have made their mark on Britain as pioneers, reformers, suffragettes, or as literary figures. She was editor of *Time and Tide* in an era when it was by far the best literary journal of its day. She was not only editor, she was the owner of the paper and she determined its policy in every detail.

Ushered into the flat by a maid in black-and-white and wearing a proper servant's cap, I at once felt awkward. This was because I was not wearing a suit. I never wore a suit unless somebody had died, or it was a City Livery dinner or something of the kind. I think this was a hang-over from Rugby days, when it was strongly borne in upon us that ordinary decent people did not wear suits on ordinary days; only Etonians indulged in such a show-off habit. A suit might be permissible after six o'clock under very exceptional circumstances, but for lunch – never. And there I was, in my grey flannels and tweed jacket, Lady Rhondda superbly dressed, Veronica equally impeccable, the table laid with solid silver and priceless porcelain and candelabra, and a bell to tinkle for the maid, and a bottle or two of superb claret. It was as unlike a Lancashire home as could be, and I felt awkward. I hoped my shoes were clean enough, and that my trousers had a reasonably visible crease.

Margaret Rhondda was short, rather square, and immensely determined. And she was so obviously knowledgable that whenever she looked at me my words became tangled. And as for her life-long friend Veronica, her head was so far up in the clouds that I had not even heard of most of the philosophers, poets, and nineteenth century or Dark Ages divines and mystics whom she quoted so easily. I was even more frightened of her than I was of Lady Rhondda. Besides, both of them were quite obviously and naturally such real ladies, not just jumped-up political dames, that I could easily appreciate their living exclusively upon the very best that Fortnum and Mason could provide. And there was I, with my hair more or less brushed, and certainly a clean handkerchief, but in my tweed jacket and grey trousers. I felt almost as though I had gone to church in bathing trunks.

But Lady Rhondda managed to put me at my ease, and she began (over the bisque) by asking me some searching questions about the current state of play between the scientists and the doctrines of the Church. By that she meant primarily Anglo-catholic practices, I think, as she was what one might have described as spikey as regards theology, and Veronica was even more so – whereas I had been reared originally in the Congregational sheepfold even if later I had a tendency to feel that the congers were busily fighting battles which had in fact been won several centuries earlier.

Over the lamb cutlets we got on to Darwin, and what people were thinking of his ideas at that time, and what about the Lysenko business in Russia – though of course he was a Communist, so what he thought did not really much matter. I had the chance to say a few things about my own pet hero Robert Boyle, a man so devout that he refused the Presidency of the Royal Society because it would mean taking an oath, so firmly did he believe that his yea should be yea and no more.

We had in fact a most interesting lunchtime, monitored by Veronica, who poured out the coffee. At the end of it, and after asking a lot of questions about a trip I had recently made to Canada with Charles Raven to discuss matters of faith with science students, she revealed the real purpose of her invitation. Would I be willing to do a series of 'Notes on the Way' on the relationship between scientific thought and religious belief?

I knew that the 'Notes on the Way' was a main item in the journal and that it was absolutely unedited, so that the writer could say what he wanted without being cowed by fear or favour of the crowd. I was almost alarmed at her suggestion, and though somewhat nervous I agreed, and over the coming weeks I wrote three successive 'Notes on the Way' for *Time and Tide*, after which I contributed regularly for several years. I got on very well with Lady Rhondda, because she was completely independent, and she knew that I was also – at least to the extent that I would not undertake any piece of writing just for the sake of the guineas. Under her command, *Time and Tide* flourished, even if its circulation was not enormous.

It (or rather she) had two enemies. The *New Statesman and Nation* was one, and to her dying day she was convinced that that left-wing weekly which so applauded everything Russian was in fact published on heavy subsidies from the Kremlin. Whether she was right or not I could not say, but it did not matter. Anything with the faintest pink tinge was anathema to her.

The other great enemy was *The Listener*. This was a quality paper which consisted largely of reprints of rather highbrow talks culled from the steam radio. I think she was right in feeling that competition from *The Listener* was unfair, in that it was obviously selling far below the cost of production, being carried on the ample and willing shoulders of the *Radio Times*, which sold by the million and had a huge advertising income. In fact it was the uneven competition with *The Listener* which eventually killed the *Time and Tide* of the Margaret Rhondda era.

Lady Rhondda had a functional deputy editor and under him there were a couple of editorial assistants. One of these was a very competent girl, Celia Henderson.

One afternoon Lady Rhondda came in, and without any preliminaries addressed Celia fiercely.

'Who was that I saw you having lunch with, Celia?'

'Oh, a friend of mine.' (Celia gave his name.) 'He's a science lecturer at London University.'

'He's a Communist.'

'I don't think . . .' Celia faltered.

'That man's a Communist. I'm not going to have members of my staff hobnobbing with Communists.'

Lady Rhondda opened her bag, counted out one month's salary in notes, handed it to Celia, and told her to take her coat and clear out at once.

Margaret Rhondda always had very decided views. One day a certain public figure was mentioned in her presence. 'Him?' she sniffed. 'He drives a Jaguar. You won't find a book in the house.'

I often recalled this statement when invited out and noting that our host had a Jaguar. Looking around, I easily came to the conclusion that her incisive remark was not altogether unjustified. Books there might be, but they were of the show-off coffee-table genus which were prominently placed so that all comers would see them, and realise how erudite their host was. They were there to be seen, but certainly not read. Large, lavishly illustrated books on great houses of England, famous gardens, royalty, antique furniture, silver, salmon rivers, anything that had an aura of wealth about it. But reading matter – no.

Since those days the status of the Jaguar – along with the fortunes of its constructors – has suffered a considerable change. Its place would nowadays be taken by a . . . well, the reader can make his own choice, and it would probably coincide with mine.

Little by little, *Time and Tide* began to get into deep water. Its contents were excellent – the weekly and often satirical diary 'Four Winds' was a very popular item to which any of us could contribute suitable material – but costs were rising, printers were beginning to be union-minded and difficult, and the circulation was not large enough to appeal to advertisers. There was the additional snag that the readership was almost entirely composed of people who shied away from advertised commodities. 'Advertised goods are Good goods' was a slogan of the publicity trade, but *Time and Tide* readers were mainly of the kind who thought (as I have always done) that if a thing had to be advertised to get rid of the stock, there was probably something wrong with it. So apart from a tiny extra income from the small personal notices, there was virtually no advertisement revenue at all.

It was about that time that Lady Rhondda was personally keeping Britain's best literary journal afloat, and she was doing so to a tune of £400 or £500 an issue, and this sum had of course had to be found weekly. That meant about £25,000 a year, and this was in the 1950s, when a sum of that order was very much larger in real terms than it would be nowadays. The drain on her resources was a serious one, and even if some of us declined to be paid the few guineas which, at that time, were considered reasonable pay for the privilege of contributing to such a journal, it obviously could not go on for ever.

Just when things looked really black, something totally unexpected happened. Lady Rhondda had a letter from a solicitor, saying that proceedings were to be instituted against her and against *Time and Tide* for libel. It happened over a competition.

Every week the paper carried a competition of a rather highbrow, literary and decidedly amusing kind. There were never more than a score or two of entries, and the circle of prize-winners was even more restricted – I noticed that the same names tended to win the competitions which at that time appeared every week in *Punch*. It so happened that Christopher Fry, who lived in Little Venice alongside the Regents Canal, had put a notice on his gate: Beware of the Doge. *Time and Tide*'s weekly competition cited this brilliant notice, and asked for notices which might well be put on the gates of certain other well-known people. There were one or two parliamentary characters of course, but one (or rather two) of those selected was the Novelda Brothers. These men, who I think were Maltese but they may have been Corsican, were particularly notorious organisers of prostitution in Soho. They were the whitest of white-slavers, and their exploits had made front page news in the kind of dailies which then as now delighted in such revelations. Some of the women the brothers ran had given evidence against them when they were on trial, and the brothers were suitably convicted.

The prize for the week's best entry was awarded to an entrant who submitted a notice for the home of the Novelda Brothers:– TRESPASSERS WILL BE PROSTITUTED. The award of a five pound book token was accordingly made, and recorded in the following issue.

It was the solicitor for the Novelda Brothers who wrote the threatening letter to Lady Rhondda, and it greatly upset her. It really had her seriously worried. She visualised having to pay out thousands of pounds for the libel, and goodness knows how much in costs. She began to lose sleep, her buoyant, forceful self became muted and depressed, and one could see that she was more worried than ever before. She thought the scandal would finish the paper, *Time and Tide* would be forced to close in ignominy and debt.

I myself and her deputy editor Tony Lejeune begged her not to worry, and not to dream of settling out of court, as was suggested. This libel case, we insisted, would be front page news in every daily in the country and delight the whole population for days on end. It would put *Time and Tide* on the map. The case would certainly be dismissed, with costs, because the Novelda Brothers who were apparently so offended by this slight upon their reputation were at that very moment doing time in the Scrubs or some such place, for running a prostitution racket. The idea of their having their reputation defamed was too hilarious for words. Go ahead, we said. Let them sue. Even if *Time and Tide* should not get full costs the publicity for the paper would be something undreamed of, and free. The whole population of Britain would, for the first time in their lives, know about *Time and Tide*. They – or at least some of them – would actually buy it. We saw the circulation soaring, and all the troubles over.

But it was not to be. Tony Lejeune phoned me one day to say that the case had been dropped, because the Noveldas' solicitor had been struck off for improper conduct. Lady Rhondda breathed a sigh of relief, but one or two of us sighed with disappointment. There would be no lawsuit, *Time and Tide* would remain a journal for a faithful but insufficiently numerous elite. Its days were surely numbered.

And so it proved. One loyal reader undertook to take it over, but he had to give up after only a few issues. A second one bravely came in and tried his luck, but to no avail. The paper was bankrupt, and the offices in Bloomsbury Street closed. The staff dispersed.

Margaret Rhondda could never overcome her disappointment, and before very long she died. Whether there was great rejoicing in the *New Statesman and Nation* I never knew.

LIFE IN THE LOWER CASE

Writing meant having to deal with printers. Such men are popularly known to have devils, but they also have a pernickety way of sorting out the alphabet and they never forget things that would escape the attention of ordinary men. For instance, that in most typefaces (but not the one used here) the letter f can stand alone on its own feet, but the moment it finds itself near another f, or an i or an l, it wants to hug it tight. Printers have their difficulties, of course, but they always remember that they are difficulties and not difficulties and no doubt this makes things easier – not that anything could present much of a problem to men who can keep two different alphabets in their heads, one for capitals and one for small letters.

Yet the difficulties with which printers have to cope may be far greater than one would imagine. My first inkling of them was when I received a short but poignant letter from my favourite printer.

Sir,
We shall unfortunately not be able to put your order on the machine until next week, as there is a wayzgoose in the works.

My first reaction was that this indicated sheer carelessness and perhaps even wilful disregard of the fencing regulations of the Factory Acts, but at the same time I was sorry for the man. My wife once had a mouse caught in the fan of the vacuum cleaner at home, so I knew how he felt. The mess . . . And a wayzgoose! I could well imagine the feathers clogging up the cogwheels, and it taking days to get the machinery going again.

I regretted the harsh words I had sometimes used toward the firm. Too easily I had imagined the head printer having nothing to do but to recline in comfort among his furniture or sit on his shooting-stick playing a game of quoins to keep his little quads happy. It was only when I received his letter that I realized how terribly I had underestimated the hazards of life in the small market town where he lived and loved and printed. I rang him up.

'I'm terribly sorry to hear about that thing . . .'

'I beg your pardon?'

'The wayzgoose. Has it interrupted your work seriously?'

'It doesn't interfere all that much in the long run,' he replied. 'The lads know it's coming and they always plan the work accordingly.'

'You mean, you've had one in the works before?'

'Well, the wayzgoose comes once a year. And once is enough, believe me.'

I certainly did. 'Does it always come about the same time?'

'Usually the end of May,' he said. 'Sometimes if the weather is really bad it may be as late as the first half of June.'

Evidently the bird was a summer migrant and came up from the Nile on the edge of an anticyclone.

'What do you do when a wayzgoose comes?' I asked sympathetically.

'Close down,' he said briefly. 'But you needn't worry. We shall start machining your job next week.' He sounded quite confident about it. 'Everything is ready for the chase.'

'It must be very unsettling,' I said.

I did not like to ask him to describe the creature, because he was already more than proud of his biological knowledge – sometimes almost to the verge of exhibitionism, I thought. He delighted in sending me proofs bearing his neat little stamp.

Marked proof, which please return with attention to queries.

And the posers were written in the margin and enclosed in tidy red rings.

Query: was not a larger sturgeon caught off Kamchatka in 1912?

Or

Query: Niersteiner, not Coteaux du Layon. Surely it was a bad year in the French vineyards on account of virus B47?

To answer these questions to his satisfaction involved considerable research in the British Library and telephone calls to the cultural attachés, fishing attachés or wine attachés concerned, before I discovered that he was right about the sturgeon but that the virus did not attack the white vine anyway.

I could see that the wayzgoose was only a caller on the way to the Arctic tundra but I wanted to know what it ate and whether it changed its plumage in spring. Yet I did not wish to reveal to the printer this gap in my ornithological information. He was already critical enough of my biological knowledge. So I thought it best to have a look at one of the birds.

'Is there a wayzgoose in the museum at South Ken?' I asked him. I couldn't remember one in the Rothschild collection, which had everything down to an albino turbot bought in Billingsgate by the second baron.

'No Sir,' he said decidedly. 'You have to be a printer to have one.' And he hung up.

Printers are sticklers for custom and etiquette, and none appeals to them more than the rule which instructs them to print in full all quantities from one to ninety-nine, but to set higher numbers in numerals except under 101 special circumstances and to abbreviate certain standards and units in a particular way, whatever the author may have written. This gives them the opportunity to rewrite such small parts of an article or book as have not already been undermined by queries.

> The storks gave the frogs no ¼. Two or 300 of them would scour the ditches, seizing the unfortunate creatures by their hind 2 ft.

And such complex sentences as

> The ferocious horde cannot have comprised a single bird less than ten thousand

is simplified to

> cannot have comprised 9,999 birds.

I asked my favourite printer what might be the advantage of this system. He explained that it was the 'Oxford Rule' and complied with the standards set by the University Press. And who am I, a mere Cambridge man, to question a practice laid down by a committee of dons at the other place, each of whom is every in. a scholar and probably has at least 4°?

*   *   *   *   *

Glossary:–
Lower case Small letters. as a, b, c, d, not capitals or small capitals. Type characters were originally held in two cases, the capitals in the upper, and the small in the lower.
Furniture Lengths of wood, plastic, steel or type-metal used in filling up the edges around the type which is to form a printed sheet in a chase (see below).
Shooting-stick Not the kind you sit on to watch a cricket match. An implement, usually of metal, used with a mallet in positioning the type and furniture in a chase. A chase containing furniture and type is known as a forme.

Quoin A metal or wooden wedge or expanding metal box used for tightening up a forme.

Quad short for quadrat, a piece of metal like a blank piece of type, used for spacing words.

Chase a frame made of iron to hold a page of type for printing.

Wayzgoose a printers' annual outing or beano. It was once the annual dinner of the journeyman printers, held around Bartholomew-tide, when the Master Printer would give a wayzgoose (a way-goose, grey-lag, harvest-goose or stubble goose, – that is, one suitable for the table) for the feast. It was generally agreed that the men refused to work by candle-light until they had enjoyed this annual repast. It was usually held at a tavern at which the Master was present, and he took the opportunity to make an after-dinner speech. In later years the beanfeast (with some other kind of main dish) took the place of the actual wayzgoose, which was difficult to obtain. But the name stuck, transferred from the dish to the occasion.

BILLY GRAHAM

That Britain is by and large a pagan country is something that bishops and clergy and Nonconformist ministers have been saying for at least half a century – even if it is only recently that the term 'post-Christian' has been applied to Britain in *The Economist*. And for decades the churches have very rightly been wondering whether they ought not to do something about it, and if so what.

Long after the Oxford Movement (not to be confused with the Oxford Group, with its titillating public confessions) there came the 'Commando Campaign', in which clergy forced their way into factories and offices armed with their convictions and a heavy barrage of argument. Town churches tried to have a wider appeal by staging ballroom dancing or handicraft classes, followed by a short homily or a brace of good old stagers from the hymnbook. Vicars spent their evenings in pubs, drawing out their drinking of a pint of beer until the head had long lost its sparkle, and some would secretly spend long hours practising a throw at double top with the ambition of being elected to represent the Plume of Feathers in a darts match against the Golden Lion. One could never tell – that was the ethic.

Quite suddenly the assault on paganism changed. A team of Yanks arrived in England, and within 6 weeks a million Londoners had trailed along the dreary Seven Sisters Road to the run-down area of Harringay to hear the team leader, Dr Billy Graham, speak in Harringay arena. They sat through sermons of 30 or 40 minutes with such attention that there was not a single cough to be heard from the congregation of 12,000. More than 20,000 people who had never previously darkened the doors of a church asked to be put in touch with one.

What had Billy Graham got that others had not? That was the question which Margaret Rhondda asked herself. And not only herself, but those of us who happened to be in the editorial office at the time. Why did he draw crowds when St Paul's could only attract a few curious overseas visitors more interested in Christopher Wren than in worship? How was it that Billy Graham attracted the mass of the population wherever he went, and not only in England? She wanted to understand his success. That was why she sent me twice in one week to the Harringay arena to observe, and to report for her.

Well, Billy had good organisation and good money behind him. He had a superb master of ceremonies in Cliff Barrows, the trombone-playing choirmaster with a thousand competent voices recruited into his gigantic choir. He had Beverly Shea, a radio singer who was popular at the time, and he had a major-general to read out the notices. Huge posters on hoardings throughout London were in the style of film publicity, with gigantic heads of the various stars floating in a mayonnaise of racy display type. There was none of the pathetic 'A Hearty Welcome to All', written by an untutored hand in ink which would run in the first shower of summer. Billy Graham had the works.

He also had the American Voice, soft and strangely romantic in the same accent which could whisper those magic words 'I love you' to the millions whose main escape from reality was provided by Twentieth Century Fox and United Artists. And he was handsome, infinitely more naturally good-looking than many a Hollywood idol. And on top of that, he had very great ability.

All these things must certainly have helped to draw the crowds, but not one of them could account for the rapt attention with which people listened to his words. Or the extraordinary sincerity with which hundreds of people each evening decided that the religion which up until then had meant nothing to them was from that moment to be such a force in their lives that they were willing to rise from their seats and traverse the length of that great arena, under the eyes of their friends and neighbours, to make with complete reverence and simple humility an act of dedication to some sort of service of God.

Dr Graham never suggested for a moment that this act of witness, or decision, bought a ticket to some special state of salvation. Very much the reverse. He would take the group aside at the end of the evening and make it abundantly clear to them that their gesture was nothing more than the first faltering step on a long and arduous road which he hoped they would follow for the rest of their lives. He spoke to them of Bible reading, of prayer, and he insisted that church membership was so vital that his own campaign was silent on Sundays so as not to distract people. 'That's the day folks ought all to be in their own churches, not here in Harringay,' he declared.

All the same, he had no use at all for a religion which was a mere cultural tradition. On the contrary, he attacked it vigorously. 'So you say to me, "That's all right Billy. I'm a Christian." And I say, "How do you know?" And you say, "I was brought up in a Christian home." Ladies and gentlemen, I might have been born in a garage, but that wouldn't make me an automobile!'

And he had a severe warning for those who had come forward. 'There's someone who'll be mad at you for what you done tonight. Hoppin' mad, I'm telling you. And you know who that is? The Devil!' And he went on to say that the Devil would do all in his power to trip them up, and he dealt out to them a series of little cards to put in their purses or wallets, each of which had a passage of scripture to counter some particular attack or temptation stated on the heading of the card. He did everything he could to consolidate the first rush of enthusiasm which his new converts had shown, and that included referral to a local church. Whether this proved successful or not depended both on the church and on his customers. But even if there were failures, there is no doubt that many of those who are clergy forty years on were first fired by attending one of Billy Graham's mass meetings, and learned much from him in the way of preaching technique.

Billy's success lay not just in the paraphernalia and style of his mission, but in what he actually said. Most preaching in Britain was defensive, and occasionally even destructive. The grounds of faith were hashed and rehashed, and the very existence of the Church desperately justified. Expounding the Bible had become only too often a matter of sowing doubts and then only partially removing them. Dr Graham, by contrast, was aggressive. He took the statements of Christianity as facts, not as things to be derided on television from the comfortable fireside of a bishop's palace. His biblical characters were always strongly drawn. 'John had plenty of bones, right enough. See how he answered the important people, the clever men who knew all the answers. He turned on them and called them a lot of snakes. "You snakes . . ." that's what he said. It takes bones to say that.' Sin he called sin, not the regrettable result of social and economic conditioning. He knew what he thought about the hydrogen bomb, and one would never have found him on a commission of the churches to investigate the situation arising from its invention. But most important of all, he declared in forthright terms what the Bible had to say about every problem of human affairs. And he hammered it home.

In spite of all the equipment of microphones and publicity, Billy Graham was strikingly humble. Again and again he stressed that what mattered was not his own opinion but what God had actually said. In this he was like an Old Testament prophet speaking to a people with precisely the same needs, but in an idiom which they could understand. With the open Bible in one hand he thumped it again and again with his other fist. 'People think . . . but God says, the Bible says . . .' He had little use for higher criticism. 'Come on now, you theological hairsplitters . . .'

If Billy was a prophet who could make the word of God real and alive to the people of a despairing civilization as something which struck forcefully in every moment of their lives, he also provided the churches with the opportunity for which they had been praying. But he was absolutely clear about one thing above all:– that it was the business of the local churches, and not of himself to take care of the future.

STANLEY SPENCER

Another small, robust, and terribly formidable woman was Amy Buller. She was South African, and she had an interest in higher education which was so forceful that she would allow nothing to stand in its way. And she was a stickler for manners, too. If anyone offended against her strict mores of behaviour – which included dress – the door was there for them to pass through, and not return.

Amy was an acquaintance of the Queen Mother, and she persuaded that wonderful lady to lend her one of the Royal Lodges in Windsor Great Part, so that she could fulfil her dream of doing something to make scientists less boorish, and arts students less airy-fairy and ignorant of what was going on in the world of technology. In the battle to achieve this she had the strong support of one or two notable Oxford dons – and occasionally of less notable ones from provincial universities.

The system was really rather simple, and consisted in organising residential weekends for twenty or thirty students, for whom there was ample accommodation in the Lodge, and mixing them in the rough proportion of half science students, probably with a well-disposed lecturer attached to them, and half classicists and humanities students, also if possible with some unobtrusive tutor or supervisor. There would be one or two lecturers also, whose task it was to tackle the interface between these two varied brands of learning. During university vacations the weekends were sometimes extended to whole weeks, so there was really a chance to make a good impact.

The weekend courses were exhilarating, and I think of great benefit to the students, whose minds were being continually more and more blinkered by the increased specialisation that seemed to be unavoidable in their chosen subjects. The course started before supper on Friday, and finished probably on Monday morning.

Much of the tonic feeling, especially for students from such places as the London School of Economics, stemmed from the peaceful and somewhat regal situation. On Sunday mornings one might go to the Chapel Royal near Royal Lodge, and look through fingers at the Queen and the Duke of Edinburgh, Pepys fashion. There was excellent walking along the rides, and the beautiful Savill Gardens were close at hand. The atmosphere was stimulating, and inspiring. And as a walk of half an hour was involved in reaching a pint of beer, there was no unseemly behaviour – apart from such misdemeanours as appearing at supper without a tie, an offence which was dealt with immediately.

Windsor Great Park was not too far removed from Cookham, and so on one of these weekends Amy invited Stanley Spencer to come and talk to the party. I knew nothing at that time of Stanley Spencer, except that I had seen in the Tate Gallery his painting of swan upping, which showed Mr Turk, the Keeper of the Royal Swans, carrying ashore from a punt a couple of birds with their wings pinioned in bottomless waste-paper baskets. I was interested in this picture, not for any special artistic reason, but because up beyond Bourne End I had once come upon a swan with a fish-hook stuck in its bill, and I had rowed ashore to report the matter by telephone to the royal swanmaster, who had to row up the river for a couple of miles in none too good a temper to try to catch the bird and attend to it.

I was familiar with the medallion crosses of Cookham bridge from the painting, and also from having steered a boat dozens of times beneath its girders. So, when I saw the same bridge in another large painting at the summer exhibition of the Royal Academy I paused to look at it. The picture was of two spinsters – at least, they looked like spinsters – apparently asleep in a punt. They looked very content and snoozy and a rug was drawn up almost to their chins, but what struck me was the title of the painting:– *Christ at Cookham Bridge*. I liked the painting, and Spencer's curious and rather medieval curving outlines of his subjects, but it was not until he came to Cumberland Lodge that I understood the remarkable title.

Spencer was a shy man and he very rarely talked about his painting, but on this occasion he did so. It was an experience which was to remain with me always, for he was so carried away that he was lifted right out of this world. He stood on the carpet by the open fire, a tiny little man who seemed no taller than the back of the chair beside him, and he began to explain, to tell us of the incident that had haunted him all his life.

During the first world war he was made to scrub the passage in a Bristol military hospital, and he was doing so when a corporal came along and simply kicked him where he knelt. Put baldly in that way it is not a very notable incident, even if a stupid one, but when Spencer spoke of it we were forty years back, right there in the long passage between the wards with its dull red brick and the smell of ether, soap, faeces, starched cuffs and death, and Spencer on his knees on the tiles, scrubbing them with carbolic.

I have never been to that Bristol hospital, and probably it has long since been pulled down by the health authority if it was not cleared away by the German raids, but I know exactly what it was like, for in an astonishing and quite unemotional way Spencer took us into that instant of experience so intimately that I could see it, and recognize it. And in fact I have seen it, at least in part, because the passage and the ugly brick of the wall made such an indelible impression on Spencer that they were never to be exorcized. In them he had glimpsed hell, and one can see it in his pictures. Perhaps if I had never heard him tell of that experience in the nightmare of a passage I would hardly have noticed the wall intruding into his paintings. Certainly I would never have realised that it was anything more than just – a wall. That it was rampant evil, and cruelty, and hopelessness, a cutting off from God, I would never have guessed at all. But there it is, and in his painting of the Last Supper, with the newly washed feet of the disciples projecting from beneath the tables, behind the setting is the wall, the Bristol passage wall right enough, and in no way like a wall one might have found in first century Jerusalem. And it is behind Christ, overcome and irrelevant.

For Stanley Spencer was a visionary, not an orthodox churchman but one who could see right through to the truth, shorn of all its accretions of ceremony and dogma. And that is how he came to paint the two ladies blissfully snoozing in the summer sunshine on the Thames. One of the students asked him about the title.

'Well, one morning I was walking over Cookham bridge, just as I often did. I think it was a morning in May. There were some people going over in the ferry from Turk's, and there were punts, and people on the river – you know, nothing out of the ordinary but just as it always was. And suddenly I saw it. *That's what the Second Coming would be like.* Christ wouldn't come to St Paul's or any of those important sort of places. It would be there, at Cookham bridge, just there by the ferry. And the people would listen. Or perhaps sleep, I don't know. But that's how it would be. *I saw it*, just in that instant.'

For the rest of his life Stanley Spencer was endeavouring to get that vision down on canvas. It was to be a huge polyptych of a score or more of panels, and the two ladies in the punt were one of those. That explained the remarkable title. But unfortunately collectors and others would persuade him to sell one of the panels when he had finished it, and the task was never to be completed. Perhaps it could not be – he seemed himself to doubt it.

'Of course you know how you want it to be,' he said. 'Because you've actually seen it, just for a moment. I think it must have been the same with St John. Some of those things in Revelation – I think he put them in just because he thought they looked rather nice, just like me with the women in the punt. I thought they would be rather fun.'

And curiously enough, ever since the evening when I heard Stanley Spencer talking of Christ coming, not in pomp and glory but just simply, like that, at Cookham bridge, I would always feel a strange sense of impatience when steering round the long bend of the shallow cut which leads up from the top of the lock to where the weir stream spills away below the blue criss-crosses of the girders. It was a strange sort of urgency, a wondering whether it might not be happening at that very moment, and I should be late. And with it there was a fear, the knowing that if it should really be like that one would be confronted by something against which no excuse or defence would stand – the face of Christ, right there on the Thames, at Cookham bridge.

TWELVE GOOD MEN AND TRUE

Or women, in these modern days. There was something about a jury that always interested me, knowing as a true Briton that this was without doubt the only real and true road to justice. Indeed, I had long wanted to be called to a jury, and when living in Highgate I was in the catchment area of the Old Bailey. So it hardly came as a surprise when I received one day a notice to attend at that formidable institution and present myself for jury service, a summons which was accompanied by the expected information that if I failed to turn up it would be at my peril and I might be subjected to almost everything except perhaps hanging, drawing and quartering.

So, expecting to be confronted by some blood-stained murderer, I attended. So did hundreds of others, and the ground floor of the Old Bailey on that morning resembled Victoria station on the eve of a bank holiday. We crowded in as best we could into a kind of lecture theatre where the hours ticked slowly away as we were summoned by name to come forward and have our credentials examined as to nationality, possible soundness of mind and so forth, and were then asked if we had any objection to serving on a jury. This question was posed by an amiable judge, who gave each of us that practised judicial regard which is a mixture of encouragement, censure and barely disguised contempt.

I had no objection but some others had. To say that they disapproved of the system, or that they found it inconvenient for their business, or had to attend their grandmother's funeral, was of course no valid objection and they were told in a benevolent but firm way that they would be summoned when required. Yet the judge was human enough, and if a potential juror really lived in the back of beyond and would have obvious difficulty in turning up at the Old Bailey by ten in the morning, that was regarded as a reasonable excuse. Even if I had to waste half a day waiting to nod my head once in assent, that was no great hardship, and I found the occasion interesting.

Two weeks later I received the real summons. I was called to attend a genuine case. I hoped it might not be a murder trial, and in fact it was not. It proved to be the prosecution of a man of late middle age who was charged with being a receiver of stolen goods. The items found in his possession had included a number of watches. His front trade was that of watchmaker, though his knowledge of watches suffered something of a blow under cross-examination by the prosecuting counsel.

One of the exhibits, a watch, was passed to him to identify. He said Yes, he recognised it, but he would like to have the back of the watch opened to make sure.

A court officer produced a pen-knife, and the watch was duly opened. The watchmaker looked at the interior and said that that was the one right enough, because he had noted the name of the maker, which was inscribed inside. Fondacier – that was the name, and there it was, engraved. The prosecuting counsel looked at him with undisguised contempt.

'Perhaps you would care to look at my watch also,' he said, taking it off his wrist. 'You can see the name of the maker on the dial?'

'Yes, Sir.' The man peered at it. 'Yes it is a Swiss watch.'

'You recognise the maker's name?'

'Yes, Sir.'

'Then kindly open the back of the watch and tell me what you see engraved there.' The man opened the watch carefully and stared at the inside.

'Well, it says Fondacier,' he said rather timidly, and also greatly puzzled.

'And that would be the maker's name? Then what about the different name on the dial? Will you kindly explain that to the jury?'

The man looked worried. Obviously he could think of no sensible explanation. But he did not have to.

'Fondacier is French for stainless steel!' The counsel gloated over him. 'And you, setting yourself up to be a watchmaker, never knew that? You thought half the watches in the world were made by Fondacier and Company, is that so?'

With the man crumpled and discredited we were free to proceed. We were shown plenty of watches, and a few silver items too, the proper identification of which took an interminable time. But the interesting thing was that the accused was also a copper's nark or police informer, and he mentioned cases in which he had assisted the police to bring a miscreant to justice. I had no doubt that he was telling the truth, for glancing up at the public gallery I could see that it was largely filled with individuals who appeared to be gloating, getting ready to meet the man outside the Old Bailey if there should by any chance be an acquittal. They were an unpleasant-looking bunch, and I divined correctly that they were the friends and relations of those who were doing time as a result of the information he had given to the police. It was clear enough that the poor man would be violently beaten up and maybe even murdered if he were set free, so I hoped that the evidence would be such that we could give a verdict that would ensure for him a decent but not overlong period in Pentonville, or some other such place so that his skin would be saved, at least for a while.

After a day and a half of inspecting exhibits and hearing the police evidence, the time came for the jury to retire. I remembered Shakespeare's words in Macbeth about how 'the jury, passing on the prisoner's life, may in the sworn twelve have a thief or two guiltier than him they try.' But I also remembered the advice I had received from a Cambridge friend who was a Fellow of St Catharine's and had recently served on a jury.

'There's only one thing to remember,' he had said to me. 'The Jury will select their oldest and maybe most stupid member as chairman. Your first job is to get him out of the chair and yourself put in his place – and then things can proceed. Otherwise you will waste hours and get nowhere.'

The jury room was just like any other committee room, with chairs around the table and a flask of water standing forlorn in the middle. We trooped in, and in a shy fashion took our places around the table, rather obviously avoiding the place at the end where the chairman might well sit. One of our number was eased toward it by others, and sat down. We then all took our seats too.

It proved to be exactly as my friend had told me. The chairman was eighty-three and rather deaf. He was a pleasant man of a churchwardenly type, with a stiff butterfly collar. He was a watch and clockmaker himself, and he pulled one of the exhibits toward him and began to scrutinize the back of it through a lens which he had produced from his pocket.

'Exquisite,' he mumbled. He turned the watch over. 'Very fine enamelling too. Some value there. Yes indeed. Exquisite workmanship. . . .'

This was obviously the time to get to work on him. 'Excuse me, Sir,' I said loudly. (I thought the 'Sir' would be suitably flattering.) 'We should be discussing whether or not the man accused is guilty of receiving stolen goods.'

'Eh? I wonder how much this cost when it was new. That would have been about eighteen-ninety, and . . .'

'Are you going to suggest how we set about the discussion, Sir?'

'What was that? Ah, yes. Very difficult. And then there's that fob-watch there . . .'

'Are you going to enquire what the other jurors think?' I had dropped the 'Sir' now.

'Enquire?'

'Yes. Start the discussion, so that we can come to a verdict,' I suggested.

'Ah, of course. But . . .'

'I think the gentleman here is right,' said a rather rough-looking character on my side of the table. 'We don't want to sit here all day looking at them watches. I got to get away in time for the two-thirty at Kempton Park.'

The poor chairman was bemused, and perhaps rather hurt. 'If you don't want me to be your foreman . . .' he began.

'We don't,' said the Kempton Park man very definitely.

'Hear, hear,' said another.

I was waiting for it, and of course it eventually came. 'I think the gentleman over there should take the chair,' one of the two women said. 'Then we can begin.'

'Well,' I said modestly. 'Of course, if you really insist.' I moved to take the chair which the old watchmaker vacated. And now we could get on with the business, I thought.

I decided that the best thing to do was to ask the jurors in clockwise order whether they thought the man guilty or not, and then we could see the lie of the land. But first I enquired how many of them had taken notes of the case. The answer was none. Except for myself.

So we began. The first, next to me, was a middle-aged woman. She said it was a terrible responsibility. Just think that we might find him guilty when he wasn't, or we might declare him not guilty when he was. It was not fair to put this burden of choice upon ordinary people.

'Quite so. Thank you.' And the next?

Next was a sensible-looking man, very likely from an accountant's office. He said he would be very happy if we could run through the evidence. Then we might be able to make up our minds. And the next?

'When the police says one thing and a feller says another, you can take it from me the police is bloody well lying, that's what I says.'

'Thank you.'

The next was the deposed chairman. He was still thinking about the watches, so I skipped over him.

'Don't care a bloody damn,' said the next. 'I could do with a drink. Nothing in here but a jug of bloody water.'

'Thank you. And you, madam?'

The madam was a young lady of about twenty-eight, I judged. She began immediately to deliver a prepared statement which she had learned, stating that trial by jury was wrong in principle and disastrous in practice. Nothing on earth would ever get her to express any opinion whatsoever, or to agree to whatever the rest of us might decide.

'Thank you madam. And you, Sir?'

'You can take it from me, that if there's a conflict of evidence it's always the same. The police is straight. The other is lying. Otherwise why would he be in the dock?'

'Thank you. And next?'

'Two-thirty at Kempton Park. I'm a bookie, see. It'll cost me a lot of money if I'm not there.'

Good man, I said to myself. That's the spirit. He can be relied upon to squash any who argue and delay us. 'Next please?'

'I don't really know. I couldn't follow all that talk, you know. I don't know what to think.'

Next, number ten. He was another ordinary and rather thoughtful man, perhaps a chief clerk in a bank. He thought, like the man opposite to him, that we should run through the evidence, and the summing-up of the judge.

And the last. 'Hang the lot, that's what I say. Instead of all this mealy-mouthed to-ing and fro-ing. Bring back the lash and clear up the lot of them.'

'Hear hear,' said Kempton Park.

It was clear that the case would be decided by myself and the two city men. We ran through the evidence, and the rest kept silent except for occasional noises of approval. The three of us took only a few minutes to decide that the verdict should in our opinion be Guilty.

I could now size up the situation easily enough. Kempton Park would obviously back anything we said. So would Hang-the-lot. The man who wanted a drink would get one soon after we delivered our verdict, so he was an ally too. The-police-is-right juror was on our side. That only left the ex-chairman, who was now virtually asleep, the police-is-liars man, and the two women. We got to work on the police-is-liars character, and he agreed that though that might be true, others could be bigger liars don't you see? Now there were the two women alone to bring in on our agreed verdict.

The terrible-responsibility lady twisted her handkerchief and said that she supposed we probably knew best. But the wrong-in-principle woman was determined to wreck the show. Nothing would ever get her to agree to any verdict at all. The whole principle . . .

'Thank you madam. Well, the rest of us seem to be agreed, are we not?'

'Agreed, yes agreed.'

The sole objector now treated us to another tirade about the principles of natural justice. I looked at Kempton Park, and he looked at his watch.

'Well, perhaps you should think about it,' I said gently to the woman. 'Please take your time. There is really no hurry. I expect you saw the memorial in the hall here to the jurors who were locked in for days rather than bring in the wrong verdict. But I think that in another two or three hours we should perhaps send a member out to ask whether we stay the night here, and what they do about supper.'

'Good idea,' said one of the city men cheerfully. 'Though I must say, that if we accepted jury service it seems reasonable that we should express an opinion on the case we have been hearing.'

'I think so, too,' the other agreed.

We all looked at the woman, who sat there like a statue but had now become rather red in the face. Kempton Park uttered a growl, and muttered something about the afternoon costing him three thousand quid, maybe more, and whose fault would that be, eh? Then we sat, silent. It was eighteen minutes before the no-jury fanatic caved in.

We filed back into court, I delivered our verdict, and the judge put the man down for two years. The court dispersed. In the corridor outside, I met the police superintendent who had collated their evidence.

'A good job, you did there Sir, if I may say so,' he said. 'Some of these juries, they'll hang on for hour after hour over nothing at all.'

And then I met the prosecuting counsel. I expressed my horror at the way in which the jury system worked. There we were, twelve good men and true (but two of us women), and only three of us were prepared to discuss the case at all. The others had fixed ideas which often had nothing whatsoever to do with the case.

'My dear chap,' he said. 'Don't you see, that's why we have twelve in a jury? Statistically the odds are that if you take twelve people at random you are reasonably certain to get two, or maybe three, who can judge the case objectively. And isn't that all we need? Even one individual would be enough. So the law wisely appoints twelve to make reasonably sure that there is at least one person with his head screwed on.'

We had been told before leaving the courtroom that we should proceed to the Taxing Office, where we would be given our expenses for travel and loss of employment time. The office proved to be a window similar to an old-style railway booking-office counter, behind which sat the taxing clerk. By a curious coincidence the man in front of me, who had come from another court, was one whom I knew. He was a City man of repute, and on various committees of the Cripplegate Ward. When he came to the window the clerk asked him who and what he was.

'I am Chairman and Managing Director of Something-or-other shoes,' he began. 'The factory is in Leicester. I have two other companies there also of which I am chairman. They are both in the boot-and-shoe industry and well-known in the trade . . .'

The clerk looked at him, then turned to a list. 'Bootmaker,' he said in a superior voice. 'Three pound fourteen shillings a day.' He counted out the money, and pushed it through the window.

I was last in the queue. 'And what do you like to make out that you do?' asked the taxing clerk, looking at me with a sarcastic grin.

'I am a writer,' I said.

'A writer? A writer, eh!' He laughed. 'Well, what you don't write today you can bloody well write tomorrow.' And he slammed the window.

But of course he was right. I could, and I did. I wrote up the story of the jury for Lady Rhondda, and although the rates of pay in *Time and Tide* were not exactly high, I ended up twice as well off as the director of three shoe factories in Leicester.

FRIENDLESS

It was a clear, happy morning of April, and the willows were breaking into leaf. Everything was so summery that it seemed almost as though the weather had made a mistake and thought it was June. The spring floods were past their peak, but the Oise was still flowing broad and strong as we ran down from Compiègne toward the confluence at Conflans Ste Honorine and turned left into the Seine, to head up for the delights of living on board for a week or two right in the centre of Paris and within a hundred yards of the Place de la Concorde.

The Seine was streaming powerfully over the weirs, but it was not so high as to make the locks unusable, so the voyage was a leisurely one. Brown and rather muddy the river swirled on its way, with ourselves forging against it and heading upstream, overcoming it by a few knots. The surface of the water carried a quantity of sticks and branches washed off the banks by the flood, so I was careful to keep an eye ahead for any pieces of floating debris large enough to damage the propellers. Once I spotted a willow branch, freshly broken off the tree and golden with catkins, and now and again a sodden log sticking its snout above the water went silently past, like a lurking crocodile.

We were not far up from Conflans when I noticed something just breaking the surface ahead, an object grey and bluish in colour. It looked like an old bolster discarded into the river so I turned slightly to avoid it. Then, as it drifted past us some twenty yards away I saw it had around it what appeared to be something like a strap. Out of sheer curiosity I took up my binoculars for a quick glance. Then I spun the wheel and swung round toward the object that was now bobbing slightly on our wake. I was almost certain that it was not a bolster. I thought I knew what it was, and a closer look convinced me. I could see the hair quite clearly now, trailing a little behind. Dark brown, it was spread out and gently waving on the ripples of the wash, like weed in a seaside rockpool.

The body had drifted past us now, so I went ahead, turned, ran downstream a little and came up with it again. With our long boathook I took a hold in the jersey, and I led it gently round to the stern. There I made a noose in one of our lines and passed it over the head and shoulders until we had the body secure and could draw it up close against the transom, still afloat.

The woman was completely clothed except for shoes, and she was floating in a frog-like posture, face downward. She was somewhat thickset, and she was wearing a skirt of greyish-blue tweed of what looked like reasonably good quality. Her jersey was of a rather darker blue, bound around her waist with the blackish belt that I had noticed when I first sighted her. One of her stockings was ripped, probably on a snag of a bankside branch, or when she had been washed over a weir.

Having dropped the anchor a little to one side of the fairway I rolled the body over in the water, and I saw that the woman had a gold wristwatch and a little octagonal medallion on a golden chain around her neck. This had slipped up over her mouth, and because of the swelling caused by the inflation of her body with the gases of internal decay it was held there tightly as though she were trying to grip it in her lips. The face had an extraordinary composure, without a trace of terror or struggle, and her absolute peacefulness – in spite of the cramped posture of her body – brought to my mind the jacket of a book I had read thirty years earlier, *L'Inconnue de la Seine*.

The next thing to be done was to take the poor woman over to some place where I could land her. Meanwhile, I would ask the passing commercial shipping to radio and report the fact of a drowning, or at the very least to ease off when running past. The response was to stare straight ahead and ignore us. It was not until a fifth ship came along that the captain gave loud blasts on his hooter of a kind calculated to arouse the attention of authorities ashore. Then I drew alongside a houseboat and informed the lady that I had found a body in the river, and in the same breath I asked her to phone the police. Her response was to go pale, retreat inside and slam the door.

Having put the nose of the boat against the bank, I called to a couple who were leaning out of their upstairs window across the road to watch. I asked them to inform the authorities. They shut the window. Another man nearby said that he had no telephone – although I could see the wires running to his eaves – and he likewise closed the window to shut out the unseemliness of death, of the fact that somebody should have been drowned. Indeed had actually, in all probability, drowned themselves.

This being France, the rather grim incident was bound to have its absurd side. Before long the police arrived, but they would only look at the body from a distance of a yard or two. It was not their business to handle bodies. That was something for the *pompiers*, the lieutenant explained. It was some time before the fire-brigade arrived to deal with that part of the operation, after which the questioning was handed over to the police. I was asked for my full name, the date of my birth, where I had been born, and . . . But at that point I held up my hand.

'No more irrelevant questions,' I said rather sharply. 'More important than to know where I was born is to discover who this woman is, and how she came to be in the river.'

The lieutenant shut his notebook, and then surprised me by asking where I had found the body.

'In the river.'

'Quite so, Sir. But precisely where?'

I said that I had not taken any precise geometrical observations against a moving stream, but explained roughly whereabouts. Greatly to my surprise, an elderly man who had joined the small group of curious bystanders now interrupted.

'The gentleman is wrong,' he said firmly. 'It was abreast of that leaning willow tree about a hundred and fifty metres upstream.'

'It wasn't,' I objected.

'Yes it was,' said the stranger, giving me a curious wink.

'I think I know best,' I said. 'It was straight out from here.'

'But . . .' he began. However, the officer cut him short.

'Certainly the Monsieur who found the body knows best,' he said. And then, turning to me, 'I regret that we cannot accept the body.'

'Not accept it? What do you expect me to do?'

The lieutenant smiled politely. 'It is not in my division.'

I now understood why the elderly man tried to intervene. He knew where the police boundary ran, and he was trying to help me by getting the incident into the area of the police who had arrived on the scene.

'The body is not mine,' the officer repeated decidedly, flicking some dust off his natty trousers. He started up the bank.

'It is certainly not mine,' I objected.

There were murmurs of approval from the few members of the public, and from the firemen, who were gathered round the body.

The lieutenant hesitated. 'As a special favour, I shall accept the body,' he said magnanimously. 'It is not my duty, but in order to assist you I shall agree to do so.'

The business with the police and the fire brigade took a considerable time, and when we continued on our way up the river we were somewhat behind our intended schedule. The locks on the River Seine were available free of charge until a certain time – I think it was six o'clock. Rather than wait until next morning at the final lock below the capital, I thought we would run ahead and have dinner somewhere in the area of the Invalides. At this final lock we had to pay forty francs for being late. The lockkeeper had already heard about the incident lower down, but he was not authorised to remit the charge for being late just because we had been helpful, he said. He was sorry, but that was that. He expressed no surprise at all about our finding the body.

'*C'est la saison,*' he said.

He went on to explain that bodies were held up behind the weirs, but when the spring floods came they floated over the top into the next reach. And so on, all the way. It was the season. There had already been several turning up that same week.

Back in London a few weeks later I wrote to the superintendent of police at Conflans Ste Honorine to assure him that I was always desirous to be helpful to the authorities in every matter whatsoever, but I was somewhat narked to have had to fork out forty francs because we had been delayed by the police over the affair at Conflans. I did not receive a reply, but six weeks later I had a phone call from the French embassy in London. Which was our nearest sub-post office, a voice asked.

I gave the address of the small sweets-and-tobacco-and-post office at the bottom of Highgate West Hill, a matter of only two or three hundred yards from where we lived, and next day a British Postal Order arrived, payable at that sub-post office in the sum of two pounds, seventeen shillings and ninepence – that being the precise equivalent of the fee for passing the lock of Suresnes after hours.

A few weeks passed, and we were forging down the Seine again toward the junction with the Oise at Conflans. I pulled in on the school barge and went up to the police station. I wanted to know what had been discovered about the poor woman whose body we had landed.

The inspector said it had taken them a week or two to identify her because she had not at once been reported missing, but they now knew her to be a certain Henriette Gillet, aged forty-nine, from Courbevoie. The family had told the police that she had tried on several occasions to throw herself into the river, but they had prevented her. This time she had succeeded.

'She was . . . how shall we say . . . *pas fou, mais* . . . ' He raised his outstretched hand, put his thumb in his ear, and moved it to and fro. '*Vous comprenez?*'

I did. Poor Henriette, not quite balanced, very possibly the victim of a depressive illness, there was no other way out. She had nothing to live for. I remembered once more the astonishing look of complete peace in her face. Perhaps it really was a fact that her troubles were over. Or was it just the swelling which had kindly removed all the tragic lines of care and worry that could otherwise have been seen in a face which had perhaps known greater troubles than I could imagine?

It was later in that same year that I was steering up the River Aisne, passing close to where the replica dining-car of Wagon-Lits stands on an abandoned siding in a clearing of the forest of Compiègne, as though the dispirited German plenipotentiaries had just left it after signing the armistice in 1918, thus bringing to an end the most stupid, unnecessary and cruel slaughter that the world has ever known. The navigable Aisne is only about thirty miles in length, and we were approaching the last lock but one before Soissons when I saw something ahead which made me cut the speed of the engines, look through the binoculars, and then go astern. I also struck the ship's bell, to alert others aboard.

The body was now floating slowly past us on the starboard side, and it was easy to hook the man by the jacket. As we rolled him over the face that confronted us was so dark that I thought at first he was an African, but in fact this was nothing more than natural discoloration. The poor man had been the victim of considerable violence, I could see. His arms were pinioned tightly by his jacket being pulled down off his shoulders, and one side of his face had been cleft away as though with a battle-axe. It was not a very pleasant sight, but I quickly had him roped in a noose round the waist, and under very slow tow.

As in the case of Henriette, the reaction of people who saw what was happening was only to avoid getting involved. We were now in the outskirts of Soissons, and the river was flanked by a straggling row of outer suburban bungalows and houses. From the upper window of one of them a woman had been watching the whole incident, but the moment I called to her to telephone the police she shut the window. Hooting repeatedly I managed to alert one of her neighbours to come to the roadway, and when I repeated the request she said she had no telephone – even if, as in the former case, I could see the wires running into her house. The same happened with the next pair of houses. They had no telephones, no; but by some extraordinary magic of telepathy they speedily informed all the houses ahead of them, so that within half a minute their occupants were streaming out to watch *Thames Commodore* towing a corpse up the river.

Below the lock I attached the line to a towpath noticeboard, for I did not want the extra complication of looking after the body in the swirl and turmoil when the paddles were opened. The keeper at once phoned the police, and a van arrived. The sergeant looked briefly at the body, and put through a call on his radio to summon the *sapeurs-pompiers*, the police not being expected to handle bodies. We waited awhile, until the radio buzzed again.

'Is it a case for artificial respiration?' the *pompiers* asked.

'If you like to,' replied the *gendarme* sergeant. 'The man has been dead for a couple of weeks and half his head is missing, but if the *pompiers* are so clever they can try mouth-to-mouth.'

A woman walking her poodle along the towpath came up to me.

'Is it a dead dog?'

'No, a man,' I replied. 'It is not a nice sight for madame.'

'*Tiens!* A man!' She walked to the edge of the bank to take a really close look. 'A man. Yes, yes, I see it is. *C'est curieux.*' She patted her poodle and walked on.

The *sapeurs* arrived, and with help from myself and the sergeant we pulled the man up to the towpath. He was wearing a striped shirt and blue trousers, apart from the jacket which pinioned his arms. He also had Wellington boots. We had just finished hauling when a couple of young lovers came strolling along the towpath, arm in arm and leaning their heads against each other with all the happy carelessness of a television shampoo advertisement or a tweedy hair-lotion. The man looked over the shoulders of the *sapeurs*, who were trying to untie my slip-knot.

'Look, *chérie!* A body!'

The girl pushed through to the front, still holding his arm.

'So it is!'

The poor man was not one of the most romantic sights to see when on an afternoon stroll with one's boyfriend, but that did not worry her in the least. She examined the corpse with great interest, then gave her companion a kiss. They continued to wander happily along the towpath beside the cornfield.

At Soissons the police were very efficient. Within twenty minutes they had the man identified from a fragment of a letter in one of his boots. They came down to the quay with a *procès-verbal* for me to sign, saying that the man was dead when I sighted him.

'The man was in his thirties. He had been out East and contracted Dengue fever, we believe. He was, well . . . useless.'

'And the injuries?' I asked.

'Ah, you thought it was murder. Perhaps it looked that way. No, the rudder of a *péniche* must have caught his jacket and pulled it back. And then the propeller – pft!' The inspector picked up the form I had signed. 'He was . . . how shall I say it?' He raised his hand, placed the thumb against the side of his head and worked it to and fro like a corkscrew. '*Pas fou, mais . . . vous comprenez?*'

I did.

It was on our final trip down the Rhone that we experienced again the same sad business, and the indifference of people close at hand. We spent a night at La Roche Glun, an ancient little village of the Rhone valley, tucked away over the bank of what used to be the course of the Rhone when I first went that way in 1962, but was now bypassed with a broad cut which carried the navigation of the Rhone toward a huge new lock. La Roche, under the actual walls of which one had formerly passed, was now situated at the edge of an idle backwater, beside a section of river cut off and motionless, except for the very slight movement of water toward the new barrage.

After breakfast next morning we cast off to head back into the river, and had not gone more than a hundred yards or so when I saw the familiar shape ahead, a low, dark object rather like a seal just breaking the surface. It was only twenty yards or so from the bank, on which sat a lugubrious-looking angler, his eye on his float.

'A body,' I called briefly to Ingrid. And I turned toward it and eased off. I merely wanted to be sure that I was right, but I did not attempt to take the corpse in tow. There was no need, because I could ask the angler to report it, and that would be that. So I drew over to the fisherman, who showed concern that I was going to run down his line, or frighten away the fish. I pointed at the body as it bobbed a little on our wash.

'*Un cadavre*,' I said. '*Un noyé.*' And I asked him to be so kind as to report it to the police station behind the bank.

The fisherman gave no answer at all. He glanced up for a moment in the direction of the body, drew in his line, picked up another maggot from the tin of bran beside him, put it on the hook and cast again before relapsing into the same non-caring stupor from which I had momentarily aroused him.

The only thing to do was to proceed down river to the next lock, where I went up the steps to the control-room. The lockkeeper asked me how the man was dressed, what colour were his shirt and trousers. I gave the necessary description.

'That is correct,' he said. 'He was expected.' And seeing my puzzled look he said that the man in question had thrown himself off the bridge at Viviers eleven days earlier. The body would sink, and probably become entangled with tree roots or other obstructions. Then after ten days or so it would float, and pass down river on the current or – as had now happened – be washed into a backwater. The police and navigation authority knew all about the man. I need not worry. He was depressed, that was all. He had been seen as he jumped off Viviers bridge, and the matter had been reported immediately. He was expected.

'*C'est triste*,' the lockkeeper said, with a shake of his head. He was the first person I had ever heard in France, or anywhere else for that matter, suggest that a deliberate drowning was sad.

Once each autumn I was invited to talk to the members of a sailing club, and tell them about the inland voyage that I had made during that summer. It was a most unusual club, which owned two ancient sailing barges of the kind that used to bring grain round to London from the ports in East Anglia, craft that were so designed that they could in their commercial days have been managed by a skipper and a lad, with no other help. The club members spent much of their spare time putting the two vessels into good order, and then at the week-ends they would go out for a day of barge-sailing in the lower estuary.

I always enjoyed these annual visits to the club. It fell to the Commodore and his wife to take me to dinner beforehand, and that was always a part of the occasion to which I especially looked forward. This couple were completely unlike the office-holders that I had come across in other boating associations – who were always pleasant enough people and easy to get on with, but to judge by their conversation mainly interested in bilge-pumps and binnacles. In this case the Commodore and his wife were not in the least inclined to talk Boat Show banalities. Probably they were just as interested in boats as I was, yet over dinner we would sit and chat of things very far removed from the dockside. We discussed prison aftercare, the question of the responsibility of young shoplifters, the shortcomings of the educational system, and what progress, if any, the ecumenical movement was making.

It was always a delight to share experiences with the Commodore, another Roger, and his wife Helen, and after the voyage on the Aisne I mentioned the two suicides that I had seen in the water and had towed in. The suicides had made a vivid impression on me, quite different from the man who had been run down by the train at the level crossing in Freiburg thirty years earlier. It was a sadness that I now felt, for it seemed at least possible that if someone had taken a real interest in Henriette and the ex-soldier in their depressed state neither might have drowned themselves. Or perhaps they would have, just the same. I did not know. And quite apart from that, I had been appalled by the apathy of people after the suicides had occurred. Shut the window, shut out the sadness of others. Don't get involved – not even to the extent of reporting the incident. That was the attitude, it seemed.

'You know, Roger,' I said. 'I've been wondering whether I could help those people who try to cope with suicidal and depressed people. You know who I mean – the Samaritans.'

His reply astonished me. 'Good idea. I'll meet you at ten o'clock tomorrow morning at St Stephen's. It's in Walbrook, next door to the Mansion House.'

ST STEPHEN'S

I think that many who become interested in the Samaritans do so for a mixture of reasons. One of these is certainly a desire to help one's fellow men or women in trouble, for if one regarded all the depressed and despairing as stupid and probably undesirable individuals who might as well jump off Waterloo Bridge, and the sooner the better, then it is not very likely that one would try to step in and change the pattern of the fate looming ahead of them. But perhaps also there might be a feeling that one has had enough of one's own problems and is getting nowhere at all by sitting and brooding over them, whereas those of others might be easier to deal with, or, if not easier, at least capable of having some dent made in them.

I might have thought – as many do – of the Samaritans as a collection of wonderful, unruffled, highly competent and loving people equipped with haloes, but I was soon to discover that this was not true. In one respect the ideal was at fault; they had no haloes, nor any desire to appear to have one. But the other qualities, competence and imperturbability, loving and caring in an objective way, these were certainly there to the brim.

Perhaps I also imagined that the Samaritans were Christians. After all, the story about the alien who helped the injured man when the clergy and officials preferred not to get involved, was one told by Christ himself. And I probably had an exaggerated idea of the benevolence of Christians compared with others. It may well be that all Christians should be capable of a genuine concern for their fellows, of whatever creed or colour mixture, but they certainly have no private monopoly in marketing the milk of human kindness. Many Samaritans that I came to know particularly well were indeed church members, but others were not. There were Jews, agnostics, humanists, all sorts and conditions working together with the same open-hearted gaiety of affection for others, and I doubt very much if our shared Father in Heaven was particularly anxious to scan their union membership cards to see if they were fully paid up, or that he was greatly saddened if they went so far as to doubt his existence. It is unlikely that these people would have been working for such a body as the Samaritans if they had no feeling at all of the ultimate worth of their fellows, a sense of something that they had in common with those others, however depressed and unattractive they might happen to be.

I am not sure what I expected to find when I presented myself at St Stephen's on the following morning. In fact I found a somewhat run-down church next door to the Mansion House, with considerable pigeon excrement on the steps. And even if I can still wonder how Sir Christopher Wren could have committed such a monstrosity of bad acoustics, disproportionate dome and cold marble, St Stephen's is probably as dear to me as any other church building in the world. This is because it was then the home of the Samaritans; or, more correctly, it lay over their home, which was under the ground.

It was an astonishing fact that within sixty yards of the busy and many-spoked crossroads of the Bank of England, with uninterrupted rush and hot roar of all the traffic of the City, one could descend half a flight of stone steps into an area so unexpectedly still, so devoid of all the noise and fumes and hurry of the external world.

This underground space was part of the long-abandoned crypt of the church, and it was known as Grocers' Gift, because one of the ancient trade guilds of the City, the Mystery (or Company) of the Grocers of London had paid for its excavation and restoration to use. This was done in a very simple manner, bits of old walls being carried further up in blockwork and white-washed, several small areas being cut off to provide interview rooms, and there was a larger central area where there was a low seat running round the walls. In one corner there was a heap of tattered magazines, and in another a huge teddy bear in a red waistcoat and green bow-tie, who was always ready to entertain the small children that visitors sometimes brought with them. It was an extraordinary place, absolutely natural, unsophisticated, and peaceful.

Grocers' Gift had nothing whatsoever in common with the sterilised, white-tiled waiting rooms of hospitals and surgeries, no smell of carbolic or chlorine. Nobody bustled about in a white overall. Quite unselfconsciously it hit just the right note to put people at ease. Not always within half a minute, for they could sometimes be very overwrought and on the brink of collapse, but certainly before long. I think the sudden replacement of the din of a successful but alien world by the slight murmur of ordinary ongoings, one person walking through, another filling the water-urn or washing up, was enormously valuable. It was probably exactly the opposite of what any client would have expected.

Clients – that is what they were called, and very rightly. Any helper who regarded one of them as a case – which was precisely how the same individuals were habitually treated by the most well-meaning of official bodies – would have been shown to the door. No, those who rang us or came to St Stephen's in person were not cases, nor were they customers, for the Samaritans had nothing to sell. They were quite simply people who came for help. Clients. And this name in itself did much to remove any feeling of superiority that one might have in trying to help them to cope with their problems.

Considering the various fixed attitudes which most of us have by the time we are adult, it often surprised me that the Samaritans were able to find as many men and women as they did who refrained from showing even a trace of judgment, who were astonishingly patient, whose love of life was infectious, and who were unflappable.

Many of our clients telephoned and were invited to come in – an invitation which a sense of guilt often made them refuse. But a great number of the London clients just came in unannounced. They were often in a state of great distress, sometimes with the law after them, occasionally pursued by imaginary enemies. Nobody asked them anything at all to start with, but just sat them down and offered them a cup of coffee, then left them alone for a while. This certainly surprised them, and it helped them to collect their wits and feel more at home, after having made the considerable effort actually to turn to us in their troubles or bewilderment. Then, after a while, a helper would take them into one of the interview rooms and just let them talk.

The first client with whom I came face to face after the weeks of training, carefully designed to show up our distastes and generally unhelpful attitudes, was a good lesson to me. All discussions were confidential – even to the extent of refusing to give information to interested parties such as irate husbands, sorrowing parents, jilted lovers, the police, or government agencies – so it may be assumed that the essentials in any description of a client that I may give are suitably altered to make any identification impossible. So, for example, if I say that this girl was named Carole, and that she lived in Stoke Newington, it may safely be assumed that she wasn't, and didn't.

Carole was twenty-three, with a pale face and long, continually combed hair which reached to her elbows and was at that time very fashionable. She was neatly dressed in a mini-skirt, and wore a good quality blouse. I noticed this as she sat down and casually rolled up her sleeves so that I could not fail to observe the slashes, old and recent, upon her wrists and arms. She meant me to count them, and I did. There were twenty-three of them.

Her parents did not understand her. When they went out they locked her in her room. She had no great contact with her father, but she told me a lot about him, from which he seemed to be rather unimaginative but in no way remarkable. Carole appeared to be reasonably fond of him, and on good terms with her mother too, except for this extraordinary business of their putting the food into her room on a tray, and then locking her in. They did this whenever they went out, which was almost every night. Even if they were at home they would not let her come downstairs. She just had to pine away in her room.

Carole told me that she had been in hospital occasionally, but she had discharged herself. They were no help to her there, they just locked her up. Her doctor was useless too. So was the privately paid female psychiatrist she went to. Carole had a health visitor too, but this woman was no help either. They just did not understand her, all these professional people. They kept on asking her why she kept trying to kill herself, Carole added, moving her sleeves a little to make sure I had not missed anything. Then she burst into tears. She looked so sweet, so helpless and ingenuous that her sobs would have melted a glacier.

I had a long session with Carole and promised to contact her next day. I went home in the evening a worried man, upset by the picture of this sweet little thing, the mere object of unmerited rejection by all who could have helped her. It was extraordinary that everyone should be so cruel to her – her mother, her father, the doctors, her private-patient psychiatrist, the health visitor. Yes, without exception, everyone. All of them as hardhearted as lumps of stone, driving her to this seemingly endless succession of attempts upon her own life. All that was needed was just what we in the Samaritans could offer; genuine friendship, befriending without strings or conditions, real understanding and love. It was a crying shame that none before would lift a finger to help Carole; but now thank heaven she had turned to us. To me.

All through supper that evening I was worrying to myself about this poor girl. Twenty-three gashes, self-inflicted – what disillusion and distress were barely concealed by those little pinkish weals. I wondered what she was doing, back at home in Stoke Newington, locked in her room whilst her parents callously went out to play bridge or visit friends. I had remembered her telephone number among the other details she had given me. I could ring her, reassure her that the Samaritans really cared and would not let her down. She could rely upon them. Upon myself.

I did not at once ring Carole. Instead I took our Welsh collie and walked out across the dam by the Highgate Ponds and up to the top of Parliament Hill. It was a fine night in February with the low, drifting clouds lit from beneath by the orange-pinkish glow of the great city. The roar of the unceasing traffic came welling up from below the heathland. Somewhere out of sight behind Highgate Hill lay Stoke Newington, and I could see vividly in my imagination this girl, staring with tear-filled unseeing eyes at a book, wondering whether to take her razor again and slash.

Something flashed a warning light inside my head. I walked over to a seat beside one of the clumps of trees and sat down, while the dog sniffed around the roots. So many experts, skilled and highly trained, had failed. Was it conceivable that I, with my blue-eyed friendly enthusiasm to listen, could make even the slightest crack in a problem against which all these able people had broken their heads? It was very unlikely, to say the least. But why, why had Carole come to us at the Samaritans?

One thing that I was certain of was that I would not telephone her that night to make sure she was safe and sound. If Carole had survived twenty-three cuts and knew enough about the circulatory system to make sure that she gashed herself where it was quite safe, a twenty-fourth would do no great harm. If I was to be of any use at all as a Samaritan I must not be carried away, least of all by a client whose skill with a razor was almost professional.

I took a turn around the ponds, succeeded in dismissing Carole from my mind, and then returned home and slept soundly. Next morning I phoned her from St Stephen's and asked if she would let me talk to her psychiatrist. She was delighted at this, and gave me the number. No doubt she thought I was going to tell the woman what she could do with herself.

'Ah, yes,' said the psychiatrist pleasantly when I rang her. 'I was wondering who she would be getting on top of next.' And she went on to reel off quite a lengthy list of doctors and welfare workers and organisations who, one after the other, had tried in vain.

'Can you tell me about her parents?' I said. 'Why do they lock her in? Is it for fear she might run off and kill herself?'

'Parents?' She laughed, but in a kind way. 'So you had that one, too. She hasn't got any parents. They died when she was quite small, I believe. She lives with a boyfriend in a bedsitter. I met him there. A nice lad, though I don't know how he puts up with it all. Of course, she's attractive. I must say I'm not sorry she's dropped me. We weren't getting anywhere. Nobody ever has done.'

I don't think we did much for Carole, either. She never came back. Perhaps she was too occupied spinning yarns to some other agency and getting them worked up into a state about her. Yet even if I resisted the temptation to become too involved with her, the sadness was inescapable that this pleasant girl was in fact so very sick that her whole activity oscillated between cutting her wrists in order to command attention, and then trying to turn against one another all those who, professionally or otherwise, were ready and anxious to help. She was one of the best scalp-hunters I ever met, and she had for a while come near to adding my own to hang around her pretty neck.

At St Stephen's, and probably in most other Samaritan branches around the country, the majority of our clients were just those who could not cope with modern life. They might be slow in decision, with the result that they could rarely secure a job, nor hold down the job if they got one.

'This is the job. These are the hours. The pay is so-and-so-much. Will you accept it? Yes? No? Please make up your mind. Sorry, but I must have an answer at once. Ah ... No, we have to fill the vacancy immediately. I'm so sorry, but that is the regulation. Thank you for calling. Next, please!'

Everything moved so fast that they could not catch up with it. The waves of modern life broke over them and bashed them on the rocks until they might wish for nothing else than to be drowned.

One client whom I saw regularly for about a year was Dorothy. She was an intelligent woman who had been a municipal librarian, and she was extremely suicidal. Aged just over fifty, she had lived a life with plenty of sadness. She had twice been engaged. Her first great love had been killed in the war, her second had died from his injuries in a car crash only a week before the wedding. For many years she had looked after an elderly mother, who had now gone. Curiously enough, Dorothy had plenty of nephews and nieces who adored her and came to see her frequently, but somehow they could not take away the great sorrow which by now had become part of her nature.

Dorothy lived in a bleak block of flats, badly soundproofed, and she could not stand the perpetual noise of her neighbours, rending the small hours of the night with the frightful sort of pop music which, as a Radio Three listener, she naturally found excruciating. Sometimes she would wander out, just to escape from the din, at other times she might decide that life was really not worth living any longer. She went occasionally to her doctor, who sent her on her way with the usual calming tablets, as so many doctors habitually did. But that only made her more depressed, she said. Besides, she disapproved of continually taking drugs.

This client had already made two deadly earnest attempts at suicide, and on both occasions chance or her guardian angel had seen to it that she was rescued, which she certainly had not intended. She was on both occasions found unconscious. The most recent was when she lay with her head in the gas oven and a neighbour came in to borrow a whisk and found her just in time.

Dorothy loved talking about books. She was very knowledgeable about them, and she could see that I was interested in the same direction, though I was careful never to tell her that I actually wrote them. All Samaritans were known only by their Christian names, to prevent their private lives being plagued by difficult or demanding clients. Once she even discussed one of my own books without realising it. Every week she would travel thirty miles up to London simply to have an hour or two of chat. Of course we were trying to deal with her immediate problems too, but the great thing for her was just the opportunity to talk, especially about books.

Between visits her spirits sank badly at times, but she survived from week to week largely because of looking forward to her next visit to St Stephen's. There were crises, but she had weathered them, partly as a result of my suggesting that she should tie a label I gave her to the gas tap of her cooker. On it I had written *Roger says ring the Samaritans*. Twice she was saved by this, and rang just to have the contact and relief she needed.

I realised only too well that Dorothy was living from one week to the next. I discussed her with the deputy director and we were both convinced that we could not make her more secure than we had done already. She was just the sort of client that we could really help – up to a point. The befriending she received made life worth living – just. It turned the scales, and in that way it was certainly successful.

I then told him what was worrying me. In two months' time I was to go for three weeks to the United States, and Dorothy would not be able to come for her weekly chats. I had tried as hard as I could to get her to accept another Samaritan while I was away, but she was not interested. She just liked chatting about books with me.

'But don't you worry, Roger,' she said. 'I know you won't be away too long. I'll be all right, really I will.'

I was not so sure. However, as Samaritans we had to live our own lives too. Dorothy herself was in any case the kind of woman who, if she thought for a moment that she was frustrating me in some way, would have killed herself at once. I was quite certain of that.

So I set about preparing Dorothy for my absence. She was extremely interested in everything about the journey. I told her which were the various cities in the United States that I was to visit, and she at once began to read about them in books from her local library. She told me a lot that I did not know. As the day came nearer I felt much more reassured. She was by now taking such an interest in my journey that it had become a major preoccupation for her. Finally she even asked what flight I was going on, and worked out that she might possibly see the aircraft climbing up the flight path. Certainly she would try to do so.

Two days before I left, Dorothy was there in the crypt as usual. We talked about herself, and about my trip. I had already decided to send her a postcard from the other side, so that she could still share in the journey. And I did. In fact I sent her three, but I do not know how many reached her. Because we never saw her again.

Dorothy's death at her own hand was a blow to me. At first I blamed myself, but when I looked at it more deeply I agreed with what the deputy director said.

'She had nearly a year more of life than she would have had if she had never rung us. And by all accounts she was very happy at times because of it.'

No, we could not keep everyone's head above water all the time. Not if we were to be able to live a life which gave us the buoyancy to be of any use at all in helping at least some of our clients to keep afloat.

It was a few weeks later that I was steering down the lower Thames tideway on a summer's night, on the way toward the North Sea and Sweden. It was a very beautiful, clear and starlit night, and the phosphorescence of the billions of tiny animalculae stirred by our wash left a path of unearthly blue. I was still occasionally thinking of our sad inability to keep Dorothy alive when somewhere beyond the Lower Hope flasher, a searchlight beam stabbed the darkness and flashed along the side of our hull. The boat with the searchlight was perhaps a quarter of a mile away on the port beam, but I heard the loud hailer clearly as it rang out across the water.

'Good luck, Roger. Have a good voyage!'

I recognised the voice at once, and flashed our masthead light in recognition. The call had come from a young steersman of a customs cutter on patrol in the watery night-time blankness of the estuary. We often shared the same shift at St Stephen's.

KICKED OUT OF BED

It was some time before I saw the body of poor Henriette floating down the river that I had an invitation to go down to Wales and give a series of three lectures on fairly basic genetics at one of their universities. I agreed to go, and when I arrived early in the evening I went round to the hotel in which a room had been booked for me.

When I checked in at the desk the head porter shook his head sadly, and said that the management was really extremely sorry but they had been obliged to cancel the booking and would transfer me to another hotel nearby. The reason was that a foreign football team was staying in the hotel, the Moscow Dynamos. They had gone into the dining room where dinner was laid for themselves and a score of others including myself, and had given each of the waitresses a handsome tip and asked them to run out and buy cigarettes. The moment the girls had gone they fell upon the food and cleared the board, not only of their own dinner but piled on top of it the food for the other hotel guests. There was nothing left to eat, not so much as a biscuit. So, very considerately I thought, my booking had been moved elsewhere.

The other hotel was a block or two away. It may have been that the better hotels were booked out by football fans who wanted the rare chance of seeing the Dynamos play on the following day, for the one where my room had been reserved was the kind of small hotel one might find in an English seaside resort – tired-looking, rather shabby and run down, and smelling of stale smoke, beer-stained carpets and boiled cabbage. A supper was awaiting me, and after I had dined I was on my way up to my room when the receptionist looked out of her office and invited me in. She was a middle-aged woman, grey and tired-looking. She said she had asked two 'commercial gentlemen' in for a cup of tea and biscuits and it would be nice if I would join them.

The prospect of sitting up over a pot of tea with two commercial travellers – the only other guests, it appeared – was not one which I found very alluring, but it was difficult to refuse. So I went into the room which served as her office and sitting-room, and sat down to join in the tea and conversation. The subject was one on which I could contribute little, the relative performances of Glamorgan's batsmen and bowlers. Even thirty years later I remember the setting very clearly, the wooden chairs, a gas fire burning cheerfully, a filing-cabinet and a safe in the corner, and the pervasive smell of cabbage. I was beginning to wonder how I could decently escape when the receptionist changed the subject.

'Before you came in we were talking about, well if someone wants, you know, wants to kill themselves. You know, puts their head in the gas oven. Do you think they suffer a lot? A lot of pain, I mean. You must know, because you're a doctor.' She was wrong there, I was not a medical man, and I said so. And as for the pain – well, I had no idea, I hadn't tried it, I said, trying to laugh it off.

So we returned to the subject of cricketers, and then moved on to the Dynamos. But after a while the woman came back with another question.

'You know how you read about someone taking a lot of aspirins and swallowing them to kill themselves. How many do you think they have to take? To be certain, I mean. These gentlemen don't know.'

'Nor do I,' I said, trying to steer the talk off the rather morbid line. 'I've never tried that either.'

And that was that. We had soon exhausted the other subjects of conversation, so we eventually bade each other goodnight and the commercial travellers went up to their rooms, and I to mine. I was tired, and very soon I was asleep.

But not for long. The sensation that woke me is almost impossible to describe. It was a tingling, something like a strong electric shock but without the pain. It made me sit up in bed, thoroughly awake, aware of something that again I cannot paint in detail, something which said, not in an external voice but insistently and within my mind, 'Get up. Quickly. Go down to the office. Now!' The order was given urgently and as a command that could not be resisted.

I was tingling all over with a strange mixture of shock and elation, and also of determination. I did not hesitate, but jumped out of bed, put on my slippers and dressing-gown and ran down the four flights of stairs to the office. The light was on, the gas fire burning, the receptionist was tidying some papers into the cabinet. I went straight in.

I can vividly recall how surprised I was at my own actions. I am not one to rush down hotel staircases in the night and burst into people's rooms, and the authority in my voice astonished me as I demanded immediately an answer.

'I want to know why you are going to kill yourself,' I declared abruptly.

'Whatever made you think . . .?'

'Never mind that. I know you are. And I give you my word that I shall not try to stop you. I promise. *But you must tell me why.*'

She sat down, then she collapsed and broke down completely. After a while she regained her composure. 'I believe your promise,' she said. 'So I'll tell you. I am going to kill myself tonight and I'll tell you why since you won't stop me.'

And then the story came out. She was an only daughter. She had lived with her father, whom she loved dearly. At the age of fifty-one he had gone blind. All the joy had gone out of his life, he had become helpless, morose, unable to do anything and had become more and more miserable until he died. It had been terrible to see the change in him, the helplessness, the decay of personality. That was many years ago, but now she herself had passed fifty. What if she should suffer the same fate, fading away in helpless misery, and with nobody to love her? She had gone to her general practitioner and asked him to tell her the truth. Would she go blind like her father? Did it run in the family?

The answer he gave her, she told me despairingly, was Yes. The condition was hereditary. Nothing could prevent her becoming blind, just like her father. It had struck him at fifty-one. She was now fifty. That was why she had decided to end it all. After our tea party in the office she had gone down and unlocked the slot-machine in the lobby and taken out all the packets of aspirin. There were about two hundred tablets. That would be enough, wouldn't it?

I said Yes, that would do the trick right enough. But I wanted to know more about the blindness of her father. So she told me all about it in enough detail for me to identify the condition very clearly. I could see that it was no more hereditary than a broken leg.

Now my research in earlier days had consisted in examining the eye defects caused by mutant genes in *Drosophila melanogaster*, the banana fly. Flies are many miles removed from humans in their structure, but nevertheless it had been useful at that time to study at least the basics of hereditary abnormalities of the eye in other species, including man, because even if their eyes were very different in structure there were certain features which might be common to both. And at that time I was giving a course of lectures on human genetics to medical students in London. I had absolute confidence in telling the receptionist that she had been misinformed by her own doctor, and I sketched out for her the whole situation of her father's blindness in some detail. The doctor had been completely mistaken. The condition was not a heritable one. She had no greater chance than anyone else of becoming blind next year.

When she spoke again her voice was very calm. 'I believe you,' she said. 'Go up to bed, now. I shall not take the tablets, ever.'

And that was that. When I came down in the morning and went in to pay my bill the woman was there. She looked quite radiant, ten years younger than the evening before.

'I'll tell you something,' she said as she made out my receipt. 'Night after night for more than a month I had been praying. "Please God, I can't face it. Tell me how I can kill myself"'. And then she added something which I have never forgotten, because it is so true. 'I think prayers are very often answered in a way you don't at all expect, and in a much wiser way than the one you wanted.'

That incident contains a number of very intriguing features. It does not in any way reflect any credit upon myself. It was just that my particular and somewhat unusual knowledge was effectively and very brilliantly used. The woman was desperate, suffering acutely and within an hour of an entirely unnecessary death, and all because of an error of diagnosis by her own general practitioner. He had given her every reason to be depressed. But she had kept her fears to herself, and prayed for something quite different, the knowledge of how to kill herself. And the only thing that could possibly have saved her was an encounter with somebody who could refute once and for all the doctor's opinion. There was no other way of saving a brave and trusting person. She had to have the intervention of a geneticist, and one who was sufficiently informed about the genetics of abnormalities of vision to be able to give her the only piece of information which could break her resolution to kill herself, and so save her.

I have no hesitation in saying that it was the Holy Spirit which kicked me out of bed and sent me flying downstairs. The sensation of being highly charged like an electric condenser was an entirely strange one to me. It would not have mattered what my particular beliefs might have been. An atheist or Marxist geneticist staying in the hotel would have been just as effective, and very probably they would have been no more able than myself to resist the impulsion to go downstairs if the Holy Spirit had pushed into the bedroom uninvited.

One is naturally tempted to try to trace the trail of events further back. The hotel booking transferred to the vital place. The decision of the original hotel manager to move me. The Russian footballers bribing the waitresses to leave the hotel for a few minutes so that they could devour all the available food. The fact that these men came over to play football in Wales at all. And so on, ad infinitum. Tied up in our curious little corner of space and time it is impossible to see where a trail begins, and I suspect we are foolish to try to do so. Instead of working on statistical improbabilities it may be much simpler to realise that we do not live entirely in a closed box, and when a person is in acute and special need, and prays persistently and desperately, there may be an answer. And that can be given in a most unexpected but brilliant way, and maybe through the agency of another person, pushed out of bed or complacency by the Holy Spirit, which perhaps can also be identified as the power of God in action. There is nothing new about that. It has happened throughout history.

SWEET REPOSE

It was a very small village, hardly more than a hamlet, and I found it at last a few miles east of Toulouse. I asked a lady who kept a little shop where the manor was to be found, but before following her directions I enquired who lived there nowadays, and she said nobody really. That is, an elderly retired officer owned it, and sometimes he was there but not very often. He had not the money to keep it up, and it was cheaper to stay away and let moth and rust corrupt. So there would certainly be no problem about visiting the chateau, at least as far as the outside was concerned, because there was neither man nor watch-dog to say me nay.

I had expected the manor of Bonrepos to have been taken over by the state or perhaps a preservation society, as it certainly would have been in England. But France had no National Trust, and when it came to preserving ancient stately homes it was hard to know where to begin and where to leave off. The whole country was seeded with chateaux and manors which once had been magnificent, but after a major revolution in which many of the aristocracy and intelligentsia were brutally slaughtered, and two world wars followed by the depredations of socialist governments, there was not much to be salvaged from most of the stately homes. And that was the case at 'Bonrepos'.

It was not just the name which had attracted me to ferret out the manor. It was my admiration for the former owner who, if he had been English, would certainly have been one of the first members of the Royal Society along with his contemporary Robert Boyle. But he was French. And he was not a scientist, though there is no doubt that he fell into that category of men that Aubrey would have described in his *Brief Lives* as *'ingeniose'*.

He had built the chateau in 1670 after pulling down an earlier one on the site. And now it was forlorn, with one or two of the windows boarded up and the shutters hanging askew on their rusted hinges. I walked through a field and approached the building by crossing a haha and plodding my way through the tall thistles which grew on what had once been a lawn *à l'anglais*. Nothing was now left of the elegant formal gardens, but on either side of the weedy drive a long band of wild purple cyclamen seemed to be bravely trying to fight against the general air of desolation.

I wandered into the woodland, through which an experimental stream had once been cut so that the Baron could make some trials with water-courses and levels. None of these works now remained, but one giant ornamental urn, almost buried in creeper, stood forlorn on a cracked pedestal as though to show me that yes, this had indeed once been a place of style and grandeur. But like the *Ichthyosaurus* of my early days, it had become outmoded, overtaken by the passage of the years, extinct.

Pierre-Paul Riquet, Baron de Bonrepos, was possessed by a dream, and determined to fulfil it, even if it were to bankrupt him – which in the end it did. Though not a scientist – he was in fact a tax-man who did well, as tax-men usually did – it was at Bonrepos that the Baron worked out some remarkable equations. Just how he did the calculations is not known, but the Baron calculated that 2 men leading 6 horses could deliver 3 tons by cart; but a boat operated by 2 men could transport no less than 300 tons. To move this quantity of goods by water would therefore save the wages of 200 men and the feed and maintenance for 600 horses – a very considerable economy. Even if wheeled transport were to be improved and the roads were to become much better than they were, the mere fact that road transport involved uphill effort and continuous friction meant that there was still a very great advantage on the side of water transport which involved neither.

The result of the Baron's calculations and his experimental trials in the park of Bonrepos were to confirm him in the determination that his real life's work was not to be in the Inland Revenue, but in joining the Mediterranean coast of France with the Atlantic ocean by means of an artificial waterway, thereby shortening the distance, reducing the cost of freight, and avoiding plunder by Moorish pirates lurking around the Straits of Gibraltar.

It had already been established that the lowest point between the two seas would be somewhere in the plain west of Carcassonne, and an Archbishop of Narbonne (another *ingeniose* individual) had actually identified the lowest point of the watershed even more exactly as being in the neighbourhood of a curious jumble of rocks some 30 miles east of Toulouse, the Pierres de Naurouze. However, this point was not only more than 600 feet above the level of either sea, but it was in an extremely dry area, and as no streams of importance could be found in the vicinity the idea of a watershed canal had been abandoned. And then Pierre-Paul Riquet came upon the scene. And he was not a man to be defeated by mere geography. He had not yet built the mansion at Bonrepos, but he was successful and wealthy, so at the age of 55 he betook himself to the curious collection of rocks near the hamlet of Naurouze, and sat down to consider. How was water to be brought to this desolate spot? Not just a trickle, but enough to provide the lockfuls of water which would be lost every time a ship passed the summit in either direction.

It seems that while haunting the neighbourhood of the rough pile of rocks thrown up by some rather inexpert giant, the Baron strayed a little from the 'chaos' and came upon a small spring, the Fontaine de la Grave. The existence of a spring was in itself not very surprising, but what immediately attracted his attention was that the water which trickled out had only gone a yard or two before its course was impeded by a lump of stone. Some of the water went to the right, and some to the left, trickling away to . . . to where? On the one hand surely to join up with streams flowing toward the Ariège, and thence the Garonne and the Atlantic; on the other to those which fed the River Aude, which flowed through Carcassonne and would eventually reach the Mediterranean. Water brought to this point would reach both seas, certainly. But how was that water to be furnished in amounts sufficient to feed the needs of a ship canal? His extraordinarily imaginative answer was to construct sixty-five kilometres of feeder channels to bring an endless supply from a forest area of high rainfall, and it was the experiments for this system which so occupied him in the woodland park of Bonrepos.

Riquet's splendid waterway, the Canal Royal en Languedoc (nowadays known as the Canal du Midi), was built by an army of 12,000 men and women working only with pick and shovel and wheelbarrows. But it was indeed completed just after his death, and even though the last commercial ship made its final passage through the waterway three centuries later, his work now provides one of the finest holiday amenities to be found in Europe.

That last of the barges to use the route was one for which we had a peculiar affection, and when it vanished we often wondered what had become of the young family on board. Her name was *Bacchus*, and she regularly filled her tanks at Sallèles with 150 tons of red Minervois plonk and carried it to Bordeaux for conversion by blending into aperitifs with well-known names. She was the last survivor of a vanishing trade. Commercial craft had, very rightly, precedence at the locks over the holiday boatmen, and these were cleared off the course when the telephone rang at a lock-house to announce the impending arrival of a wine-tanker or grain barge.

The *Bacchus*, like other *péniches*, had a crew of two, the man and his wife, and between them they had to manoeuvre a ship of a few hundred tons, look to the warps, and shut or open the paddles and gates on one side of a lock while the keeper attended to the other. There would usually be a number of holiday boatmen standing around with their hands in their pockets, irritated that mere working folk had taken precedence over them, but they never seemed inclined to lend a hand. Knowing what hard work it could be in a staircase lock, Ingrid and myself would usually help without being invited to do so, and on this particular occasion I was standing on the gates of the triple lock at Trèbes, ready to wind the paddles as soon as the bottom gates had been closed behind the newly arrived *Bacchus*.

The barge skipper was young, and had not yet learned to take things easily. He was also sullen and rather dirty, and the strong odour of wine did not come exclusively from his cargo. He shut his gate, came racing up the steps, and began to wind the paddle-gear furiously, stopping only to shout curses and orders to his wife, a pale and frightened young thing who had to manage the motor, tend the wheel, and tighten the aft warp. I judged her to be about seven months advanced in pregnancy.

Roughly he yelled at her as she just stood there looking crushed, miserable and resigned, and not daring to answer. After another bout or two of his cursing and swearing I could hold back no longer.

'Is that your wife?'

'Of course,' he snarled.

Reprimanding bargees for their behaviour had never been one of my regular habits, but this time I thought I would risk it.

'You must not speak to her like that,' I said. 'Especially now when she is having a baby, she needs to have kindness, gentleness, love, and everything to make her time easier. It is hard enough work for a woman on a *péniche* even if she is not seven months pregnant. You are not to behave like that toward her. Never. Never again.'

The bargee turned toward me, but he did not attempt either to punch me in the face or push me into the lock-pen. He simply stared at me in speechless amazement that an elderly stranger, and a foreigner too, could reprimand him in such a way, calmly but firmly. Then with a shrug he resumed working his paddle to fill the pen.

'It is the wine,' he muttered by way of excuse. But he had stopped his shouting, and as the barge chugged out of the top lock he gave me a slight nod of his head and a vestige of a smile.

A few months later we were lying at the bank near another lock when the *Bacchus* came into view, running light from Bordeaux to fetch another load of Minervois for blending. The skipper saw us, and eased off.

'It's a girl! You must come aboard and see her,' he exclaimed as he drew alongside.

I had never seen a man so transformed. He was washed and tidy, and as we jumped aboard to his open steering position he called to his wife in a gentle voice to let us see the baby. I duly expressed my admiration – though in truth I find small babies something less than attractive – but what we both of us particularly noticed was the change in the mother. The hunted, terrified look had vanished, and everything about her showed that his treatment of her had completely altered from what I had seen earlier in the triple lock of Trèbes.

Over the last year or two of our voyaging we often met this couple. Once the skipper insisted that we pass him, and that he would work the lock for us. Another time a loud blast on his hooter announced that he was coming by, and as the ship came gliding past he leaned far out, holding the rail in one hand while he passed over with the other a bottle of *brut* from the cargo as he went on his way as cheerfully as anyone – and especially his young wife – could ever have wished.

It was more than thirty years ago that I first passed through the Canal du Midi. East of Carcassonne there is one long level or *bief* (a stretch between two locks) of fifty-three kilometres, a winding track of water of astonishing beauty. It passes through the length of the Minervois, a vast wine-growing area (because it is too dry to grow anything else), a district my wife and I came to love on the many occasions when we passed slowly along the waterway lined by the reflection of its yellow irises and edged by an endless band of huge plane-trees on either side – originally planted by Riquet to give shade to the tow-horses. Gradually the area became a second home to us, and one day when we passed close to the village of Argeliers we drew in beside a hump-backed bridge from Riquet's days, and from the top of the arch surveyed the quietly beautiful countryside to the north.

About two miles distant a small hill was crowned with a little village of faded stone, topped by the three giant arches of an ancient *chateau-fort*. The sight was so appealing that we set out at once to follow the tracks across the vineyards to see it at close quarters. When an hour later we arrived, there was not a soul to be seen, not even a dog. It was the holy hour of the long-drawn-out French lunch.

That village struck us immediately as one of the most beautiful in the whole of the Languedoc, and when the time came to retire from exploring by boat – for lock-winding could with increasing years prove quite hard work – it seemed the one place that was inviting us to accept its offer of a gentle and sweet repose, a Bonrepos of our own.

We never called our house Bonrepos. It already had a name of its own, and Bonrepos would in any case have seemed rather suburban. Besides, even if we were happy to have occasional repose – particularly in the hot noontide of the Languedocian summer with the thermometer at thirty-six degrees in the shade – we were only retiring from waterways and not from life. Not in the least.

To be accepted with such kindness in a French village was something we could never have expected. But it happened. And quite soon we were involved in the life of that small community of only 170 people and a few lazy dogs. The sun shone, and so did the faces of the villagers. There were no pretensions to being anything other than what they were, hardworking *vigneron* families, happy to live in that community.

It was several years later that I attended one evening at a village meeting, as usual. This time I was not in the chair, but I took a seat among the audience gathered in the *Mairie*.

Monsieur Horthala beamed, and thumped upon the table. He was a retired wine-grower and the first President of the Association for the Preservation of Montouliers, a society which had been formed three years previously to frustrate the intentions of some English purchasers to buy the thirteenth century *chateau-fort*, the pride of the community. The society was determined to see that it was bought for the village instead, and they would set about restoring it and converting some of it into very high quality *gîtes* – an undertaking of great difficulty and great courage for so small a community.

This was the second open meeting of the members of the Preservation Society in the current year, and the gathering had several important matters to discuss, such as how many open days the village would have, and what special activities could be thought up to add to the prestige of Montouliers, and whether we could win the prize for the best *village fleuri* for the third year in succession.

At the President's thump, the members gradually subsided into silence. Madame Meunier, the very competent secretary of the association, said that before the other business began Monsieur Pilkington had something that he wished to say. And she looked at me encouragingly.

I said Yes, that was quite correct. I had. The fact was, I explained, that I was rather hard of hearing (but I did not add that even if I were not hard of hearing I found it difficult to understand what most of the local people said). More importantly, within a very few months I would be eighty, and people of such an age were too old, I thought, to be office holders of any association. So I had decided that the time had come for me to hand over the Vice-presidency of the association. That was my wish, and I was sure all would agree that it was a sensible one.

But surely, somebody asked, I would not think of resigning from membership of the association?

I said No, certainly not. The village could count upon my continuing membership, and that of my wife. And upon our aid in any undertaking where we had any competence.

So that was agreed, and the resignation was received with kindness by everyone present, and after we had dealt with the rest of the business I was free to walk up the village street and home for supper.

Home. Yes, my wife and I both had our hearts in this village of Montouliers, even if from the official point of view of residence and nationality it was not our documented home. That was elsewhere and would have to remain so – because nobody in their senses would get into a situation in which they were regarded as French residents and subjected to all the red tape, inheritance laws and the rest of the code of curious regulations devised, perhaps, by Napoleon in an off-moment.

Our house was on the edge of the village, and on its property there was a cave in a cliff of orange-coloured stone, water-worn and showing a number of fossil forms of plant life as well as some stalagmitic incrustations. The fossils were obviously of later date than my *Ichthyosaurus*, and the cave was only a few yards deep. It had been used in recent years by tramps as a dormitory, and further back in time by the early hunters of the area. It seemed likely that they had driven wild animals over the edge of the wedge-shaped cliff as a means of slaughtering them for food. But that was only conjecture.

Sometimes we would sit in the mouth of the cave and look out across the miles of vineyards. In the middle distance was the line of trees of the Canal du Midi and beyond that, the plain extending to Narbonne, with its cathedral towers standing out against the background of the Massif de la Clape.

Sometimes a giant emerald lizard would come and stand warily outside the cave, eyeing us with suspicion. Late in April the nightingales returned to sing for us, and the frogs rattled away in the stream. A hoopoe among our cypresses would call to its mate below the church, and loveliest of all the sounds was that of the dwarf or Scops owl. 'Poop!' it would cry from our cliff, and half a mile distant its mate would answer. And from the second week in June we had the constant company until September of what sounded like a whole factory full of sewing-machines, the busy scissor-grinding cicadas which are such a delight of the Mediterranean area.

The cave itself was home to many creatures. There were spiders, ant-lions in their craters in the sandy floor, and maybe a beautiful black scorpion hiding under a flower-pot, harmless, and like a baby black lobster as it ran over the cave floor with its claws stretched out on either side sweeping the road clear of ants. There was a hole which housed a rabbit family until they left, bequeathing the premises to a handsome Montpellier snake.

All these delightful creatures shared with us the happiness of the domain, and the wild brilliance of the broom and pink cistus, blue linum and red antirrhinum which spread up the rocky slope. And, delight of delights, a large wild boar accompanied by a young one would descend our bank on their nocturnal raiding of the village allotments, leaving their piggy tracks in the clay of our upper vineyard.

And among the smallest of creatures was a species for which I always had a special affection. That was the fruit fly, *Drosophila melanogaster*, which liked to throng in its hundreds the neighbourhood of the barrel from which I was bottling our amateur but decidedly drinkable white wine. They liked to siphon up the wine-flavoured drips. It was as though these little creatures recognized me as well as I recognized them from the years long ago in the zoological laboratory at Cambridge. I could never find it in my heart to trap these little insects on a fly-paper, or spray them with chemical warfare. They were friends, clad in the nostalgia of early days, and with them they always seemed to bring that exhilarating, curiously indefinable smell of laboratory.

In the peace, the kind friendliness of the village people and the shy presence of so many lovely creatures, we felt a great contentment, a thankfulness which we could express every morning in the brilliant early sunshine on our terrace, and also in the ancient church that crowned the village mound. We had been given undeserved a wonderful and eventful life, and if this were indeed to be the gentle beginning of the end we could never have wished for a finer place in which to ease off and accept our share of sweet repose.